Their Bones Are Scattered

A History of the Old Head of Kinsale and Surrounding Area

Raymond White

First published in 2003
by Kilmore Enterprises
Mill House
Kilmore
Ballinspittle
Kinsale
Co. Cork
Ireland

British Library Cataloguing in Publication Data
A CIP catalogue record for this book is available from the British Library

ISBN: 0 9544398 0 5

To Mary and our children, Adelaide and Denis
For I believe only for the past there would not be a present

Contents

The Old Head of Kinsale: Ancient Irish kings once ruled here. It was the seat of Cermna, a stronghold for the Vikings and Normans. The shear, awesome headland made the Old Head of Kinsale easy to defend.

Acknowledgements

I take this opportunity to thank all those who helped whilst I was compiling this book. When I was seeking information and sources, whoever I approached was only too willing to help, and if I have omitted anyone it is not intentional and I do apologise.

I would like to express my gratitude to the following: the Buttimore family, late of Kilmore mill and Garrettstown and who now reside in Coventry, the Isle of Man, Drogheda and Dublin, to whom I am most grateful for permission to publish the 1900 photo of their grandfather, Robert Buttimore (cover picture); Frank and Maybelle Buttimore, and their late aunt, Marie (Polly) Buttimore, the late Miss (Nora) Holland, and the late June and Anglin Buttimore, whose stories I listened to on those long winter nights so many years ago; Bill, Jack, Maureen and Freddie Buttimore (all deceased), who were always an interesting source of history and information about the locality; Patrick O'Sullivan of Bandon, never wanting when I needed help, and for access to his early letters on the Albion, and for his encouragement; Philip McCarthy of Kilgobbin, Ballinadee, descendent of the McCarthy clan and a brilliant historian, for his perseverance and research on the McCarthy clan, Dr Milner Barry and for other papers supplied, and without whom this book would never have been written; Charles O'Sullivan of Scarborough, Ontario, Canada, to whom I am most grateful for initial help on the Anne Powell letters and the Robinson family papers and for his kind letters; the director of the Hotel des Invelides, Musee de Armee, Paris, for allowing me to photo Lefebvre Desnouettes' portrait, and the staff of the museum for the courtesy afforded to me on my visit at Easter 2001; my great friend, Terry J. Senior, Marazion, Cornwall, author of the French Commanders Study Group, for his initial research on Charles Lefebvre Desnouettes, and his wife, Joy, two of the most considerate people I have ever dealt with; John Cotter, Old Head, who called on my behalf to Cheltenham Museum regarding General Lefebvre Desnouettes; Sophia Wilson of Cheltenham Museum and her colleague, Steve Blake, who were most helpful at all times and who arranged to have General Lefebvre Desnouettes' ring photographed; the late Fr Gus O'Regan, an historian to whom I was protégé and who led me to put pen to paper – may God bless him; Mrs Eibhlin MacPháidin, Rathfarnham, Dublin, that great Gaelic scholar, for her contribution on Drum Ceatt and who was always willing to help out when needed; Betty L. Krimminger, NC, USA, for her research; the

Commissioners of Irish Lights, Dublin who afforded me every assistance; Alan Boyers of the Old Head, who accommodated me on so many trips to the present lighthouse; Finbarr O'Connell, Old Head, and Jimmy Nyhan, Ballycatten, who were most helpful with information about the rocket; Gerard Wrixon; Michelle Manning; a late friend of mine, Patrick Arundel of Boston and formally of Garrettstown, who always gave me encouragement on all things historical; Francis Dempsey (deceased) of the Old Head – many a story he told; my uncle, Daniel White, late of Garrettstown, and his family; Kathleen O'Donovan of Ballinspittle; Martin Moir, who kindly came up with a photo of Ballycatten fort; John and Patrick O'Connor, Old Head of Kinsale Golf Links, for their efforts in preserving the ancient sites at the Old Head and to their staff for the courtesy extended to me at all times.

Thanks to Alan Roddie for his early research on the *Albion*; the Manning family, Garrylucas; Dominic White; James Downey, that great survivor of World War II; Tom McHugh, who answered my questions on the workings of the computer; Geraldine O'Donovan, who was a great help with the photographs and always willing to help; Oliver O'Dwyer of Bandon; Jack Healy, Old Head; the late Fr Christy Walsh; Eamon McKenna of Upton, who always came forward with old papers; Christine Harte; Joe Harrington White; Denis Murphy Coolmain (the Castle); Gerard Collins; Dave O'Mahoney; Captain Paul Bullen; Nora M. Hickey; Evelyn Draper; Francis Healy; Timmy White; Dermot Collins; Dan O'Callaghan; John Kiely, who willingly translated early nineteenth-century writings; Anne McCarthy; Peter Kelly, who set me on the road with my computer and guided me safely throughout my historic trip to France in Easter 2001; Margaret Herriott; Bernice Murphy; Canon Thomas Kelleher; Colm Lankford, Dublin; John Dukelow; the Bowen family of Coolbawn; Clair Doherty; Graham Maddocks; Peader O'Donovan's article in the *Southern Star;* Kieran Burke; Murris MacPháidin, who was always willing to help with the Gaelic; the late Donie Buckley and his family, Old Head; Judith Ann Schiff; Suzanne Warner of Yale University for courtesy extended to me; Finbarr Carroll on Donncha Dubh; Gerard Harrington on Timmy McCarthy; Pat Dineen; Patrick O'Donovan; Cornelius O'Donovan; Pat McNulty of Coilte who assisted me in every way and for his efforts in preserving the local antiquities under his control; Albert Murphy of Ballycatten

I am grateful to Finbarr Mawe, present owner of Garrettstown House, who has tried to keep buildings intact where possible; Conrad Payling Wright, for his letters to Paddy O'Sullivan and Alan Roddie on their earlier research on the Albion; Leo Bowes; Tim Cadogan; Ann Collins, who always showed great interest; John R. Hailey, Croydon, Surrey; Eli Lilly, Dunderrow, my employers, who always gave me great encouragement; Denis Fahy; Charles Dolan; Pádraig O'Donovan, Boxtown; Canon David Williams; Gerard Long, National Library; J.J. Hayes; Kenneth W. Nicholls, on the development of lordship in Co. Cork and for the courtesy he extended me; Ruth O'Connell; Vivion Hoary; the Hurley family at Ballinadee, for allowing me to encroach on their property to photograph the standing stones; Jeremiah O'Brien, Kinsale, for his co-operation with the Oldcourt graveyard; Tim Feen of Ardfield and John O'Donovan, formally of Ardfield and now Ballinspittle, to whom I am most grateful as they were always there when needed; Anthony Moir; John Murphy; Jerry O'Callaghan and Tadhg O'Shea, for their help with the Peninsular War headstone; Tim O'Leary, Douglas; Historical Society members in Kinsale, Bandon and Cork, for their encouragement down through the years; Erika Ainger, Kinsale and Dominic Carroll, Ardfield, who prepared this work for publication.

Thanks to my mother, Jean; Aunt Mabel in London, Uncle Bob, Ned and the late Sidney, who always mumbled something about Garrettstown estate to send me on a further search. Thanks also to my sister, Terry, and my brother, John, with whom I have fond memories of growing up together and who has gone to great effort to restore part of the Serpentine lake at Garrettstown; my aunts, Joan, Kitty and Mary, who always had some story to tell; my late Uncle David, who was always good with the yarns, my late Uncle George and my late Uncle John of Boston. Whilst writing this book, my late father, Denis, and my late brother, also Denis, were often brought to mind, as were my late grandfathers, Johnny White and George Moir, who helped preserve some of the papers of Garrettstown.

I would like to thank my wife, Mary, for putting up with the inconvenience of books and papers scattered all over the house and for the many cups of tea supplied over the long winter nights – the silence is now broken. And to our son, Denis, and daughter, Adelaide, who helped me with corrections and always bought the right book for me at Christmas, thanks. My young grandchildren, Isabelle and John – and their father, Fergal – should be thanked for providing some of the motivation for writing this book, for we must pass onto the next generations what we have learned.

To all my extended family and other friends who unknowingly helped in some way, my sincere thanks.

Raymond White
January 2003

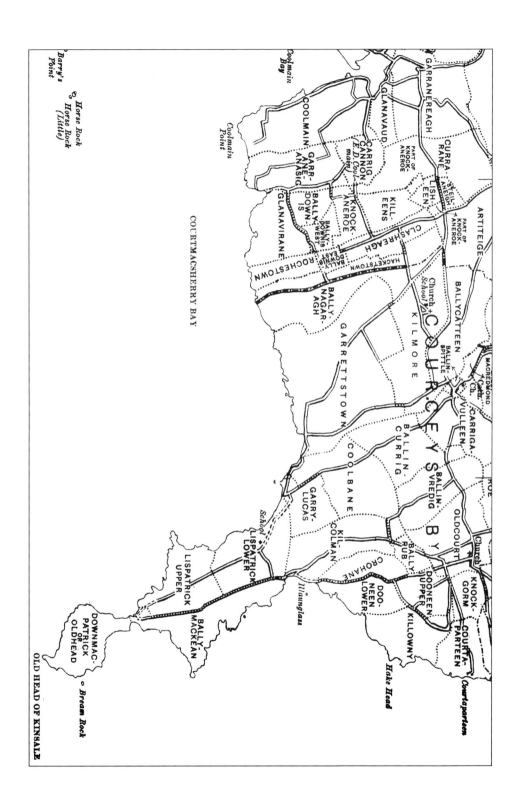

Foreword

On putting this compendium history of south Munster to the reader, one cannot fail to note the continuous brutality of the native Irish clans toward one other before Christianity took hold in Ireland. Upon the arrival of the Vikings, there was a brief respite and a coming together of the natives to drive the northern invaders from our shores. Yet, very soon, Irish and Viking alliances would be concluded, and battles for supremacy by the Irish kings – most of whom were mendicant patriots – would be commonplace. Invitations were even issued to the Anglo-French Normans who subsequently became the conquerors. With the gradual introduction of the English, warfare persisted between Gael, Irish, British, Anglo-French and landlord.

Down through the centuries, religion provided a pretext for the pursuit of territorial advantage and as justification for the often brutal oppression by the leaders of clans of their neighbours. Violence, both imposed and reactive, remains a chilling inheritance. The quest for land and territory was the most important contributory factor to the infighting, and brought about the eventual destruction of the native Irish clans. The imposing of a religious code of beliefs is, to this day, decisive in the polarisation of some groups on this island.

Today, we stand proud as a nation; we are a caring, independent people. Although dispersed by famine and eviction, Irishmen and women have achieved greatness at home and in many a foreign land over the last 500 years.

The Celts and the Old Irish

Ireland has been inhabited for nearly 10,000 years. The first Irishmen probably came across the narrow north channel from Scotland and settled in Ulster. Prehistoric Ireland produced some of the most remarkable human artefacts in Europe, many of which are still visible today. In particular, the extraordinary burial chambers and passage graves in the Boyne valley in Co. Meath – of which Newgrange is the most spectacular – testify to the sophistication of ancient Irish life.

The Irish as we know ourselves today are a very mixed race, composed initially of Phoenician, Albanian Celtic, Spanish, old Briton and Roman. Later, the Vikings, Normans, Angles, Saxons, Scots, English and Huguenot were added to the mix.

Gods with long hands, such as Lugh Lamhfhada and Oenghus Olmuchada, are recorded as ruling in Ireland in 800 BC. One of the most notable modern symbols in recent years has been the Red Hand of Ulster – seen as a rather threatening symbol of the Ulster loyalist planter tradition, it in fact goes back long before that. It was the heraldic badge of the Uí Neill dynasty, the symbol of the Celtic kings of Ulster. It also appears on the seal of Aedh O'Neill, king of Ulster in 1334–64. The Uí Neill dynasty would rush to their foes with the war cry 'Leamh Dearg Abu' ('The Red Hand forever'). However, it goes back further still to the Milesian invasion. Eremon had taken an oath that he would be the first to land on the shores of Éireann. When he saw that his ship was not going to make it first, he cut off his hand and threw it onto the shore. In this legend we find an echo of the symbolism of the reaching out of the hand. Eremon, according to the Druid Amairgen, became the first king of Ireland. (In Irish mythology, the Milesians were people from a royal Spanish family who invaded Ireland about 1300 BC and are the ancestors of the modern Irish. The name is after Milesius, the legendary head of the family.)

It is interesting to note that around the thirteenth century, the McCarthy Riabhach clan of Kilbrittain Co. Cork would sound the war cry, 'Lamh Laidir Abu' ('Victory to the strong hand').

It is said that the six sons of Milesius – Eberus, Eremon, Ir, Don, Amergius and Calptha landed in Ireland. From Eberus sprang the Momonia (the people of Munster); from Erimon were derived the people of Lethlenn and the Lagenii, or people of Leinster; the Ulides, or people of Ulster, sprang from Ir; from Don, the territory of Teach Duin in the western parts of Ireland; and from

Calpatha, the River Inber Calpatha was the name of where the Bodanus empties itself. Ancient accounts differ from one other: some claim only three sons of Milesius landed in Ireland, and Keating says the landings were in Bantry Bay, which they called Inber Sceine. In Bantry Bay in west Cork, there is a place called Adrigole, most likely named after the clan of the Gauls or Celtiberi who landed there. Adrigole and Argyll in Scotland is the same name. A colony of the clan of Gaul or Celtiberi sailed over from Ireland to the western isles and gave that part of Scotland, Argyll, its name. They called that country Gael Albenich, from old Albania, and until a few years ago, the clothes worn by the men and women of Ireland were the same, and today both nations retain the same language, manners and customs.

Gaelic chieftains would take as many as four wives. Each had equal status under Brehon law, the elaborate codified system of social order, and the concept of illegitimacy was not recognised. Man's first marriage was for dynastic reasons, to unite powerful families; his second was to supply a head for his household, to be in charge of his domestic affairs. The third wife was chosen to be his companion and confidante. The fourth wife would be very young and would be there to spur him on in old age.

We know that in AD 506, the three sons of Erc – Fergus, Angus and Loarn – crossed over to Scotland and colonised that part of the country now known as Argyllshire. That name signifies Airer-Gaedhil (arrer-gale) – the territory of the Gael or Irish. The name Scotia originally belonged to Ireland and the Irish were called Scoti or Scots. Scotland was in ancient times called Albania and subsequently named Scotia Minor, as being peopled by Scots from Ireland, while the parent country was for distinction often called Scotia Major. This continued down to about the eleventh century, when Ireland returned to the native name Éire and Scotia was from then on exclusively applied to Scotland; the word 'land' in both cases was added on later.

The people who inhabited the more western parts of Co. Cork were known as Uterini and Iberni. Their origin was Iberi or Spain, and they are said to have sent early colonies to Ireland. That is very probable because that part of west Cork is almost directly opposite Spain and about 150 leagues distant – ancient sailors had no navigational aid other than the sun by day and the stars by night. The people on the western end of the counties of Cork and Kerry are tall and thin with black hair, this being very different than the squat, short-limbed people from the eastern coast who resemble the Welsh from whom they are descended.

In about 550 BC, the Celts from the heartland of Europe – what is now France, southern Germany, Austria, Yugoslavia and the northern mountains of Italy – began to migrate towards Spain, Portugal, Turkey, Greece and northern Europe. The Celtic chieftains had built up riches in hilltop palaces throughout Europe; their wealth was buried with them, including gold and bronze artefacts. The Celts were part of a military aristocracy and from their fortified dwellings on strategic points on hilltops, they controlled the trading routes between Europe and the Mediterranean. It may be noted that most of the ringforts in Ireland are built on hilltops and most of them in sight of each other.

The Irish are usually thought of as Celts, but Ireland was inhabited for many thousands of years before the arrival of the Celts, which occurred around 450 BC. They crossed the narrow channel between Britain and Europe, as they were being driven north from central Europe as a result of the wars in the Mediterranean area.

In 113 BC, Celts – who by now had migrated to the eastern Alps – put up fierce resistance to Rome, and in 58 BC, Caesar opened a military campaign in Gaul – now France – conquering the Celtic tribe known as the Helvetii. In the year 279 BC, we find Celtic tribesmen invading Macedonia where they kill Ptolemy Caraunus. But fierce tribesmen from the mountains force them to move east ahead of advancing Romans. Gaulish Celts crossed to Britain around 400 BC – they themselves later becoming the Britons. Years later, they would be pushed out by the Angles and the Saxons into Cornwall, where they would become the Cornish, and into Wales, where they would become the Welsh.

About 350 BC, the Celts arrived in Ireland; some came by way of Britain, which they named Albion, while more crossed from the Iberian peninsula. Their language was a little different than that of the British Celts. Today, the old native tongue of the Scots, Welsh, Cornish, Irish and other parts of Britain along with the western part of France have quite a few words in common with one another.

It is possible that there were several Celtic conquests, though we are not at all sure of the timing. Pytheas, the Greek mathematician, astronomer, and explorer (300 BC), refers to the British Isles as the 'Pretanic Islands'. This term is Celtic and comes from Priteni. When they arrived in the British Isles, they settled in the south-east of Britain before fanning out to the farthest extremities of the British Isles. It was in these areas that they became dominant; their power was not challenged, let alone broken, for over a thousand years.

The Roman Influence

In 54 BC, Julius Caesar made an expedition to Britain, followed in AD 40 by Claudius, who lead an expedition to conquer Britain. Lonndinium (London) is founded by the Romans and they surround it with a high wall. It is certain that many of the ancient British people retired to Ireland upon the invasion of the Romans under Vespasian (AD 9–79), who became emperor in AD 69. Some of them came to Ireland for the sake of peace and quiet, others to keep their eyes untainted by the Roman insolence, and others again to preserve their liberty.

As the Roman Empire began to crumble by the fifth century, new settlers arrived from northern Europe and settled in the south-east region of Britain. This new group were Angles, and gave Britain its name: Angland or England. It was this group that pushed the Celts out of the region, but they left many names after them which are still in use – rivers such as the Avon, Dee, Don, Severn and Thames; hills and forests such as Barr, Brent, Cannock; and areas such as Kent, Carlisle, Dover and Leeds. The Celts were a warlike people and their tribal divisions led to constant warfare between local petty chieftains.

In AD 48, Wales is taken by Roman legions; in AD 79, Chester is founded. In AD 83, Agricolas and his legions are fighting in northern Britain, where they defeat the Caledonians. It was around this time – AD 84 – that Agricolas, the Roman governor of Britain, considers the conquest of Ireland. Later, in AD 122, Hadrian's Wall is constructed across northern Britain. A further wall is built in AD 140, known as the Antonine wall, after emperor Antoninus Pius who reigned from AD 138–61; this wall connected the Forth and the Clyde and was constructed mainly of turf. Antoninus was the successor of Hadrian, and this was his attempt to stop the Picts and the Caledonians from breaching southward to Britain.

In AD 333, the Roman grip on Britain was weakening as they began to withdraw their legions and, by AD 367, Britain had been devastated by attacks by the Irish, Picts (from Scotland) and the Saxons from Germany. In the year AD 407, the final Roman withdrawal took place, as the garrisons were needed to defend Rome from the barbarians. After 360 years of Roman domination, the British Isles reverted to native rule. But by now something else was beginning to happen that would bring about a major change to the once prosperous empire. In Europe, on the last days of December AD 406, over the frozen River Rhine stormed thousands of hungry men, women and children. The barbarians had arrived in huge numbers, the likes of which had never before happened despite migration from the east having gone on for centuries. The Roman side of the river was prosperous but, until now, the widest river in Europe had been a natural barrier against those undisciplined and illiterate hoards of people. The Danube and the Rhine had long been considered the natural barriers between the civilised world and the northern barbarians, and the Eternal City of Rome had remained free from attack since the Celts from Gaul sacked it in 390 BC. But it was now in danger.

The Roman Empire had stretched to the Scottish border, the rich plains of Gaul, to North Africa and the rich Nile valley, all the way to the coasts of Asia Minor; in the middle was Medi-Terra-nea, which they called the Sea of Middle Earth (Mediterranean). The Romans were now up against the barbarian hoards of wild, hairy, shabbily dressed, undisciplined individuals with painted bodies – a stark contrast to the clean, well-dressed Roman soldiers who faced them on the opposite side. Rome was again sacked by Alaric in AD 410, and its last Western emperor died in AD 476.

The straight, paved Roman road that ran up the length of Europe was for many centuries safe for travel; now it was full of highway robbers. Extortion was ripe and bribery was the order of the day. By AD 441, Saxon settlers from the Rhineland had established a colony in southern Britain, and in AD 446, Britain appeals to Rome for help to defend itself from the Saxon invaders. The Roman emperor, Honorius, told them to defend themselves.

The Roman Empire never stretched as far as Ireland, but Romanised Britons traded freely and set up trading posts on the east, south-east and south coasts. Though evidence has emerged of Roman remains north of Dublin, the Irish Celts were left to themselves politically.

The Irish Attacks on Britain

The first notable transaction that I can find mentioned by historians in this part of the country is an account of a memorable battle fought at Árd-Neimheidh (the Great Island) in AD 125 between Niadh Nuaget and Engus, who was the monarch of Ireland. In this conflict, the former recovered the crown of Munster from the latter.

Several ancient writers mention frequent excursions of the inhabitants of these parts of Ireland into Britain around AD 306, during the rule of Constantine. In the fourth and fifth centuries, large Irish colonies were set up in Britain. One such group of colonists were called Uí Liatháin and these were probably the Érainn who were at one time settled in the Old Head region of Cork. The power of the Irish over the British was great; they divided large parts of Britain between them into estates, and it is said that, at that time, the Irish lived as much east of what is now known as the Irish sea as they did in Ireland.

The *Annals of the Four Masters* mentions that from AD 125 onwards, the area where Cork city is now situated and most of Munster was afflicted with several plagues. It also mentions that a great plague raged all during the year AD 685, leading us to believe that trade in both slave and commerce was alive between Ireland, Britain and Europe and bringing with it this pestilence.

The Eóghanacht, who wrested the kingship of Munster from the early Érainn, were colonists who had returned from Britain, more than likely driven out by the Romans. The people who lived near what is now Cork city seemed to be derived from the ancient Coritani, a British tribe from Leicestershire or Lincolnshire – hence the Latin name for those people: Coriondi. Around 500 BC, the Greek philosopher, Marcianus Heraclitus, wrote that Ireland had sixteen nations, eleven famous cities, five remarkable promontories and fifteen principal rivers. It is almost certain that one of those promontories was the Old Head of Kinsale.

The Irish call all marshy places corcass grounds. The boats they used were made of wattles covered over with rawhides, and these were the type of craft that the ancient Irish and Britons used to sail in. In the Irish tongue, these are *curraghs*, and in the old British, *corcog*, which comes very near to the name Cork, *viz.* Corcach, or marshy place (or it could be the place of the curraghs, i.e. this type of boat was used in the western shores off the more remote parts of Ireland up until the end of the twentieth century). The ancient name for the river Lee was Luvius.

Ogham: The Written Word

Standing stones are everywhere around Ireland but more so in Co. Cork. Some are small, more are large – as much as ten feet tall. Dating from Neolithic times (8–5000 BC), they appear to have been used in three different ways: as memorials to the dead, to mark the site of a great battle or to establish a boundary. In most cases, they had no markings – these were simple unchiselled slabs or pillars – but the most interesting ones are inscribed in what is known as the *Ogham* alphabet. Only about 400 of these memorials are known, and of that number, approximately fifty were also found where the Irish had settled in Britain, Cornwall, Devon, south and north Wales, and also in the Isle of Man.

The vast majority of them in Ireland are to be found in Kerry, Cork and Waterford. This was the earliest form of written Irish – an alphabet of lines and notches cut out on the edges of stone. Based on the Latin alphabet (again, the Roman influence), they would seem to date from about the middle of the fifth century to the latter part of the seventh century. It has been suggested

Standing stones, north of Ballinadee village.

that the characters were derived from an alphabet of finger signs. Early Irish manuscripts tell of messages in *Ogham* cut on pieces of wood and sent from one important person to another; the primitive people of remote areas of the world used such methods well in the twentieth century.

On his travels around Ireland in 1944, Robert Gibbings of Cork, when writing his book *Lovely is the Lee*, came across an *Ogham* stone in a loose stone wall at the Mizen Head and, even closer to this area, he discovered one near Kilbrittain, leaning against a cottage wall. He asked the owner what he was going to do with the stone, to which the man replied, 'I'll put it in my rockery.' Gibbings told him to put it in the museum where it belongs and the man agreed. The author then lifted the stone and found on the reverse side a carved cross, suggesting that *Ogham* writing was contemporary with Christianity or that the stone had been a pagan monument which was converted at a later date for Christian use. The stone was donated to the museum in Cork city, where it can now be viewed. It carries an inscription which translates as T E C O R M A Q (Cormac).

The Arrival of St Patrick

By the middle of the fifth century, the borders of the empire of Rome were closing in north Africa. The empire's breadbasket fell to the Vandals as did large parts of Gaul and Spain, leading to panic and desolation. By now, the Roman garrison in Britain was depleted, leaving Britain exposed to the Germanic Angles and Saxons on its eastern and western shore. This was a time of wholesale enslavement and barbaric acts, and saw the most terrifying slave raids by the Celts of Ireland. It was the beginning of the end of the Roman Empire, and changed the face of Europe. The only reference to that great empire today is its capital city, still known as the Eternal City, and the impoverished country called Romania.

There was no tribe more feared than the Irish. With their sailing skills in skin-covered boats, they would move to isolated coves and their war parties would pounce before dawn on some remote farmhouse. They would pillage, rape and slaughter the elderly, and grab sleeping children. They would be well across the Irish Sea before it was realised what had happened.

Around AD 401, a large fleet of these light skin-covered boats sailed up the River Severn estuary in western Britain and seized hundreds of young prisoners for the slave market in Ireland. One such boy was called Patricius. Around sixteen years old, his father, Calpurnius, was a nobleman and his grandfather a priest. This middle-class lad was a Romanised Briton but was not interested in following in his father's footsteps. Now tied in chains, he was brought to a pagan land and sold to a king named Miliucc in the district of north-east Ireland – more than likely Antrim or the hills of Tyrone. At the time, sheep and goats were the main animals kept in the hills, where there was an abundance of wild fodder. The sheep needed protection from wolves, and it was in this environment that Patricius became a shepherd boy and obedient to the whims of his master.

Partricius spent at least six to seven long years in this isolation, giving him ample time for meditating on the Christian faith, thinking of his parents and wondering how he might escape from the clutches of Miliucc. Eventually, he did escape. Walking for days on end, he covered nearly 200 miles until he reached the coast – we believe this to be around Wexford or Waterford. Here, he came across a group of sailors loading up their boat with Irish wolfhounds and other goods which they were going to sell on the Continent. These dogs were much prized and would fetch good money when sold. Partricius approached the ship's captain – who eyed him with suspicion – and asked could he take passage with them; the captain turned him down, saying Partricius was wasting his time travelling with them. Partricius turned away in despair, pulling his cape over his face in a bid to hide himself in case he might be spotted as a fugitive in this little seaside hamlet. Suddenly, he heard a call from one of the sailors: 'Come on board – we'll take you on trust.'

They reached the Continent and it was here that Patrick became a priest and later a bishop. He could never forget the Irish, and had visions of the long days and nights he spent on the lonely hills. So he returned to them, only this time to teach the pagan Irish the Christian faith. It was about this time that Ireland's isolation from Britain and Europe was coming to an end. When Patrick arrived – around AD 432 – with his group of Christian missionaries, the Romanised Briton's influence was stamped on subsequent Irish history forevermore.

In Muskerry, Co. Cork, there was a church called Ecclesia Dentis, its name derived from a tooth of Saint Patrick that was kept there. This church and its ruins have long since disappeared. At a spot near Sandycove village, a well known as Patrick's well still exists. Patrick would certainly have called to the Old Head and district with his missionaries, and to Ballycatten village.

With Christianity gaining a firm grip, thanks to Patrick and his dedicated band of preachers, the Irish were beginning to learn and write. Even before Patrick, other monks had made some attempts to bring about this change but with little success. The six years spent on the lonely hills and mountains by this educated Roman was about to pay off, and this was the event that ushered in Ireland's golden age. For over 200 years, Ireland was a beacon of culture and learning at a time when Europe was sunk in the misery of the Dark Ages. Great manuscripts were written, including the *Book of Kells*, which still survives.

By now, the pagan Saxon settlements in southern England had cut off Ireland from easy commerce with the Continent. Rome and its ancient empire was fading from memory, the illiterate Europe rose from its ruins and a literary culture was blooming in Ireland and in the northern part of England. All along its Celtic fringe, it was what you would call scribal Ireland. Eventually, Irish monks would colonise the barbarised Europe, bringing their learning with them. In AD 564, the Irish missionary, Colmcille, and his small band set up a monastery in Iona, off the Scottish coast – their first outpost.

Scotland was already colonised by the indigenous Picts and by the Irish, who had established themselves in Patrick's time. The Irish monks were never interested in edifices and preferred to spend their time in study, prayer, farming and, most of all, copying. So a basic plan of a monastery was executed which consisted mainly of a small hut for each monk – the head abbot had a larger hut which was elevated a little on higher ground. The commune contained a kitchen, refectory, a scriptorium and library. To survive the harsh winters, they built barns to house their stock, a little kiln and mill, a smithy to forge their irons and a small church. In later years, further additions were added, such as a guest-house for the influx of students who came to study. These consisted of Scots, Picts, Irish, Britons and Anglo-Saxons. Some of them were never to return from this remote island. Quite a number of the monks would be sent off to set up other religious communities around the rugged coasts of Scotland, England and Ireland. Colmcille's reputation spread and, by AD 790, Irish monks reached Iceland in skin-framed boats.

After the Synod of Whitby in AD 663 – at which the controversy raged about the rule for the keeping of Easter and where Roman Christianity prevailed over Celtic Christianity – St Coleman, Abbot of Lindisfarne in north-east England, left that monastery, taking with him all of the Irish monks and thirty of the English monks. They initially settled on the island of Iona, but later some of them came to Inishbofin off the Mayo coast in the west of Ireland. Here, they founded a monastery, built on a narrow isthmus between two pre-cipitous chasms, with cells balanced on the edge of the cliff-face. One of these cells would have been the scriptorium, and for hundreds of years, students flocked to Inishbofin to learn the arts of calligraphy and illumination which were taught by the disciples of St Colmcille. It was his school that produced the *Book of Kells*, the *Book of Durrow*, the *Book of Lindisfarne* and other great Irish art – the most illuminated manuscripts of the world, yet to be surpassed. The famous *Book of Kells* was written in Lindisfarne during the period of Viking raids; it was brought over to Kells for safekeeping where it was subse-quently found.

Johannes Scotus Eriugena (b. 815), an Irish born scholar, crossed over to France in his early thirties. He took up a position at the Palatine School, which was under the patronage of Charlemangne's successor, Charles the Bald. John Scotus, who more than likely was a layman, was the first true Christian philosopher since the death of Augustine in AD 430. Scotus had a great mind and also a great since of humour. In Europe in those times, it was wine-soaked lavish dinner parties, and it was at one such gathering that the emperor asked John Scotus what separates a fool from an Irishman: 'Only the table' was his reply. The witty John Scotus is reputed to have been stabbed to death with the pens of his students.

The Ancient History of the Old Head

The famous landmark known as the Old Head of Kinsale, familiar to travellers in the Old and New World, was known to the Syrians and Phoenicians and to all who sailed the seas in the early ages of mankind. According to the *Chronicles of Eri Cermna*, brother of Schairce, who reigned in this rock-bound stronghold as king of southern Ireland from 893–54 BC, the headland became known as Dún Cermna, or Cermna's Fort. We are told that this Cermna was slain at Dún Cermna by Eochaid Faeburglas, grandson of Eber, suggesting Dún Cermna had been attacked by the southern Goidels. It is also possible that around this time, the Old Head had passed out of the hands of the original owners over to the Eóghanacht. Dún Cermna was built during the reign of Eremon by Manthan Mac Cachir. The names of Mac Cachir's sons are given as Mael, Umai, Falbe and Garban.

The genealogy of the Érainn begins with Duline, son of Mael Umai, son of Cachir (who built Dún Cermna), son of Eterscéil, son of Eóghan. Duline in Mael Umai in Cachir Casa n'Dernad Dún Cermna, Mac Eterscéil in Eógain (ancestor of the O'Driscoll's).

In a poem dated AD 887 by Mael Mura Othna, commemorating the victories of Tuathal Techtmar over the ailing non-Goidels, we are told of the battle of Cermna against Caicher.

An entry in the glossary of Cormac (AD 908) tells how Caier, king of Connacht, having been disfigured as the result of a satire directed against him by Néde, left his kingdom and betook to Cacher Mac Eterscéil of Dún Cermna (Sonas Cormaic AD 698). This Cacher Mac Eterscéil (or Etersciol) who, in the forgoing passages is closely connected with Dún Cermna, is further represented as ancestor of several branches of the Érainn. From a son of his named Laoehri descended the Érainn of Dún Cermna, and from another son, Duifne, came the Corcu Duifne. From the third son came Mael Uinae, the Érainn of mid-Munster. In the poem of Mael Mura Othna, Lugaid Loígde, divine ancestor of the Corcu Loígde, is called king of Dún Cermna and Bérre.

A contemporary enumeration in a verse about the leaders who fell in the Battle of Belach Magua (AD 908) includes Domhnall of Dún Cermna. Three fragments of the *Irish Annals* include a prose account of Domhnall Rí Dún Cermna. It is likely that he was king of Corcu Loígde and might in verse aptly be described as coming from Dún Cermna even though the actual *dún* was no longer in his territory.

A poem written at the convention of Drom Ceatt in AD 537 gives the names of the twelve kings, all called Aed, who attended the convention, among them Aed Bolge, Rí Dún Cermna (that is, Aed of the Bulig = Érainn, king of Dún Cermna).

The Árd-Rí (High King) of Ireland, Aodh (Hugh) Mac Ainmire, summoned by his royal mandate, the princes, the nobility and clergy of the kingdom to meet at the parliament of Drom Ceatt.

> The Irish monarch summon'd by his writs
> The parliament of Drom Ceatt; the subjects in debate
> Were, the expulsion of the poets, the ancient tribute
> Of the Dailraids, and the just disposing
> Of Scanlan, prince of Ossory

Those summoned were Criomthan Ciar, king of Leinster; Iollan, son of Scanlan, king of Osraí (Ossory); Maoldúin, son of Aodhna or Hugh Dubh, son of Coleman, king of Clan Fiachadh; Firghin (Florence), son of Aodhna or Hugh Dubh, son of Criomthan, king of the whole province of Munster; Raghallach, son of Uadhach, king of Tuatha Taighdean and Breifne Ó Ruairc to Claibhan Modhuirn; Ceallach, son of Cearnach, son of Dubh Dortha at Breifne Uí Raghallaigh, Congallach Ceanmhaguir Tírconconuill; Fearguill, son of Maoldúin on Oilioch; Guaire, son of Conguill of Ulster; the two kings of Oirghialla – Dimhín, son of Aongus, from Colchar Deasa to Fionn Carn at Sliabh Fuaid and Hugh, son of Duach Gallach from Fionn Carn at Sliabh Fuaid to the river Boyne; Aodhan, son of Gabhrán, son of Domanguirt; Conall, son of Aodh Mac Ainmire; Dónal, son of Aodh Mac Ainmire; St Colmcille, who was summoned from Scotland by the high king and was accompanied by a great number of religious persons who were allowed to sit in the assembly: twenty bishops, fifty deacons and thirty students of divinity who had not yet taken holy orders.

> St Colmcille arrived at Drom Ceatt
> Followed by a retinue of his clergy
> By twenty prelates of superior order
> By forty presbyters and fifty deacons
> And thirty students of divinity
> Not yet ordained.

Aodh Mac Ainmire had three reasons for appointing this convention. The principal reason was to discuss the position of the poets in Ireland. Poets had always been held in great esteem in the country. The chief poets were regarded as equal in rank to kings. They received great rewards in land and goods, and wherever they went, they and their servants were entertained free of cost. Many of them had become very grasping and overbearing. People were so afraid of having satires in verse made against them that they dare not refuse a poet anything. Aodh Mac Ainmire was in favour of taking away their privileges and banishing some of them from the country. Colmcille, who loved

13

poetry, used his influence and this was not done. The number of poets was reduced and stricter rules were laid down for their conduct.

> The poets were secur'd from banishment
> By Colmcille, who, by his sage advice
> Soften'd the king's resentment and prevail'd
> That every Irish monarch should retain
> A learn'd poet; every provincial prince
> And lord of a cantred, were by right allowed
> The same privilege and honour.

The second reason for the king summoning the great assembly of Drom Ceatt was to settle a constant tribute upon the tribe of the Dailraids in Scotland. They owed homage to the crown of Ireland and paid a ransom called 'Eiric' to the king. They had of late refused to contribute their portion to Aodh Mac Ainmire.

> The Dailraids, I ordain shall pay
> Eiric, as tribute to the Irish crown
> And with their troops endeavour to support
> The king by sea and land

Dál Riada was a small kingdom in north Antrim which also encompassed a little part of Scotland and was, at this time, ruled by an Irish prince, Aedan. At Drom Ceatt, it was agreed that the portion of Dál Riada which lay in Ireland should serve the high king with its land forces and King Aedan with its sea forces.

The third reason for the assembly was the request by Colmcille for the release of Scanlan Mór, king of Osraí (Ossory), who had been imprisoned by the high king. Aodh Mac Ainmire refused to release him. Tradition has it, however, that Colmcille miraculously had him freed from his captivity and restored to his kingdom. Thus ended the parliament of Drom Ceatt.

This account was compiled from Keating's *General History of Ireland*, translated by Dermod O'Connor, and from *Beatha Cholm Cille* le Séamus Ó Searcaigh. The verses are from *Amhráin Cholmcille*, and are a rough translation.

The territory of Carbery took its name from an ancient Irish chief. According to the *Irish Annals*, there were three brothers: Carbry Riada, Carbry Muse and Carbry Bascoin, and they are said to have been sons of Fiachad, brother of Eana Aighnach, Monarch of Munster. From the first son is supposed to come the race Dailriadi, in Scotland. The second brother gave his name to Muskerry, and the youngest son gave the name Corca Bascoin, the area where Cork city now stands.

The town of Cashel was the seat of all the Munster kings – 'Upon this rock I shall build my church'. This must have inspired the building of the monastery on the Rock of Cashel. Cormac Mac Cullinan was born in AD 837 and was once king and Archbishop of Cashel. The Dál Riada territories were north Antrim,

The lighthouse at the Old Head of Kinsale stands guard over the grave of the *Lusitania*. In the foreground lie the outline remains of Cermna's Dún.

and the ancient kingdom of Ossory was around the Kilkenny area and part of it is still known by that name today.

It has been argued that a great Celtic group was in the third century BC based upon Dún Cermna, the promontory fort on the Old Head of Kinsale. These people, who represented the southern Érainn or Iverni, are thought to have possessed lands which extended westward as far as Beara.

We can only speculate but there is good reason to believe that the Érainn, the tribe that once dominated the area at the Old Head, gave its name to what we know today as Éire.

By the first century AD, their important stronghold at the Old Head had been taken from them and a new Celtic group had become dominant. This new group represented the race that by now retained the undisputed possession of the land of Ireland until the Anglo-Norman invasion around 1171.

This Celtic Christian civilisation was disturbed next by the Vikings from Scandinavia in the eighth century. The first Viking raids happened around the coast in the years AD 793–94. Forts and monasteries were looted and burned. In 795 Ratlin, Iona, Inishboffin and Inishmurray were attacked. The city of Cork and adjacent country was ransacked in 820. In the same year, marauding bands of Vikings sailed into the mouth of the Bandon river and also landed around the shores at the Old Head and further west at the Galley Head – so called after a Viking longboat, or galleon, was wrecked off the headland during a violent squall after its crew had plundered and burned Ross Abbey.

In March 830, during the rein of Hugh Dorndighe, who was monarch of Ireland, there were terrible shocks of thunder and lightning, the likes of it never before mentioned, and over a thousand people were killed in the Cork region. Large clan gatherings on high-elevated ground preparing to face the Viking hoards – equipped with body armour, spears, daggers, copper shields and swords – made them like earth bars and magnets for the lightning to ground.

About this time, the sea rose and cut across many low marshy areas to make several islands – Little Island, Great Island, Inchydoney Island and several more in west Cork. The Old Head peninsula was cut off several times from the mainland by the sea but the shifting sands gradually built natural embankments.

The Vikings moored their boats at the beaches and inlets of Garrettstown at the west and also at Duneen on the eastern side of the Old Head. The small forts and settlements at the base of the Old Head were soon overrun, and from there they made a two-pronged attack from land and sea. After a short struggle, they had wrested the stronghold at the Old Head from the ancient Irish. Later, they set up a large settlement north of the Bandon river in a place known today as Dunderrow. Kinsale Harbour was thought to be safe sanctuary as was the Bandon river, being tidal as far as Innishannon, yet, in the *Book of Leinster* – written in the twelfth century – it is reported that in AD 837, Innishannon was plundered by Viking pirates who had sailed up the estuary. This waterway also gave the raiders easy access to other large settlements, one such being the great fort at Garranes – situated close to Bandon town, it is one of the largest forts in Ireland and dates back to the second century AD. This fort is nearly 200 metres in diameter and is reputed to have been the ruling seat of the Eóghanacht dynasty. Innishannon must have been a very important place; this is highlighted by the fact that in 1291 the village was taxed more than five times that of Kinsale. The Vikings were the founders of all our major cities around the coasts, including Dublin in AD 841.

In 913, Cork was burned and plundered by the Danes and, by the year 915, the greatest part of Munster was again wasted by them. In 916, according to the *Annals*, the Munstermen defeated them in a pitched battle.

By 918, the Danes of Dunderrow, the Old Head region and other parts of Munster were in peaceable possession, but a little later, some of them joined a party of their countrymen from Scandinavia and sailed to Albania (Alba, i.e. Scotland) and committed great ravages over there.

The Danes were at continuous war with the Irish during the following years: 1012, 1016, 1026, 1048 and up until 1081. The Danes of Dublin, Waterford and Wicklow united their forces in the year 1089 to attack Cork, but they were overthrown in the battle by the Irish of the Eóghanacht, who were part of south Carbery.

After consolidating their stronghold at the Old Head, the Vikings cut and hacked their way up the valley following the little river known as the Lucha, which flowed out the centre of what is now Garrettstown beach. At that time, the land protruded a half-mile out on either side of the present beach, which was a shaking morass with a turf bed.

The river cut through the turf, making it navigable in between the tall reeds. After a distance of two miles, the Vikings came upon the sleepy hamlet of Ballycatten which lay outside the perimeter of its great defensive fort. The dwellers of the village fled to the sanctuary of the fort. Most, if not all, the early Viking raids were around the coast where rivers and inlets accommodated their fast-moving boats, their main mode of transport. Otherwise, they travelled on foot. In later raids, they ventured more inland. The name

Ballycatten comes from the 'Home of the Battle', although some dispute this.

The fearsome Scandinavian warriors, with their painted bodies and long flowing hair crowned with a set of horns, drove fear into the natives as their swift crafts made their way up the waterways and rivers. Standing in the front of the craft, often dwarfed by a huge dragon or some other pagan demon, was a scantly clad, red-headed female – her body painted – urging her male counterparts forward with a frenzy of screams which drove terror and consternation into all those who stood in their path. Perhaps from this was derived the modern superstition whereby a sailor considers the sight of a red-headed woman as he walks the gangway a bad omen, making him reluctant to go to sea for fear of some tragedy.

The huge, three-ring embankment fort at Ballycatten, which had its perimeter and inner embankments reinforced to defend it from attack, was achieved with several palisade rings of tall sharpened timbers, which formed a complete circle around the existing outer embankment. The inner circle consisted of a walkway at a high level which gave the defenders a great advantage, especially as Ballycatten fort was well elevated on high ground. On the inside access, ladders or timber ramps lead up to the parapets which had several crenellated openings. Most of the inhabitants living in the numerous small forts in the area would have sought the sanctuary of the much larger fort at Ballycatten. With its underground souterrains, the women and children crawled to safety. Approximately twenty-five of these small forts of the single-embankment type were in existence within a three-mile radius of Ballycatten (any area or townland beginning with *Lios* or *Lis* derives its name from a fort of some kind that once stood there). Fort Arthur, being larger with two embankments, was situated on high ground approximately one mile directly to the east of Ballycatten. A Viking attack on Fort Arthur was repulsed and, after several escalade attempts on Ballycatten and a battle which lasted several days and caused much spilling of blood, the Vikings were beaten back and Ballycatten survived the onslaught. The Vikings were unable to penetrate its defences nor triumph over the determination of the ancient Irish.

On their retreat from Ballycatten, the Vikings sacked, looted and burned the big church situated just south of the fort. That place is called today Kilmore – 'Big Church'. This church was in a vulnerable position because it stood outside the defensive walls of the fort, as was the tiny hamlet of Ballycatten – with its mud-walled houses thatched with reeds, the village was looted and razed to the ground. The defenders of Ballycatten and Fort Arthur fought and chased the Vikings back down the valley towards the Old Head. It was here that the Vikings consolidated their position and rebuilt a defensive line at the lower, narrow part of the peninsula; this caused a logistical problem for the marauding Vikings. The headland, with its high and rugged coastline, was easy to defend but to get supplies and equipment ashore in inclement weather posed a problem for the invaders. Their fuel had to be retrieved from a bog situated in open ground at the bottom of the headland, and venturing further inland to fetch timber for the repair and making of new craft made the invaders open and vulnerable to attack from the Irish. Their boats, which were their main mode of transport, had to be hauled back for safe keeping to the

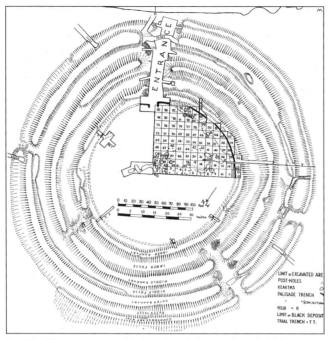

Sketch of the excavation of Ballycatten Fort, a portion of which was explored in 1942.

headland from the sandy and sheltered coves at the bottom of the headland. These problems and the continued harassment of the natives caused the Scandinavian invaders to stay at the Old Head a few short years. They managed to hold out a few years longer at Dunderrow, north of the Bandon river, where they settled and fortified. Some of the Vikings stayed at the Old Head and Dunderrow, as they did in several other areas, and became peaceful traders. It is interesting to note that several family names of Norse origin still exist today, including Coppinger, Copithorne, Arthur, Sweetman and O'Beirne, from the Norse forename Bjorn.

Ballycatten's famous fort, with its triple ramparts, is in near perfect condition and can still be seen today, standing as a grim reminder of the slaughter it must have endured over the last 2,000 years.

Ringforts were a settlement of early Celtic times – some date from 800 BC and they were a common dwelling place up to AD 1200. Thousands of these forts existed, mostly on hilltops around the country. In early Christian times, Ireland was ruled by over 150 small kingdoms called *tuatha*, and each *tuatha* would consist of a large fort and several smaller ones in close proximity, under the control of a petty king. Under him would be nobles, lords, farmers, labourers and slaves. The kings and lords had several wives to make sure that male heirs continued the line, something considered very important. With the coming of the Normans, towers and castles replaced the forts although some farmsteads used them up to the 1700s.

In 1942, part of Ballycatten Fort was excavated under the guidance of the Royal Irish Academy, supervised and documented by Seán P. O. Riordan and P.J. Hartnett. The survey revealed underground passages and turned up some artefacts. Only a small quadrant on the south-west corner was exposed, and here are some of the findings. Ballycatten fort is not only the largest in the locality but is also the best protected. While other smaller forts in the hills around it would command a better view of the country, Ballycatten is well

Three-ring embankment fort at Ballycatten: its moats – in near-perfect condition – saw many a battle.
The Vikings are reputed to been first defeated here and repulsed in south Munster by the native Irish.
During their retreat, the Vikings burned Ballycatten village and the nearby church at Kilmore.
Photo: Martin Moir

placed to provide a central vantage point of a large area. Its defences consists
of three concentric banks and three fosses, the inner diameter is about 200 feet
while the total outer diameter is around 390 feet. The whole earthworks cover
approximately three statute acres. It had at one time a fourth outer embankment which was not fossed, and more than likely it was here that it carried the
first line of defence as previously mentioned. The excavation showed that the
inner bank was not itself regarded as sufficient defence for it was here that
they discovered that a palisade of wooden posts were put in position about six
feet inside the crest of the inner bank and, after the survey team removed
nearly four and a half feet of fill, they found that the builders had to cut
through nearly six feet of rock. The defences must have been formidable in
their original state.

The entrance to the fort was on the south-east side and consisted of two
gates, one inner and one outer. The centre of the fort was tilled and corn grown
there in 1790, and was also very much used as a grazing paddock for horses
and cattle over the last several hundred years. Top dressing with farmyard
manure would explain why the excavation on the upper turf levels found so
many nails, horseshoes and other items. Black deposits were found, and it was
here that some unglazed pottery and some bronze pieces came to light. At the
edge of this black deposit, a stone-built kiln was located. At a depth of nineteen

inches, the stones averaged twelve inches in height and five inches thick. The material – a close-grained sandstone – showed signs of intense heat. The whole area of this activity was about nineteen feet by five feet. The flue of the kiln was covered with slate and sealed with clay.

The kiln is similar to the Romano British pottery kilns found at Dorchester and Oxfordshire in England. The kiln at Ballycatten more than likely was used for making pottery.

Twelve hearths were found, as were post-holes which indicated possible round, thatched huts. Three elaborate souterrains were found consisting of several small chambers. In most cases, the roofs had caved in, and on the floor of the passages a quantity of seeds were found, identified as abundant on sea coasts. The souterrain stone walls were dry-built.

Bronze pieces more than likely used on a horse bridle were found at a depth of sixteen inches. These were believed to date from the eighth century: AD 700–800. There was evidence to show that this find was similar to a find at Vendel in Uppland in Sweden. Yellow glass was also found as was a penannular brooch, complete with pin. The inside diameter of the ring was 25mm, the barrel of which was 3mm and tapered to a total length of about 52mm. It was dated about to the late sixth or early seventh century. Two dark-blue glass beads were found in a pocket of ashes near a stone hearth; these beads had a hollow cylinder (diameter 8mm, height 6mm, diameter of boring 5.5mm). These were found at a depth of sixteen inches.

A small, lead spinning top with a central bronze core (diameter of top was 25mm) was believed to be from early Roman times. A total of twenty-three iron objects were found – some modern, some ancient – including an axe head which was located on the floor of a souterrain. This type of axe was widely used by the Teutonic peoples and became very popular in Ireland when introduced by the Scandinavians.

Twenty whetstones were found; these close-grained, water-rolled sandstones were more than likely obtained from the sea. The stones were polished from use and one stone looked like it could be held in the hand and used as a pestle for crushing or pounding grain. Two fragments of rotary querns and one spindle whorl were found (about 400mm diameter). Around thirty pieces of flint were located: these black flint stones looked like that they might have been picked up at the seashore and some of them seemed to have been deliberately brought to a point.

Nine crucible fragments were found, made of clay and baked to a hard stone-like quality. Some were glazed on the outside and partially inside the rim. About sixty pieces of unglazed pottery came from the black deposit. A small quantity of animal bones was discovered, as were several piles of limpet and periwinkles. The excavation team estimated the main occupation date of Ballycatten Fort at around AD 550.

Ancient Churches and Cells

There are more than 6,000 places in Ireland whose name begins with the word Bally, from *baile* – a town. There are about 1,400 townlands or villages with names beginning with the word *Lis*, and half that number again beginning with *Dún*. Another 700 or so begin with *Rath*. All three words signify fortifications of one kind or another. *Ceall*, *cill* or *kil* refers to the existence of an ancient church or cell, but is often confused with *coill* – a wood – and with *ceal* or *keel* – a burial ground.

At Kilnacloona, close to the Bandon river, a church once stood, and according to tradition was built by St Finbarr, the patron saint of Cork. Finbarr, the son of Amargein, a master smith, was born near Bandon in Co. Cork in the year AD 560. It's probably around this time that the church buildings which were to flourish in the region were built.

Overlooking the outer harbour of Kinsale, close to the village of Sandycove, can be found the remains of a seventeenth-century village. Several of its mud and stone walls survive, and close by is Kilroan (St Rohan's church), now known as Cuirt a Poirtin – the 'Court of the Little Bog'. One of its holy water fonts, possibly of Cornish or Celtic design, was found in the nearby spray field and subseqently placed in the refurbished Ballinspittle church. The church stands roofless at the very edge of a shaley cliff severely affected by sea erosion. The church was built of rough stone, and possibly had a cobbled roof. Given its round-tower windows, it probably dates back to the sixth or seventh century. A rectangular building measuring thirty-two feet by twenty feet (external dimension), its walls are about two feet and eight inches thick. Its narrow entrance door, only two feet and six inches wide, is in its western gable. The narrow slits that let in the rays of sunshine are on the eastern gable, so that the head monk or abbot preaching on an elevated platform in a small darkened room with the rays of the early morning sunshine beaming through the tiny slits would have his outline projected onto the wall.

Nearby is Kilooney, where once stood a pre-tenth-century church. Called Killuna, after a saint of the O'Driscoll clan, it was taxed as a chapel of ease in the Taxation Roll of 1302. A chapel of ease was a church built for people who lived a long distance from a parish church.

At Kilcoleman, closer to the sea, another little church braved the elements. Around 150 years ago, a gold ring was found here. On its inside was an inscription: 'Brek not thie promis to pleas thine eie but feare God and learne to die i.h.s.'

Kilroan church, believed to be sixth century. A rough-stone building, with only slits for windows, looks across at the outer confines of Kinsale Harbour.

Another church mentioned in the Taxation Roll of 1302 was the nearby Kilkerrin church, in the townland of Kilgobbin, called after Gobhan, the saint from Kinsale. In Kilanetig could be found a small Mass house which was desecrated by Donncha Dubh (McCarthy), a highwayman who would stable his horses within. Both of these churches were in the parish of Ballinadee, a little, well-kept hamlet whose old name we believe was Templemichael, after the Knights Templar. Within the Ballinadee area can also be found Pairc a Cille (Field of the Church) and Cill an Faoitig (White's Church).

At Ballycatten, an ancient church was situated just south of the present fort at what is today called Kilmore, meaning 'Big Church'. This church was in a vulnerable position because it stood outside the defensive walls of the fort, and was destroyed by the Vikings. All that remains today are a few stones and the name of the church lawn – Faitche Cill Mór. Later, another small church was built not far from Kilmore and was to serve the village of Ballycatten for several hundred years. A survey map of 1650 shows the townland of Kilbeg (Small Church), where the former little church once stood. In the late thirteenth century, with its thatched roof in a bad state of repair, it was decided to replace it with a new, larger church high on a hilltop. This Norman-style church, built at Templetrine, was dedicated to St Treun (Trinity), a disciple of

St Finbarr. In 1302, we see this church taxed at four-and-a-half marks.

In the sixteenth century, a large portion of the Christian church was reformed by breaking away from Rome. This resulted in two sets of Christian values, each believing in the same God. The Reformed Christian Church had its origins in Henry VIII's disagreement with the pope over marriage laws. The Reformed Church attempted to stamp its ideals on its fellow Christians, and

'Slit' window at Kilroan church.

confiscated and reformed the vast majority of churches in England, Ireland and Europe. Templetrine church was reformed in 1588, one of the first in this area. In most cases, the burial places around the confiscated churches were still used by both sets of Christians. However, Penal Laws were enforced, and anyone caught practising the Christian belief of Rome could suffer a sever sentence, including the death penalty. Those driven from their place of worship continued to practise their beliefs in remote valleys, glens and rock outcrops, known as Mass rocks. Several of these places of worship were in the parish of Courceys. Religious services were conducted at the western approaches of the Old Head, in a place known as File an Aifreann (the Cliff of the Mass), and just north of the village of Ballinspittle, at Carraig an Oigin (or an Neidin – the Rock of the Ivy). This latter Mass rock was unmarked for years, but towards the end of the twentieth century, the holy place was again brought to life by Canon Thomas Kelleher who erected a great, white cross to mark the place where long ago so many Christians worshiped, some of whom payed the ultimate price for their beliefs. Another place used for worship in those days was Cablac an Aifrinn, which can be found down the cliffs, south of Sandycove Island on the western edge of Kinsale Harbour.

When Templetrine was reformed around 1588, the now disused site of Kilbeg – which I believe to be at the elevated point at Garrettstown upper – was used by the Kearney family, who were driven out of Limerick by Queen Elizabeth around the year 1588. They then settled in Garrettstown. Later, some of the Kearneys changed to the Reformed Church and used Templetrine as their place of worship.

Templetrine became disused in 1781. A new church, with a neat edifice and a square tower, was built in 1821 on the summit of a hill. A glebe house was built in 1822 as was a schoolhouse with a residence for a master. At the same time, a female schoolhouse – supported by Miss Cuthbert of the Kearneys – was built at Garrettstown by the waterfall on the main road to the beach.

All that remains of the old Norman church at Templetrine is part of its south gable wall, which is now the tomb and resting place for some of the Kearneys. In the aftermath of the decrees of 1750–51, Bishop Richard Walsh affected at least eight parochial reorganisations. In his erection of a new church in Ballinspittle and his appointment of Denis McCarthy as parish priest in 1750, he formed the new parish of Courceys by uniting the ancient parishes of Ringrone, Kilroan, Templetrine and Ballinadee. The name Courceys did not come into use until 1810. The new church in Ballinspittle was completed in 1752, the Penal Laws by now very much relaxed. Most of the local Catholic landlords had survived with their estates relatively intact; among these were the Kearney family of Garrettstown and Gerald Gibbons of Ballymacredmond. These were very influential in the area and probably helped Rev. Denis McCarthy in getting the church built in Ballinspittle.

The Vikings

There is an ancient Irish chronicle which relates the actions of Brian Boruma, king of Munster. In the second year of his reign, the bloodthirsty Brian sent a challenge to Miles Mac Broiu, chief of the Mahoneys and king of the Eóghanacht – a part of south Carbery in west Cork. Brian would fight Mac Broiu in a pitched battle on the plains of Beallagh Leachta – the road of St Leachta, the patron saint of Donnaghmore, near Macroom and Mallow – so as to avenge the death of his brother, Mahon, who had been murdered by O'Donovan Mac Cahill, chief of that sept and a dependant on O'Mahoney. The king of Carbery accepted the challenge, and besides his own and O'Donovan's forces, brought 1,500 Danes to assist him. A fierce battle was fought but Brian Boruma's forces, being superior in number, broke through the enemy. There followed a great slaughter in which huge numbers of O'Mahoneys and O'Donovans were slain, along with most of the Danes.

In AD 997, Brian Boruma (Boru) and his rival Máel Sechnaill II – over-king of the Uí Neills – met at Clonfert and divided Ireland between them. The agreement made Brian master of Dublin and Leinster. Two years later, Brian – now high king of Ireland – and Máel Morda, king of Leinster, defeated the Norsemen occupying Dublin. Later, Mael Morda formed an alliance with Sitric Silkenbeard, the Norse ruler of Dublin. Such alliances were common – the first Viking–Irish alliance was reported in AD 842, when Sitric summoned Sigurd of Orkney, Brodir of Man, and even Thorstein Hallson of Iceland for the Battle of Clontarf. The battle raged all day long on Good Friday 1014; the eighty-seven-year-old Boru was in his tent when Mael Morda broke through Boru's bodyguard and stabbed the high king of Ireland and leader of the Dál gCais dynasty to death. He died at the hands of a fellow Irish king, Mael Morda, who was captured, tied to a stake, tortured and had his testicles removed and hung around his neck. Boru's furious army got its revenge with its defeat of the Vikings.

Though the Vikings ultimately failed, they established a number of settlements and were the founders of all our major cities as we know them today. Quite a number of Scandinavian words are mingled in the present Irish language, many of them associated with sailing, fishing and trading – words such as *ancaire* (anchor), *bád* (boat), *scód* (rudder) *stiúr* (sheet) *dorgha* (fishing line), *langa* (ling), *trosc* (cod), *margad* (market), *pinginn* (penny), *scilling* (shilling) and *gate* (street).

The Normans

The one and only true conquest of Ireland was that of the Anglo-French Normans. It was swift and they stamped their authority throughout the island of Ireland.

Within a short time of landing, the Normans set up strong-points and, at first, erected wooden towers surrounded by an outer stockade. Foremost among them were the Arundels of Ring, the Barrys of Barryroe, the Hodnets of Lislee, Carews at Bantry, Barretts at Glandore, the Fitzgibbons, Fitzgeralds, de Cogan on the east, Powers and de Courceys. After consolidating their position, the Norman craftsmen were set to work constructing stone fortifications, evidence of which we can still see today. The castle at the Old Head was a fine example of such buildings. In 1215, Nicholas Buidhe de Barrie built a castle at Timoleague, and other Barry castles sprung up, such as Castlefreke and Dún Deide at the Galley Head.

In 1260, the McCarthys wreaked havoc; they burned, spoiled and slaughtered, and many an innocent person fell before them. Norman castles all over south Munster became targets – some were destroyed and more occupied. Their first reverse was at the siege of Timoleague castle. The Norman family of the Barrys now ruled Ibane, Barryroe and, further west, the area of Ardfield – but their land was cut in two by a belt of McCarthy's land which reached the sea at Clonakilty, and the McCarthy Riabhachs had by now established themselves in Kilbrittain. They suppressed many native Irish families including the O'Heas, O'Floinns and Cowhigs. The Barrys, Hodnets and even Lord Arundel of the strand at Ring Castle all now owed allegiance to McCarthy.

The stonemason was the man of this era and given plenty of scope to carry out his trade. The little walled town of Timoleague grew around the friary in the Norman fashion. The first friars reached Ireland and landed in Youghal, Co. Cork in 1214. Their first Irish house was founded in 1231 and, according to the *Annals of the Four Masters*, the foundation of the abbey at Timoleague was in 1240. For surely Timoleague was of Norman creation – it boasted urban officials with courts of law, fairs and markets and, when Bandon was a shaking morass, Timoleague was a town with more than a dozen taverns and resthouses where Irish merchants and Spanish traders did their business, and ladies of leisure did a brisk trade.

With such a sparse population in Ireland at this time, to find a mating partner was difficult, prompting the aristocratic Anglo-French Normans to marry into quite a number of the noble Irish families. Margaret de Courcey, eldest daughter of Milo de Courcey, married Lord William Barry. Lawrence Barryroe married Orla, daughter of O'Brien, Lord of Thomond (Thomond: Tuathmuhumhan; this area was what is now most of Co. Clare and the adjacent parts of Co. Limerick and Co. Tipperary). Later, the McCarthys and de Courcey were bonded in marriage, but the bickering continued and family feuds hindered the growth of unity. In 1507, Barryroe and his chiefs went on a pilgrimage to Spain but were all drowned on their journey home.

In the middle of the sixteenth century, the Barry Roe lordship was racked by a succession dispute in which James Fitz Richard Barry, whose father had been bastardised by an annulment, slew or exiled his cousins and made himself lord.

Edmund de Courcey, who was bishop of Ross (Ross was the old ecclesiastical See now known as Rosscarbery, west Cork), resigned his See in 1517. De Courcey acted as papal legate and the English King Henry VII had great confidence in him. He retired to Timoleague Abbey where he died in 1518. Many great and noble families are buried in Timoleague, such as the McCarthy Reaghs, O'Sullivans, O'Heas, O'Mahoneys, O'Donovans and O'Dalys. William Barry and his wife, Margaret, were buried there in 1373. When the republican Oliver Cromwell arrived in 1640, the graves of the noble Irish lords were desecrated and their bones scattered in the bay of Timoleague estuary and washed by the waters of the Arigideen river. During Pococke's tour of south-west Ireland in 1752, he describes Timoleague as a poor place – 'a village with one short street, of very indifferent buildings; on the east end of it are the ruins of a castle, and near it the monastery of Franciscans of which there are great remains.'

The effect of the Goidelic conquests in the south of Ireland was to shatter the power of the once dominant Érainn. One section of them was henceforth confined to the west and south of the Bandon river; in ancient times, this area was called Laoidhe, and came to be known as the Corca Laoidhe. But even this restricted territory was not left to them intact; the district between Courtmacsherry Bay and Kinsale Harbour, including the Old Head of Kinsale, had been wrested from them by one of the branches of the Goidels. This branch, the Eóghanacht (the clan-name of the descendants of Eóghan, son of Oilioll Olum to which many of the main families of south Munster belonged) of Raithlinn (later Gurranes, Templemartin) near Bandon had apparently no use for Dún Cermna, the great fortress and city of the Érainn, and from then on it lost its importance. Writing around AD 150, Ptolemy – in his description of Ireland – places the Iverni, or Érainn, in what is now Co. Cork (and perhaps Co. Kerry as well), and mentions a city called Ivernis, presumably the capital of Érainn. In the same region, Ptolemy, although writing in the second century AD, was using older material for his account of Ireland.

Early tradition in Ireland, says the historian O'Rahilly, unmistakably connects Dún Cermna with the Érainn, and we may justifiably equate it with the town of Ivernis which Ptolemy, or rather his earlier sources, place in this very district. The Érainn group did not, however, disappear, and in various districts throughout the south, and particularly in counties Cork and Kerry, remained for centuries and formed the Gaels, the roots from which the later population grew. At some future date, a scientific excavation should be carried out to throw light on the predecessors of the Goidels in Munster and, one might say, the capital of the Érainn.

Oilioll Olum was king of Munster in the third century AD. After his death, his son Eóghan inherited south Munster. The group of families that descended from this Eóghan was known before the introduction of surnames as the Eóghanacht (Magh Feimin). This is where the surname McCarthy came from, with its various branches in the Kinsale region. It was from here that tribal divisions came into being. Two more branches were formed: the Uí Eachach, one of whose branches had Aedh as its founder. They adopted the surname O'Mahony and occupied the present barony of Kinalea (Cineal Aedh), to the east of Kinsale.

The de Courceys, the great Anglo-Norman family after whom this barony is called, changed their name – as did many other Norman families – from de Courcey to Mac Patrick, and the Old Head fortress became Dún Mhic Phádraig (Mac Patrick's Fort); it had sometimes been known as Cape Courcey during its occupation by that family, and today, amongst local Irish-speakers, it is referred to as Seana Cheann (the Old Head).

In old Spanish, Portuguese, Italian and Dutch maps, the Old Head is marked and named in their various languages: Cap Veco, Cap Pucis, Cauo Antiquo, Cauo Vechio and Cauo Bechi. In a Spanish document, it is described as Cabo de Velbo – the 'Cape of the Light, or Beacon', which burned on its summit from time immemorial. Just north-west of the present lighthouse can still be seen the mounds of Cermna's Dún – approximately twenty-five-yards square – and more remains lie under the present castle foundations and fortifications.

William Shakespeare once fittingly described the Old Head: 'It is a cliff whose high and bending head looks fearfully on the confined deep'. A poem by Bligh Talbot Crosbie describes it thus:

> This old world coast of fiord and promontory
> Whose off sets rude with placid inlets draw
> Has many a lovely cove with friendly Shaw
> Of bright arbutus hushed as purgatory
> Has many a buttressed coign above the hoary
> And never resting surf, with vapours raw
> And chill as breathed from some sea monsters naw
> Blinded, but none more stupid in plangent story
> Than this vast hammer head, with fluty work
> Fashioned for dispertions utmost throw
> This old Kinsale in whose stark cranium lurk
> The legion presidents of war and woe
> Known to the Dane, the Saxon, and the Turk,
> Called by the Spaniards Cabo de Velbo.

Clinging to the Remote Outcrops

With the wholesale destruction of the Western way of life by the barbarians that followed the fall of the Roman Empire, Irish monks retreated to remote outcrops. The Skellig Rocks off the coast of Kerry is typical of such places, as was Glendalough in Co. Wicklow, where St Kevin established a monastery.

Another such place exists at the Old Head of Kinsale. This is a barren rock or island, which at one time was only accessible from the sea. A well-constructed wall in the Romanesque style now connects it. Certainly, what is now Kinsale Harbour would be no stranger to Roman traders who we believe used the port quite frequently. The wall, which is about midway on the eastern side of the peninsula of the Old Head, is about fifty feet high and contains an archway complete with a keystone. However, the underside of the archway is built up, and the architecture would suggest it dates from around the sixth or

Cush Wall with its prominent Romanesque arch. Possibly of the fifth or sixth century – or earlier – this wall joins a small island on the eastern side of the Old Head of Kinsale.

seventh century. It is unclear as to why the archway was constructed with such a prominent keystone. There seems to have been a similar wall running parallel, a piece of which can still be seen. More than likely, the two walls supported a wooden bridge of some sort.

The present wall at the top is about two feet wide, just enough for one person to pass, thus making it very easy to defend. Clearly visible is the hand-cut track leading to and from it. This little rock outcrop rolls down to the sea facing the south-east, and with no protection or shelter in a storm, the conditions here must have been severe, especially in wintertime. It is bare and barren except for some wild grass, and there is no sign of any type of shelter such as the beehive huts found on the remote Kerry coast. But noticeable on the land side on its higher elevation are a few small indentations in the ground: half-circular in shape, perhaps the only sign that some dedicated people could have lived there. As the men of God meditated in their remote locations following the fall of Rome, they felt safe from the hands of the barbarous hoards sweeping across Europe. The present name on this little track is the Cush Wall. This phonetic spelling of the Irish word *cois* means 'foot'. However, it is nearly impossible to pin down why the wall was built and by whom. In pre-Christian times, it is mentioned that the Phoenicians knew of the area which we now know as the Old Head of Kinsale. The Bible (Genesis) refers to a people called Cush who lived in the north-east of Africa, around

Cush Wall.

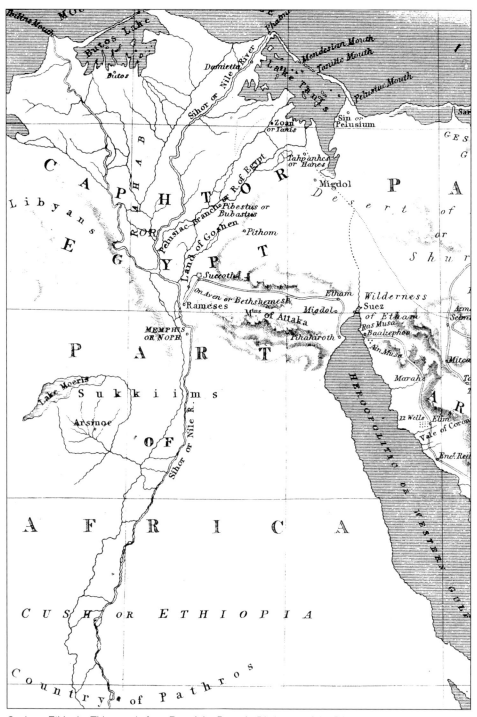

Cush, or Ethiopia: This map is from Rev. John Brown's *Dictionary of the Bible.*

Ethiopia and southern Egypt. Cush was the oldest son of Ham, brother of Canaan. The Cush descended from the Phoenicians, the ancient peoples who occupied a coastal area known as Phoenicia, today called Syria, and it was here that they set up trading posts, pushing their trade as far as Britain and, perhaps, to Ireland, too. Famed for learning, they are said to have been the inventors of letters. They were also noted for wall-building, and built small cities on islands joined by an isthmus.

The Rev. John Brown's *Dictionary of the Bible* contains the following:

> Cush, *blackness*: (1) The eldest son of Ham, and father of Nimrod, Seba, Havilah, Sabtah, Ramah, and Sabtecha. and the grandfather of Sheba and Dedan. His posterity took up their primitive abodes, on the east and west and of the lower part of the Euphrates; and in Arabia, chiefly that part of it called The Happy, Gen. x. 6–8.
>
> (2) The name of some countries where Cush or his posterity dwelt, called Ethiopia by the Greeks and other translators . . .
>
> (3) Cush, Ethopia or Abyssinia, a country on the south-west of the Red sea, and south of Egypt . . .

Close by the Old Head, not far from the Cush Wall, lies Black Head. Why, I have never been able to ascertain, but is there some connection with the Cush, meaning 'blackness'? Could these have been our first traders, with their outpost at the eastern side of the Old Head guarding the entrance to the Bandon estuary?

Cush Wall.

Famine

The terrible fate that befell so many during the Famine of 1845–47 was not visited on the families of Garrettstown estate. Here, each household was provided with a cottage or lodge for which a small fee was deducted from the householder's wages at the end of the week. Thirteen of these dwellings graced the hill of Laherne near the sea. Each had a plot of land for vegetables and received a few stone of wheat each month, with plenty of milk and butter. Most held onto their small fishing boats as the sea abounded with fish. In other areas around the coast, the poor souls sold their boats. Contrary to teaching, the Famine was not caused by the English but by the Anglo-Irish: most of our grain was exported for want of a better price. The best grain in this part of Ireland was grown at Garrettstown and, when it was dried, contained nearly 700 grains to the ounce. Farm labourers in the area were paid sixpence a day, without food – at best, they might get a light breakfast. But at the Kearney estate, they were paid six-and-a-half pence per day complete with breakfast which consisted of bread, butter and milk, and for dinner, bread, milk and potatoes.

The pay list for workers in Garrettstown estate on the week ending Saturday 22 October 1864, compiled by Abraham Foster (land steward), illustrates what a typical family lived on. A single man earned 5 shillings a week. He started work at 6am and finished around 9pm, Monday to Saturday. If lucky, he might finish early – around 7pm – on Saturday night. The milkers

Pay list of Garrettstown estate from January 1864, made out by Abraham Thomas Foster JP, steward of Garrettstown estate.

had a rota for working Sundays. Fathers, sons and daughters all worked on the estate and were paid each Saturday night. The forty-seven employees on this pay list were due a weekly total of £10/6s./9d.; stoppages were £2/13s./5d., leaving a pay-out of £7/13s./4d. According to the list, John White and his son were paid 9 shillings, of which 1s./10d. was stopped; Jim Long was due 5 shillings but stopped 3s./6d. and owed 2 shillings for pigs; Jerry Sullivan was paid 5 shillings but stopped 4 shillings and owed for wool to the tune of 2s./6d.; Tom Coveney was paid 5 shillings and stopped 5 shillings – the poor man worked the week for nothing; Daniel Meenig (McCarthy), his son and three daughters were paid 15s./5d. and stopped 1s./8d.; Jack White and his three sons were paid 16s./6d. and stopped 8s./4d., and he had a debt of 5 shillings.

There were several famines down through the ages, caused by harsh winters and either dry or very wet summers. The choice of food was limited and most of the population depended on the soil for survival. In 1683, one of the hardest winters hit this general area; the River Lee was frozen for many weeks – so much so that horses and carriages passed over from the ferry slip to the east marsh. In late 1739, the River Lee again froze solid, as did all the other major rivers in the county and throughout most of the country. Wheat was very scarce and during the following summer the poor perished in their hundreds. All rank of people came together and many thousands of the lower class were saved by being daily fed in Cork city and other towns.

During the Famine of 1847, the Irish middle class played a big part in the whole sorry saga for in came the middleman at the fairs and markets, known as the tangler, which means to twist and to trap somebody in a difficult situation.

The outline of eighteenth-century mud-walled cabins of the poor cliff-dwellers at the edge of the cliff-face between Garrettstown and Courtmacsherry. Numerous such dwellings dotted the shoreline. Their small plots of land, on which they grew their crops, were fertilised with kelp from the shoreline. The locals used to throw vast amounts of stones into the sea which would be retrieved when kelp had attached itself to them.

When the poor unfortunate man or woman went to sell their fowl and stock, and tried to get the best price they could so they could pay their rent and support their starving families, they were beaten down to the lowest price and sometimes in pure desperation sold their stock for a mere nothing to the tangler. Unable to pay their rent, a number of families were evicted from their homes by unscrupulous landlords.

Large Famine cooking pot. These cast-iron pots were used to cook the gruel to feed the starving during the Famine years of 1845–47.

I had the privilege in the mid-1970s of speaking to a good friend of mine who had emigrated to America during the late 1920s; when he was a little boy living at the Old Head, his grandmother told him a true story of the great Famine. This lady was born in 1837 and lived at the Old Head in a little house up against the present castle wall. Young and pretty that she was in 1847, and barely ten years old, she witnessed the horrors of the Famine. She mentioned going bare-foot to Kilmore mill near Garrettstown to get a handout of meal, which was doled out to the hungry and starving people; she also mentioned seeing some poor wretched creatures crawling and begging on the dusty roadside. The local beaches and rocks at Garrettstown were swarming with people she did not know – they had come from the towns and surrounding countryside picking and gathering limpets, mussels, periwinkles and even seaweed of the green type – anything that they could get to eat among the rocks which were laid bare. She knew one farmer by name who had a fine field of turnips guarded by a man and a dog; it was all to no avail – the turnips were lifted and eaten where they grew.

At least twenty years before the great hunger of the 1840s, emigration was on the rise and, with a growing population, the need for food was great. Maize was introduced but many of the poor people did not know how to cook it.

On an island off the Cork coast, a ship foundered carrying gold of all sorts, some of which was found by the natives. Tea was new to the area at that time and when it was introduced to the island, it was paid for in gold balanced on a scales. The tea was boiled, the water thrown away and the leaves eaten – this was from force of habit since the root crops they were use to were boiled and the water dumped.

Though the Old Head and district endured great suffering during the Famine, very little is documented about this great tragedy. Most of the small landholders, with their plots and stone or mud cottages, either starved to death or departed their homeland for a foreign land. The larger landholder held out and most, if not all, the plots of land left behind were absorbed into the larger holding. A great-grand-uncle of mine from my father's side was hired in this locality to bury the dead and to give them a dignified funeral. This man had a large horse and cart, sometimes draped with a black cloth, and in this cart was a wide box with two handles – one on each end. There was no such thing as going to the church for a service or Mass; a dead person went straight from his house or in some cases the body was picked up from the field or roadside and put into this box with several others. The horse and cart would make its way along the dusty road or track to some lonely graveyard, watched by residents peering out from their humble shacks – malnourished mothers clutching and holding their starving babies, suckling the last drop from their breast, and children peering – some so weak they could hardly walk at all – wondering who would be next. In most cases, it was the poor and uneducated who perished.

In the graveyard, a larger than normal grave would be opened up. When the cart reached its destination, a number of men would lift out the large, plain coffin-like box and placed it over the open grave. The box had a sliding bottom and when this was pulled all the bodies fell into the hole. This sequence of events was repeated several times until the grave was full – it was then closed up. Very few markings were left and no names recorded or etched on stone to indicate the spot where they lay. Old Henry White carried on collecting bodies, for he was under pay of Garrettstown estate, and it was there also that several of the rough coffins were made; more were made at Kilmore mill.

For some, it was an embarrassment as neighbours watched their fellow human beings beg, starve and eventually pay the ultimate price – death.

Ruin of a 'Famine' village at Courtaparteen.

Etched forever in the solid rock and laid bare by the constant erosion of the sea are the tracks of horse-drawn carts. Close to the Old Head, this was once a dust-covered track that weaved its way around the rocky coastline.

Very little was handed down or spoken about concerning this tragic time in our sad history in case the skeletons might fall out of the cupboard, for that is surely what happened. After the big winter storms of 1989, a number of human remains were found at a garden patch close to a gable end of an old mud cabin which became exposed by the exceptionally high seas. This was at the western end of the Old Head, an area which before the Famine was littered with mud cabins of the poor cliff dwellers. These were driven to the extremities of existence, their backs to the land of their forefathers and nothing in front of them but the vast Atlantic Ocean that so many of them would eventually cross, and with many of them paying the ultimate price on their hazardous journey to the Promised Land.

Some of those who stayed at home would eventually succumb to the horrors of the Famine, only to be buried in a pauper's grave. One family from the Old Head was saved that humiliation, for they buried their loved ones in the little garden of their house facing the sea.

The Cores and the Kearneys

It's known that John Core lived in Garrettstown around the 1600s, and that successive members of that family were called Garrett – hence Garrettstown. There is a place in Liscaroll in north Cork in the barony of Orrery where a celebrated battle was fought on 3 September in the year 1642 at the site of an old Danish fort, now called Lis-Garret. It was here that eighteen of these Cores, with 1,500 other brave Irishmen under the command of Lord Mountgarret, were slain whilst defending the fort against the English under the command of Lord Inchiquin. They were buried close to where they fell.

Edmund Kearney came to Garrettstown around the 1620s, during the rein of James I, and the family resided at Garrettstown for close to 250 years. They were forced from Co. Limerick by the oppression of the Earl of Desmond (Desmond Deasmhumhan consisted of all of what is now known as Kerry and a big portion of Co. Cork) during the reign of Queen Elizabeth. The original name of the family was Eoin Ní Chearna, and they hailed from the Six Mile Bridge area of Co. Clare.

The Kearney family first lived in lower Garrettstown where they had succeeded in dislocating the occupiers, the Cores, who by now had become outlaws. This once fine and handsome fortified house – looking down the valley with a view of the Old Head in the distance – became a century later too costly to keep and was in a bad state of repair, prompting the Kearneys to build a new and more modern house in an elevated position – the present Garrettstown House. Before the family left the old site, they planted a grove of oak trees to the north – consisting of about three acres – and to the south of the house, in the lawn, they planted a single oak tree and surrounded it with a circular stone wall. About three foot high and thirty yards in diameter, an oval plaque was placed at its base bearing the inscription:

> This oak is the produce of an acorn set here in February 1759 and at three feet above the ground measures now in October 1794 forty-two inches girth. Most of the lower branches trail along the ground and covered a circumference of sixty-nine feet. This shows how much a finer tree an oak makes that had when young sufficient room to spread.

Sadly, this tree and the oak grove were cut down in the late Fifties. Ironically, the marble plaque survived and can be seen embedded in the wall of an entrance to a modern bungalow very close to its original spot. One reminder of the Cores that remains to the present day is their messenger house, which is in near-perfect state. It was from here that the trained carrier pigeons flew far and wide, their masters' messages attached to their legs. Weeks later, they would return to their houses – in most cases, their messages delivered. The slate ledges upon which they used to perch were removed about fifty years ago.

In the period around 1571, Maurice Roche, mayor of Cork, was presented with a silver collar of the order of St Simplicius for able services rendered against the Desmond insurgents. This collar was preserved by Roche's descendent – Thomas C. Kearney esq. of Garrettstown – and today it resides in the Fitzgerald Museum in Cork city.

In 1730, Francis Kearney, described as a landlord from nearby Garrettstown, offered the friars of Kinsale a site for their church in the poorer section of the town, among the weavers on Lower Catholic Walk which was just below their old residence. In 1735, the friars built a friary, a storehouse, a garden and a small church on the site. Fr Patrick O'Mahoney O'Carm purchased the plot in 1737 and was appointed prior in 1739. An attempt was made in 1744 to imprison Fr O'Mahoney for owning land, but he was exonerated through Kearney claiming ownership of the property. Later, in 1747, Fr O'Mahoney was appointed Town Almoner.

James Kearney was MP for the Kinsale area from 1768–97 and, in 1799, James was made escheator of Munster. He died unmarried in 1812. This family was the undisputed owner of Garrettstown estate and its 1,865 acres.

Garrettstown House. Though now roofless – a testimony to the destruction of the 1960s – it still stands defiant, its pineapple finials on the entrance gate pointing to the sky.

After his death, his first cousin, Thomas Rochford, came into possession of the estate. James Kearney's two spinster sisters continued to reside at Kilmore house near Ballycatten. In 1833, one of the sisters – Mary Kearney – still held property at Kilmore in her name: 3 acres and 2 roods of waste and 66 acres of arable land; the total value of her land was £74/5s. All that remains of the house today are its square entrance pillars and beach-lined drive.

The Kearney family, like other families along the south-west coast of Ireland, are reputed to have become rich through smuggling. They built for themselves a grand house with two wings facing each other across the fore-court in the Palladian manner, levelling the site out of solid rock and at great expense, the evidence of which can be still seen today. The two wings, constructed with an attractive golden stone, featured handsome pediment façades, each with a rusticated doorway, and faced each other across the fore-court.

The two wings continued to serve their respective purposes of house and stable right down through the years. The house had seventeen bedrooms and large reception rooms, and was complete with a library. There was also a vast kitchen with a huge open fire. A very unusual feature in the house was a dog spit: a dog would walk around in circles, working a series of bars moving over the fire so that the huge joint of meat was cooked in an even manner.

Surrounding the house were a beautiful garden and grounds. Handsome stone-gate piers with pineapple finials and wrought-iron gates guarded the entrance. Inside the main gate stood a huge yew tree, five foot in diameter, its trailing branches shading the kitchen windows.

On passing through the main white-painted door, one would enter a large hall with two rooms on either side. The hall floor was covered with reindeer skins which came from the deer that roamed the two parks close by. On the walls hung guns, swords, pikes and a few knives, all with a story to tell. Scenes from the plays of Shakespeare graced the sides of the huge winding staircase that led to the rooms above. In the dining-room hung many a painting of its former owners, their eagle eyes bearing upon you.

Outside were a bake-house, brew-house and many other smaller houses. Its cobblestone yard consisted of a well where a large banded timber bucket was winched up and down. In the shade of the yard, a large food safe stood. Pork was smoked in a large, upturned barrel from which sides of pork were hung while a boy kept sawdust burning around the barrel, suspended a foot above the cobblestones.

The stables, still intact to this day, lay across the large and once gravelled yard from its now roofless dwelling house; the façade of each was the same. Part of these stables once housed the very ancient carriages in which the Kearneys and the Rochforts travelled with their riders and outriders. Four horses – two white, two black – drew the carriages.

The Kearneys enclosed the estate with approximately ten miles of stone walls, some as high as nine feet. They used up to 40,000 tons of stone, a huge proportion of which was cut and faced by the stonemasons. Thousands of tons of stone more were used to construct two farmyards with all sorts of outhouses and dwellings. Several miles of smaller walls, about four foot high, were built with a type of slate stone which was stood on edge. All in all, an enormous feat of engineering for its day.

At the western edge of Garrettstown beach are the ruins of a lonely house. The rocks here were cut out so boats could be launched and brought ashore after a day's fishing, for this was the bathing house of the Kearneys, Cuthberts and Rochforts. Their clothes were looked after while they bathed in the pools nearby. Still to be seen today is the little pathway cut over the rocks and the few steps that lead down to the water's edge. Until recent times, this house was occupied by the Hayes family and they had the privilege of having Robert Gibbings – author of *Sweet Cork of Thee* and *How Lovely is the Lee* – stay there in peace and tranquillity so as to write.

In the latter part of the eighteenth century, this house was occupied by a family of Donovans, one of whom was a blacksmith. It was he who made the beautiful entrance gates and grille work with the Kearneys' initials and the date of 1775. This man left Garrettstown for America during the Famine.

At the rear entrance to Garrettstown House, over the archway, stood two eagles with outstretched wings – as if waiting to fend off intruders – and towards the south was a handsome orchard and gardens, very well laid out in the eighteenth-century style; the west part of the garden contained a handsome amphitheatre, the ground being naturally suited for that purpose.

To the west of the house, there is a chalybeate saline spring; this was discovered during excavation for a new canal on the north end of the present pond. The water is a crimson colour and has a strong taste. In 1750, a sample was taken to Cork where it preserved these qualities for several weeks. Upon evaporation, a failed attempt was made to move with a magnet the nine grains

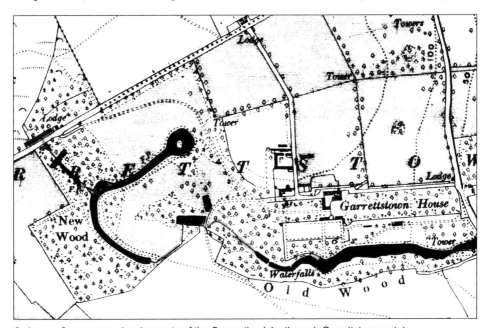

Ordnance Survey map showing route of the Serpentine lake through Garrettstown estate.

Serpentine lake, once graced by black swans, was constructed by the Kearney family in 1750. Great thought was put into its design: at the head of the lake is a small island and, with its long narrow sweeping tail, it depicts a serpent.

One of the several waterfalls that cascaded down the valley onto cobblestone bases and through at least four small ponds.

43

Remains of an eighteenth-century round tower on the Kearney estate at Garrettstown. Six of these towers graced the estate and were known as look-outs. Several other gazebos, tree-houses and statues lined the wooded pebble walks that followed the cascading stream down the valley. One such walk was known as the Crinoline Walk.

of ochry (a brownish yellow colour) sediment. It dissolved soap without any difficulty and a few drops of 'ol tart' turned it milky. It had no symptoms of any sulphurous quality. It is good for the appetite and all other complaints of which chalybeates are normally recommended; a more modern sampling might come up with other findings. Its remains, with its beehive covering, can still be seen today.

A number of lakes and ponds were formed, one such called the Serpentine lake which was complete with a small island and black swans. The stream cascaded in several rivulet falls which had cobblestone bases, and could be followed down the wooded valley by way of the Crinoline Walk, constructed wide enough to allow two ladies in their huge skirts to walk side by side. This walk led down to the sea and to the bathing house. The Kearney estate was surrounded by high walls and round towers, known as look-outs, each of which had a set of steps leading up to an elevation of ten feet. A total of six towers covered the approaches. It was here that the servants, with their giggling young female helpers, served evening tea on a silver tray, along with home-baked light ginger biscuits. All the towers were in line of site of one other – a near perfect example of one can be seen today on the main road in upper Garrettstown. The estate contained two walled deer parks with special embankments – these had protruding pointed stones to deter the deer from escaping. Three gate lodges controlled all entry points, and at one time the building of an access road from the south and a viaduct to cross the valley was considered. Some of this work got underway but was abandoned due to the expense – all that remains of the effort are the two garden pillars looking in a southerly direction; at the far side, one mile from the house at the top of Laharne hill are the bases for the other entrance pillars.

The Kearney family also constructed a rabbit warren, surrounded by walls that went deep into the ground and which were divided into several enclosures. In one of these enclosures, the earth was piled up into an embankment so the rabbits could dig their burrows. The other two enclosures were used for grazing. These were connected by a long, narrow passage through which the rabbits had to pass in order to return to their burrows. In the evening or early morning, dogs would be released into the pasturage enclosures, causing the poor rabbits to flee towards the doors and passageway connecting with their burrows. But those leading to the first enclosure would have been closed and the rabbits were held up in the passage. Having no escape, they would bury themselves in the square holes cut out in the foot of the walls in the passageway, from where they could be taken out by hand. The young ones would then be selected for slaughter.

In the summer, grass abounded in the grazing paddocks and, by the end of autumn, the increase in the rabbit population ensured nothing was left but the vegetation – unpalatable ground ivy, briers, nettles, thistles, ragworth and violets. In the winter, turnips and hay would be thrown into the rabbits; their favourite food was parsley and when the turnips were first introduced to them, three weeks passed before they took to eating them. The rabbits in the warren at Garrettstown were under constant attack from weasels, grey crows, hawks and magpies. Cats were another problem as every household in the district kept several, mainly as a deterrent to rodents.

When rabbits were first introduced into Ireland, it was mainly close to the coast where there was sand. The fur was used for making elegant gloves. Rabbits spread like wildfire through the countryside and, during the first half of the last century, they were trapped in all sorts of ways. In most cases, their fate was a cruel, slow lingering death, snared by the neck with a sliding wire, their feet caught in an open trap for hours on end. Nets were put on burrows and a ferret introduced into the hole – the rabbits scattered to escape only to get caught in the nets on the way out. Dazzling them with a light on a windy night with a greyhound in tow, the poor creatures stood no chance. Their meat went for export and the damaged ones were kept for home use where they were skinned in a very unusual way – the woman of the house pulled the skin from the ass out over the head. When the price was high, a rabbit with a broken back would not be accepted, so an old bicycle spoke would be pushed into position to replace his broken backbone.

In the early 1960s, a huge proportion of the farmers' root crops was being gobbled up by these furry little fellows, so a disease was deliberately introduced into the species, bringing about a decline of the rabbit population.

In 1790, Michael Kearney of Garrettstown had over 200 sheep which, in that year, gave him 960 pounds of good-quality wool; the much tougher wool was taken off the black rams. Kearney sold his wool to a man in Kinsale who knitted socks; this man made about 3,000 pairs each year at 2 shillings a pair, mostly for soldiers. The sheep at Garrettstown weighed around seventy-two pounds, while in the general district they weighed only forty pounds. Better feeding and the crossing with the English breeds made Kearney's sheep much heavier. Another interesting point to note is that in 1790, most of the cattle in the Garrettstown estate were never housed – even in winter – primarily because there was very little straw in the district and the scarcity of fuel meant people had to use it for fires. Very little wheat was cultivated in the region close to the sea so that in the south of Ireland bread was made with oats, in the eastern part of the country bread was made with rye, and in the Midlands they used a mixture of rye and wheat; it was beaten in the fields, on the roadside and in the village streets by means of a flail.

Sir Walter Raleigh was supposed to have introduced the potato to Ireland. The historic house where he lived is in Youghal, Co. Cork. The well-known story goes as follows:

> In the garden attached to his residence it was there that he planted the first potatoes. The man entrusted with the care of the garden, in the absence of Sir Walter, supposed that the apple, or seed, was the esculent part of the novel production, but finding the taste unpleasant, he bestowed no further thought on the plantation, until, upon digging the ground for some other crop, the root was found to yield a wholesome and palatable species of food.

Various dates have been ascribed to the first planting of the humble spud. Dr Campbell, in his survey of Ireland, asserts that Sir Walter first planted the potato in Ireland in 1610 but some disagree with this, not least because in 1603, Raleigh was tried for high treason and on conviction confined to the Tower of London for fourteen years. The prosecuting lawyer, Edward Coke, who was also the attorney general at the time, addressed the prisoner in the following style: 'Nay, I will prove all: thou art a monster; thou hath an English face but a Spanish heart. You are the absolutest traitor that ever lived. All that he did was by thy instigation, thou viper; for I "thou" thee, thou Traitor.' So how could Raleigh have planted the spud in this part of the world? After all that jargon was said, he was clapped in irons and put behind the walls of the Tower.

In the summer of 1580, Raleigh – then Captain Raleigh – was based in Cork when he heard that David Barry was at Cloyne with several hundred Irish rebels. Raleigh had at his disposal eight horse and fourscore foot soldiers and set out to attack them. On his journey, he observed a company of Irish on a plain close to a wood, and he immediately attacked them with six of his horse – his foot soldiers had not yet reached that spot. The Irish, seeing so few persons to fight, killed five of the horse including Captain Raleigh's. One soldier – a Yorkshireman named Nicholas Wright – saw his master's horse take the plunge after being hit with a spear and shouted out to an Irishman by the name of Patrick Fagan to assist his captain, which he did. Wright himself then furiously attacked six of the rebels and killed one of them.

By this time, James Fitz-Richard had arrived with a kern (medieval Irish or Scottish light infantryman) and came to Raleigh's assistance. The kern was slain and Fitz-Richard was in great danger. Raleigh cried out: 'Wright, if thou be man, charge above hand, and save the gentleman.' Wright, at his master's command, pressed among the Irish and killed five of them, and thereby saved Fitz-Richard.

In the year 1586, Raleigh obtained a huge tract of land in Waterford and also land in Co. Cork which had been forfeited by the Earl of Desmond. He was made mayor of Youghal in 1588 and it is possible that it was at this time – when he was expanding his property and living in tranquillity in Ireland – that the potato was introduced. The famous Sir Walter lost his head, for it departed from his body in the old palace yard in 1618.

It is also said that Spanish potatoes were planted in Ireland in 1565 by the navigator, Hawkins, who brought them from Santa Fe. Either way, the introduction of the potato to Ireland was a blessing as it became the staple diet for the masses, but 250 years later it would become the death knell of the poor of the island of Erin.

In 1760, nothing was grown in Garrettstown but hemp, used for the making of canvas and ropes. This was abandoned as a crop though flax was still retted in the turf bogs in the locality, which contained the softest water in the country.

The real beginning of Ballinspittle village was when several corn and flour-mills were constructed, first by the Cores and later by the Kearneys. The old mud-wall houses of Ballycatten village were then in disuse, so the masses moved into the valley where there was plenty of work and constructed rough dwellings. Unfortunately, they brought with them all sorts of disease. A small hospital was constructed at Ballymacredmond, close to the present village, to treat the sick and dying, and to keep them isolated from the workforce. This hospital would eventually give the village its name. It had two small ale taverns to serve the thirsty workforce; whiskey was regarded as a peasant's drink, cheap and crude. On a recent renovation of a part of one of these taverns,

An artist's impression of how Kilmore mill would have looked in 1906. *Painting courtesy of Buttimore family*

the mud and stonewalls were evident. There were also at least two blacksmith shops. Then, in 1750, it was decided to build a decent church as a place of worship and some good houses were constructed to house the craftsmen: weavers, millers, carpenters, blacksmiths, masons and millwrights. In the 1830s, a square of houses with good slate roofs was built, and most of them can be seen to this day.

Near Ballinspittle village in the early part of the eighteenth century, in the townland of Kilmore, a tuck and scutching mill was constructed for weaving the flax, which was retted in the local bogs. A long, man-made canal drove the looms and also drove a flour-mill and all sorts of other machinery that came with the Industrial Revolution. During renovation work at the end of the last century, a stone roller for stretching the woven flax at Kilmore was discovered. After flax is harvested, it's steeped in water for a number of days in order to rot the woody part of the stem; this is called 'retting'. It is then spread out to dry. When ready, it's sent for 'scutching' whereby rotted straw is removed from the fibre. The scutch-mill machinery consists of revolving wooden blades driven by water-power. The dried flax stems are taken in handfuls called 'beats' and are held against the blades which beat the rotten straw – called 'shives' – off the fibre and leave the latter unharmed. In this process, two kinds of fibre are produced: the long fibre, called 'line' remains in the beats in the hand of the scutcher, while the short or broken fibres are beaten off with the shives, but fall into a separate container; this is called 'tow' and is capable of being spun into

Cutting the harvest in upper Garrettstown at the end of the nineteenth century. Sitting on the reaper and binder is Thomas McCarthy Meenig; on horseback is Jerry Quinn; kneeling on the left with stick and soft hat is Tady White, under-steward of western Garrettstown; lying on the grass on the left is Dan Stanley Murphy; kneeling with back to binder is Jack (Johnny) White, gamekeeper; lying on the grass in front of him is John Hayes, herdsman; man standing close to binder is Jack Forde; lying on the grass in front wearing soft hat is Thomas Hayes, coachman; standing out in front with large beard is George Moir, overall land steward of Garrettstown estate.

coarse or heavy yarn for sailcloth, while the line is spun into better-quality and fine yarns. The spinning, with its attendant processes, is carried out in a spinning mill after which the yarn goes to a weaver to be woven into cloth. The cloth is bleached and laid out in long lengths on the grass for natural bleaching.

These small scutch mills, such as the one which operated at Kilmore, employed about two dozen people. The Kilmore mill was at one time under contract for the Besnards of Douglas. In 1775, the average heckler worker earned a shilling per day, a weaver about 8 pence per day. A family loaf cost 3d., beef was 2d. per pound, a large salmon was 1 shilling, a score of herrings could be had for a penny and a pair of ducks could be purchased for 1 shilling. Table beer was a halfpenny per pint and stronger brew cost a penny a pint. A large goose cost 8d. The goose grease could be used to waterproof boots and was also used for sprains, aches and pains. Before the poor bird was killed, it was used to clean large chimneys by lifting it up and down, tied by the legs – its flapping wings swept the chimney. In 1808, women spinning yarn earned 2 shillings per week but in times of depression that fell to 2d. per day. Quite an amount of the spinning was contracted out to the homes of families.

The tuck mill at Kilmore ceased to operate in the 1820s, and the flour-mill – with its large overshot water-wheel – served the countryside well up until before World War II. The records show that de Courcey had a mill at Ballymacredmond in the thirteenth century and that the Cores sold their mill to Kearney around 1620. No remains of these ancient mills are to be seen today. Much later, in around the early part of the seventeenth century, more modern mills were constructed in much the same locations. One of these mills was at the spot where Ballinspittle bridge stands – this corn-mill had an undershot water-wheel. The river here is flat and the water was diverted into a sluice so as to hit the paddles at the bottom; in a severe flood the wheel was prone to being washed away and the gears damaged.

The second mill was constructed at Kilmore lower – this dates back to 1610. These small flour-mills flourished prior to the much larger ones of the Industrial Revolution. A canal was constructed from the bottom of Gortnachrusha hill by diverting the river so as to give a controlled water supply. A number of sluice gates were fitted – a remarkable feat of engineering for its time. This four-foot wide canal was approximately two miles long and drove a fourteen-foot overshot water-wheel. In summer, water was scarce so another stream from the Templetrine hill was also diverted into the canal, giving it an added boost. This mill ceased to operate in late 1930 and was demolished during World War II. The canal banks were breached and the river was re-routed to its original source. The outline of a large part of this canal can still be seen today.

The dressing of the millstones was an art in itself. After the Great War, this was done by a man who had lost one leg during the conflict. Dressing the millstones was a very cumbersome job, and he used to remove his leg and place it close by. One day, some of the young children of the family that owned the mill took his leg and were cutting it with a saw when discovered by their mother. So a new leg had to be made for him which came from an old, large mahogany table and was spun down on a lathe. No longer in need of the damaged leg, the

Kilmore mill served the hungry masses during the great Famine of the 1840s. Demolished in the 1940s, its structure arose from the ashes at the end of the twentieth century.

man discarded it. A reconstruction programme on this mill was started in 1994 and during the excavation I found the dumped leg, and have it now as a memento of the man who once dressed the millstones at Kilmore.

Michael Kearney introduced furze to Garrettstown and cultivated it in windrows in the less-arable part of the area, and when this furze was cut it was eaten with pleasure by cattle and horses, who preferred it to oats. Furze was planted on all the high and poor land between Kilbrittain and the Old Head, and after about four years would have gained a height of around five feet. The method for cutting the furze was to take a short timber fork in one hand – to straighten the furze up – while in the second hand, a sickle was wielded. Only the young shoots were used for fodder and they were chopped or bruised in a special machine. Years later, the furze went wild and was used for firewood.

The nearest lime quarries were nearly twenty miles away in the Lee valley. Coquebert's description is of an immense furnace in which lime is burned with turf taken from a local bog, and at night – when seen from the distance – this furnace produces a remarkable effect. He notes how on Sunday, the peasants were going to a patron church, each carrying a thick cudgel and most of them dressed in blue. The lime was mainly used for building and was sold for between 2 shillings and 3 shillings a barrel. The farmers in this area used the resources provided by the sea, such as sand – which was used to open the ground – and vast amounts of varec, kelp or seaweed, which grows on rocks and stones and is thrown up on the beach after the equinoctial gales. This was used mainly as fertiliser for potatoes. To encourage the growing of this seaweed, the people living close to the coast threw vast amounts of stones into the sea which would be retrieved when the seaweed had attached itself to them. In 1790, potatoes in the Old Head area were planted from February to June, with April being the best month. In Garrettstown, the ground was opened with a conical iron ploughshare drawn by two horses. The harrows for breaking up the ground were all made at the forge, the ruins of which still stand today. In preparing the ground, varec was spread before or after ploughing, and then the lumps would be broken and beds up to four-and-a-half-foot wide would be made. The potatoes would be cut into large pieces, each piece containing an eye, and were placed in the beds about six inches apart and covered with earth. This work was done by children from the ages of ten to thirteen, wearing no footwear. The potatoes were again earthed up when they began to grow. Ten to twelve hundredweight of cut potatoes per English acre were planted. The average yield from this amount was about

The little humpback bridge over the River Lucha near Kilmore mill, Ballinspittle. This footbridge was demolished in the 1960s. *Photo: Buttimore family*

eight to ten tons per acre but Michael Kearney got over ten and a half tons per acre at Garrettstown: varieties such as the kidney – of Spanish origin and fit for use in July – and Surprise, fit for use in September. The average price was about 2 shillings per hundredweight and sometimes falling to 1 shilling. The potatoes from Garrettstown were sold as far away as Dublin. Starch was also extracted from them, and some were dried and then exported to America. This was achieved by first boiling and leaving them out in the sun to dry, and fetched about 24 old pence per hundredweight. It was forbidden to sell potatoes by bulk rather than weight. Some fifty years later, in 1840, most of Ireland and some parts of England would experience starvation and mass emigration due to the failure of the potato crop.

At Templetrine, the resting place for some of the Kearneys, a headstone reads: 'Edward Kearney esq. died March 8th 1723 aged 29 years and 29 days. James his brother died February 18th 1723 aged 23 years and 11 days. This was made by their father and mother. Remember the good man minister.' The stone features their coat of arms, a standing lion with the words 'Semrer et Denis'. This was the start of the end of the line of succession for the Kearney family at Garrettstown. Another branch of this Kearney family have their tomb in Courtaparteen (Kilroan). This monument was erected by Miss Anne Kearney of Duneen over 'the regretted remains of her deceased relatives, her parents, Edward and Ellen, her brothers, Michael, Patrick, Frank and James, her sisters, Catherine, Drinan and Mary Kearney. The latter departed this life March 8th 1838 aged 59 years. Her days were filled with deeds of charity and

in death her lamp was not extinguished (Requicat et-in pace).'

These headstones and the few remaining pieces of architecture of Garretts-town estate are the only reminders of the proud and prominent family forced out of Limerick in the six-teenth century and who settled with distinction in the barony of Courceys.

Top: Kearney headstone at Templetrine. Below: Kearney family burial plot at Courtaparteen (Kilroan).

Coquebert de Montbert Visit: 1790

In his 'Cornets de Voyage', the French consul, Coquebert de Montbert, on his visit to Garrettstown and the Old Head district in 1790, describes a fishing trip taken with Francis Kearney of Garrettstown. Their trip takes place on 14 September and they set sail from a small cove in a boat rowed by seven men and equipped with small sails. It was at this cove that coal from England was landed for Michael Kearney. There was a house close by named Doras Brack, or 'La Porte de Differentes Couleurs'. Coquebert describes the fishing in great detail: there was plenty of herring, mackerel and lobster, and he describes Duneen at the Old Head as being littered with small boats pulled up on the shore. Next, they landed at a place called Bream Rock or Cuas Cannon (*cuas* being the Irish for 'small cove'), named after a ninety-gun warship that foundered there a few years earlier. The pilots of Kinsale Harbour would leave their boats in this cove when they climbed up the promontory to watch out for vessels that may have needed their services. From there, Coquebert and his fishing party make their way to the lighthouse (now disused) and come across a family with a small garden, pigs, sheep and a coal fire maintained at the cost of twelve pounds per year.

On the grill over the live coals, Coquebert and his friends are allowed to cook mackerel, mussels and red potatoes with white eyes. They wash down the meal with grog (rum and water) for no other drink is available in the district since the decline of the smuggling trade. Besides mackerel, they find in that house deargan (gurnet) and pollack, or 'coal' fish, and graduas carbonarius, called in Irish *gour*, meaning a goat. Fortified by their meal, they leave the lighthouse to see more of the surrounding district.

Perhaps the strangest building seen in the Old Head is the school – a sight greeted by Coquebert with the words 'Quelle Chaumiere!' The pupils are often seen taking their lessons in the ditches. Coquebert describes the Old Head in 1790 as being mostly inhabited by old sailors better able to communicate with a stranger than with those living on the Head who cannot speak a single word of English. From fishermen, he was told about a cove at Blackhead. Close by was a house called Chateau du Nialadore, a *nialadore* being a man in command of a group of men engaged in herring fishing.

According to Coquebert's account, the weather in September 1790 must have been very pleasant. He describes a place about a half a mile south-east of Garrettstown House where a small stream enters the sea. Here, they left their clothes in a grotto and bathed. The grotto is described as more beautiful than the grotto of Apollo in Versailles (this, we believe, is where the present stream enters the sea which, at the time, was much further out to the sea; the roof has now fallen in and close examination reveals it to be naturally cut out at its base). Next, they visited an underground cave a little to the west of the present beach at Garrettstown and finished up having their evening meal with a farmer named Nahan.

Coquebert left Michael Kearney and Garrettstown, and made a brief call to Innishannon and Bandon. His host, Michael Kearney, had a lot of contacts in these two towns as this was where he used to dispose of some of his produce. Kinsale was a long trek by road and there was no bridge crossing the river which had to be traversed by ferry from Castlepark. In the year 1750, a French colony of some thirty houses was founded by a Mr Aderley who brought the French to Innishannon to manufacture cotton, dimity, etc. However, as soon as the Irish had acquired their skills, the French were so neglected and plagued that they departed for London.

Other items of interest noted by Coquebert in his diary are hurling and faction fights, sometimes waged for the honour of Munster and Leinster. A popular activity in this part of the country was the throwing of an iron bar from the shoulder; another past-time that rendered the roads dangerous was the launching of a ball made from lead weighing two to four pounds – after four or five throws, the man whose ball had travelled the farthest was declared the winner.

Of Bandon, he speaks of Castle Bernard, once the seat of the O'Mahoneys but then owned by Mr Bernard, a very rich man who had recently married the daughter of Lord Shannon. The town at that time was very industrious with twisting mills where 100 bobbins were worked by a belt set in motion by a women operating a treadmill. Female winders earned as much as 16–26d. a week, depending on their diligence. In the years 1750–80, Manchester alone took Irish cotton to the tune of £36,000. Spinning was one third cheaper in Ireland than in England. The town also contained a barracks and a very productive slate quarry. At that time, the town was walled and divided by a swift-flowing river. Coquebert also notes that Catholics were not permitted inside its gates, but that very many lived outside in its seven suburbs. Coquebert adds that the town was full of beggars. The most important businessmen in the town at that time were George Ormond (the principal manufacturer of cotton), John and Joseph Wheeler, Isaac and Christopher Dowden (thread and cotton); wool manufactures were Hazell (father and son), Moacley, Barret, Baker, Sullivan and Chambers, all of whom exported.

It is told of the witty Jonathan Dean Swift (1667–1745) that when he and his servant were entering Bandon, the Dean, being a little in advance, wrote on the gate of the town the following lines: 'Jew, Turk, or Atheist, May enter here, But not a Papist'. The servant, on arriving at the spot read the inscription, and concluded that it was the Dean's composition, added the following rejoinder: 'Whoever wrote this did it well, The same is posted in the gates of hell.'

Coquebert left Bandon on 3 October 1790 for the west of Ireland, only to return again to Michael Kearney for the Christmas season. He told Kearney that on a visit to the Bath district of England the previous Christmas, he had come across mistletoe hanging in the houses and that it gave rise to all sorts of small pranks. There was no known mistletoe in Garrettstown and Michael Kearney said that he never saw the Bath custom in Ireland; however, the Irish do use holly to decorate their houses during the Christmas season.

In his 'Cornets de Voyage', Coquebert de Montbert, a liberal in outlook, sums up the Irish situation as he saw it in 1790:

> I picture England and Ireland as two sisters, the elder steady, thrifty, attentive to her business, thoughtful but over exacting and a little jealous, and so treating her younger sister rather badly at times. The younger less poised, a little giddy and inconsistent, fickle, scarcely per- turbed about the morrow, by no means quarrelsome – for though easily roused to anger she is just as easily conciliated – heedless, careless in her dress, curious, talkative, loving entertainment, witty sayings, good cheer, dancing and games, not too much work, above all else ever ready to make promises never fulfilled all without evil intentions; in short an amiable child full of spirit and with good heart but needing another few years to attain her sister's good sense. If the English are pleased to refer to their country as Old England this land should be known as Young Ireland.

The Kearneys of Garrettstown were very powerful and, generally speaking, not harsh or vindictive towards their poorer neighbours.

Prior to inheriting the Kearney estate, Thomas Rochfort was living on lean means so that, when the estate fell to him, he found himself very rich. He made a will consisting of sixteen pages and, with his new-found wealth, donated various sums of money to different charities. One such was the even- tual building of the old school at Ballinspittle (which still stands today, as a guest-house). A small plaque on its south wall states: 'Ballinspittle Parochial Schoolhouse Erected by Bequest from the late Thomas Rochford of Garrettstown Esq. AD 1833.' He had married a Jane Cuthbert in 1802 but his courtship of Jane had been a long, drawn-out affair so that both were advanced in years at the time of their marriage. Jane died in Blackrock, Cork in 1830 while Thomas died in 1831.

The estate passed to his brother-in-law, Thomas Cuthbert, but the will was challenged. Thomas Cuthbert went to Garrettstown to take possession of the house and lands and left it in the care of a servant of Rochforts by the name of Purcell. While Purcell was attending Rochfort's funeral in Cork, a mob – led by Dominic Sarsfield and Bartholomew Verling – broke into the house. Cuthbert assumed the name and arms of Cuthbert Kearney, and had to go to court to have them evicted; Daniel O'Connell represented them.

In 1834, Thomas Cuthbert Kearney's daughter, Mary Anne, married Thomas Franks of Mallow and Dublin – this was how the estate passed to the Franks family. Matthew Henry, born in 1835, married Gertrude Priscilla Despard in 1869, and they had three sons and one daughter, Lucy, who was born 12 July 1876 and never married. She spent Christmas, Easter and the

Garrettstown House, its roofless condition testimony to the destruction of the 1960s.

The coach-house of Garrettstown House is still intact. It once housed the four-wheeled carriages of the Kearneys, Cuthberts, Rochforts and the Franks. A large double door was at the side. Its façade mimics the dwelling house.

long summer months at Garrettstown House and also stayed with her two maiden aunts, Jane and Catherine Cuthbert, who lived at Kilmore House. At the entrance gate lived their shepherd, Morris Cosgrove.

As Lucy grew older, she used to organise the picking of primroses at Kilmore meadows and at Garrettstown, and have them transported by train to Dublin to the hospitals for sick children and the aged. Being the only daughter, Lucy used to keep the house for her aged father, who was now deaf and deteriorating with each passing day. When Matthew Henry died, the estate passed to his brother, Harry. Lucy missed out because it was only the male line that could inherit.

During their stay and visits at Garrettstown House, they used to keep a full house of guests, English and Irish, Anglican and Roman Catholic – all were welcome, including the local medic, Dr O'Leary, and Fr Murphy, the rector of Templetrine. Fr Willie Murphy was instrumental in getting the present local co-op up and running in 1928.

Lucy Franks was a founding member of the Irish Country Women's Association, and did much for Ireland and for Irish women in general. She was interested in persuading women to take up spinning, weaving and other crafts. As a result, Ireland today has a strong women's organisation. Lucy's brother, Harry, died in 1942 and the estate passed to her nephew, Cecil Franks. In 1964, at the ripe old age of eighty-eight, Lucy Franks passed away and is buried in Deans Grange Cemetery in Dublin.

Henry Cecil Franks died in Blackrock, Cork in 1981 and is survived by his two daughters, Charlotte, who resides in England, and Bridget Kearney Franks, who is married to a Franks (no relation) – their home is in Canada.

So ended the Kearney family line at Garrettstown House, for they who were driven out of Limerick nearly forty years before the Battle of Kinsale during the reign of Queen Elizabeth are no more. They had found refuge close to the land of the powerful Irish McCarthy clan and under the watchful eye of the Norman conqueror, de Courcey, after whom the barony is named.

Kearney's tomb is at Templetrine, and commemorates the proud family that lived in Garrettstown for over 250 years.

> Roofless houses where ivy crawl
> The night owl lurks high upon their mist
> That once was ruled with an iron fist
> Their parks where deer once roamed free
> Alas no more for the eye to see
> Where pillars still cradle their pineapples
> A new breed of family is born
> Their high walls and proud round towers
> Some still stand there as if not to die
> The only call now is the seagull's cry
> Their baneful gates, and once fine walks
> Where ladies strolled in crinoline attire
> With garden beauty and exotic roses
> The lakes and ponds in revolute falls

Where black swans glided and to feed did call
Their lodge houses now in decay
That once held back many a fray
Their tombstones leaning and faded
While underneath is now degraded.

Things were changing fast in Europe and its impact on the British Isles would be enormous. In AD 911, Charles the Simple, king of France, ceded Normandy to a Viking chieftain named Rollo, who promised that he would protect the coast against the avaricious Norsemen. By the eleventh century, aristocratic Vikings had set up the dukedom of Normandy which included the northern part of France and the Low Countries. When Harold II was crowned king of England, two Viking descendants waited in the wings – one, the ruthless King Harald Hardrada of Norway; the other, William of Normandy who was descended from Rollo. Their attacks came days apart: the English army beat back the forces of Harald Hardrada at the Battle of Stamford Bridge near York but then had to about-turn and head south to confront the Normans who had in the meantime streamed across the channel – Duke William of Normandy had landed in southern England with a large invasion fleet. King Harold of England confronted the enemy, the Battle of Hastings ensued and the Normans were victorious. Harold was killed and William – William the Conqueror – crowned himself King William I of England in Westminster Abbey. By 1169, the Norman conquest of England was complete.

When Rory O'Connor advanced on Dublin in 1166, he had himself made king there, but he had his eyes set on the high kingship of all Ireland. The provincial kingdom of Leinster was then ruled by Dermot MacMurrough. Disagreement and squabbling over the kingship forced King Dermot to travel overseas in search of mercenary troops to retrieve his position. At this time, Henry II's hold on England was insecure and he was dissuaded by his mother, Empress Matilda, from getting involved. He was busy quelling uprisings from the Saxons and the Picts, but he did authorise his subjects to come to MacMurrough's aid.

Using Bristol as his base – where he had been given a civic reception – King Dermot then recruited Richard FitzGilbert de Clare and a group of cambro Norman knights that included Maurice Fitzgerald and his half-brother, Robert FitzStephen – both sons of the Welsh princess, Nesta. These knights were all promised land in the Wexford area for their services. De Clare – better known as Strongbow – was offered Dermot's daughter, Aoife, in marriage and the whole province of Leinster on Dermot's death. From 1169 to 1171, the Normans reconquered all of Leinster, including Dublin, for Dermot. Romantic Irish historical writers over the last two centuries shivered and cringed at the idea of an Irish king seeking help from the Normans who had conquered Britain, and it would come back and haunt them, for it was the Anglo-French Normans who conquered Ireland for Henry II and, like it or not, they were eventually accepted; it is said that they became more Irish than the Irish themselves.

Near Waterford city, there is a place known as the Valley of the Lamentation – its name derived from the tremendous conflicts between the Danes and the

Irish. The original name for Waterford was Port of the Thigh, because of its shape. It was founded in AD 155 and became a considerable town in 853 under the Norse ruler, Sitric. On the lower end of the harbour, a Danish tower was built in 1003. It was known as Reginald's Tower after the founder Reginald, son of Imar. In 1171, when Strongbow and Raymond le Gros took Waterford, it was inhabited by Danes who, with the exception of the prince of the Danes and a few more, were all put to death. It was here also that Earl Strongbow was married to Eva, daughter of the king of Leinster. In the National Gallery of Ireland, a watercolour study by Daniel Maclise, painted in 1854, depicts a grandiloquent representation of a theme from Irish history: the lamenting harpist in the foreground and Strongbow's foot planted on a broken cross symbolise the oppression of native Irish culture by the Anglo-French Normans. It was in Waterford that the Norman king of the conquered Britain, Henry II, first landed in Ireland to take possession of the country which had been granted to him by the bull of Pope Adrian and conquered for him by Richard FitzGilbert de Clare (Strongbow). The Norman stamp is still evident in the south-east of Ireland – the name Power (de Paoir) is synonymous with Waterford. Cork, before the arrival of the Strongbownian conquerors, was a kingdom of its own, the kings of which were the McCarthys. In the year 1172, Diarmuid (Dermot) who was McCarthy Mór, king of Cork, handed over the city, swore fealty, gave up hostages and subjected his kingdom to a yearly tribute to King Henry II.

Six years later, in 1177, Strongbow's army, under Raymond le Gros, had plundered the neighbouring country and were shipping the booty to Wexford when they were attacked; Gilbert, their commander, was slain. Henry granted the surrounding territory to Milo de Cogan and Robert Fitz-Stephen, excluding the city of Cork which was occupied by the Ostmen, or the settled Vikings. Henry kept Cork for himself. In 1185, the city came under siege from the Irish under McCarthy. Fitz-Stephen, shut up within the walls, sent for help to Raymond le Gros who was based at this time in Wexford. Le Gros came by sea and brought with him some twenty knights and 100 archers. They attacked and routed the Irish on the first onslaught. One year later, while McCarthy was holding conference with other Irish chiefs near the city, he was slain by Theobald Fitz-Walter, who later founded the noble house of Ormonde.

This was the beginning of a long connection between the Anglo-French Normans and Irish, evidence of which are the Norman names still common in Ireland: de Cogan, de Rourke, de Barra, Fitzgerald, Fitzgarrett, Desmond, de Faiote and de Courcey, to name but a few. They invaded the neighbouring province of Meath and O'Rourke's kingdom of Breifne. When Henry II learned the scale of their activities, he withdrew his consent and placed an embargo on exports to Ireland, cutting off supplies to Strongbow and his invaders. When Dermot died in May 1171, Strongbow succeeded in crushing a revolt of the Leinster Irish and made himself lord of that province. Their task was made easy because the Ostmen, or settled Vikings, were their brethren, so to speak, as said Normans were the settled Vikings from France two centuries before.

With the threat of an independent Norman kingdom on his western seaboard, and with the appeals for help from the other Irish kings and chieftains, who had suffered greatly at the hands of the conquering Normans, the Norman king of England came to Ireland at the head of a large army that landed in Waterford in 1171. Such kings as Dermot McCarthy, king of Cork, Dónal Mór O'Brien, king of Limerick and several other Irish chiefs paid great tributes to King Henry at the Rock of Cashel. As it turned out, the army was not needed as Strongbow had conquered all the important provinces for Henry. Later, the Norman knight, Richard de Clare (Strongbow) and Archbishop (later saint) Laurence O'Toole were the co-founders of Christchurch Cathedral in Dublin (as it is called today) and, in 1172, they began to reform and expand the cathedral's Celtic tradition along the European lines. The original Viking church was built in 1038. When designing the chapel, Strongbow and his knights showed strong dedication to St Edmund (king of East Anglia 855–70), and the chapels echoed those in Laud, their original home in Normandy.

Strongbow, the Norman conqueror of Ireland for Henry II, died in June 1176. His original tomb was destroyed when a wall above the roof collapsed in 1562, and it was replaced later. Archbishop St Laurence O'Toole, his co-builder, died in Normandy in 1180.

In 1177, Henry II granted to the Norman knight, Milo de Cogan, a large area south of Cork, taking in the whole of the Kinsale region. The conquest here was shaky as the McCarthys continued to exercise their authority in the outlying parts.

Soon after the Norman invasion, the Old Head and the surrounding district came into the possession of the de Courcey family whose descendants later appear to have used Mac Phádraig as the Irish equivalent of their surname. The south-western part of the region south of the Bandon river was given by de Cogan as a dowry for his daughter when she married Milo de Courcey. He was created first Baron of Kinsale in 1223, and built himself a fine fortified castle close to the old Celtic site of Dún Cermna at the Old Head of Kinsale.

In 1397, King Richard II granted letters patent to William de Courcey, baron of Kinsale, to buy a ship to pass whenever he pleased between England and Ireland. In 1412, King Henry V granted the town of Innishannon and its ferry by letters patent to Philip de Barry.

The Norman castle at the Old Head was built at the narrowest point of the headland, and it had a deep, dry moat and drawbridge, making it impossible to breach from the land side. It would be defended by people using sharpened poles and crossbows. The first Norman castles and defences in Britain were built of wood – oak, in fact, of which there was an abundance in the western isles. Oak, when freshly cut, was easy to form, and when it seasons it becomes extremely hard and sturdy. However, this posed a problem for the early Normans as, when their castles were attacked and set on fire, the oak became impossible to quench. So they changed their building material to stone.

In a fortified castle such as that at the Old Head, the headman lived at the higher level (the beautiful arch on the top floor of what now remains of the present castle at the Old Head is proof of its existence). Tapestries and different kinds of furs would decorate the walls of the living-room, while at the lower level and rear of the castle would live the defenders and their families. When all was quiet and there was no threat to the castle, hunting parties would head inland on a couple of days' hunt. Trained falcons would be used to catch different types of game.

The castle was always defended, with lookouts posted at various points. When the hunting party returned, the huge drawbridge would be lowered, it being the only access to and from the fortified headland. The embankment leading up to the castle walls would be shaved clean and, with its high wall running to the extreme edge on either side, some turrets were in place in case cannon were needed as another line of defence from northerly attacks.

The Jacobite (supporter of King James II) Lord Kingsale (Almericus de Courcey) had escaped outlawry during 1689–91. It was north of his old castle that the twenty-fourth Baron de Courcey commanded the Kinsale horse militia in 1748, but soon afterwards went to reside elsewhere, and the ruins of his manor at the Old Head almost disappeared in the nineteenth century.

Very little now remains of the famous de Courcey castle at the Old Head; one of the two huge towers still stands, while the other was demolished for road building in the 1920s. The moat and the drawbridge, which once admitted the powerful and the mighty, is now no more. Part of the fortified wall that runs from east to west, with the remains of its smaller towers, can still be seen. Until recent times, some families lived up against the south wall of the castle.

In the summer of the year 1887, some students and two reverend gentlemen – on holiday in the Kinsale area – visited the castle at the Old Head. They noticed the ruins of little houses up against the castle walls; they described these ruins as being on the left-hand side as you approach the castle and not more than thirty feet from the precipice. On some of the walls, various scenes had been painted. Some of the subjects depicted were of singular character – trees and foliage, possibly a forest scene – but what excited them to the highest degree was to find in such a place a representation of the stage in the Passion of Our Lord. As well as they could make out, the soldiers were leading him from Pilate's house to Cavalry. The figures were very well drawn – about eighteen inches to two feet high – and the colouring was beautiful. They were particularly struck by a soldier in Roman military garb.

The students and their peers said at the time that they had no special knowledge or judgement as regards sculpture or painting, and they could not say to which school they belonged, but that what they saw at the Old Head in the summer of 1887 was of high artistic merit, and they were lost for words as to why such paintings were exhibited in such wretched, perishable buildings. No explanation was evident. They mentioned the paintings to a Mr Shenkel; when he saw them, he too was surprised. There has been no trace of those buildings for more than seventy years.

On the steep and craggy rocks beneath the castle, there is a bird colony. The breeding place of so many birds – guillemots, razorbills, kittiwakes, fulmars, cormorants, herring and black-backed gulls to name but a few. One must not forget the chough, a member of the crow family often mistaken for the jackdaw. Its yellow legs and beak distinguished it, and several pairs nest in the high cliff and castle walls. Seal colonies abound around the shores of the Old Head and, on a fine summer's day, the basking shark is a sight to behold. Under the castle, huge caverns are hewn out of the rock and, in fair weather, one might pass from east to west in a small boat as was the case several years ago when boats were rowed – this reduced the long and often dangerous trip around the point of the Head. Just a little south-west of the castle ruins can be seen a mound of white clay; this, when mixed with water, became the washing powder used by the women from the region to clean clothes and utensils. Of de Courcey's other two castles, one was at the edge of the Bandon river near Kilgobbin and later fell into the hands of the McCarthys. Not being in an elevated position, it was vulnerable to surprise attacks from the land side. The Norman builders, taking this into consideration, had constructed it to a height of eighty-four feet, with walls seven-and-a-half-foot thick. It was built close to an earlier tower that had been constructed by the McCarthys. In 1824, a great hoard of gold coins was found close to the ruined base of this old tower.

De Courcey also had a castle in Ringrone and it was here that Finghin McCarthy was slain by John de Courcey's grandson, Milo de Courcey, in the year 1261. Many of McCarthy's followers were drowned in the Bandon river during the onslaught. This castle stood high on the hill overlooking the estuary of the Bandon river and was built by de Courcey during the reign of Richard II (who reigned 1367–99). It was twenty-five-foot wide at the base with walls four-and-a-half-foot thick, and with a fifty-foot-high parapet. In its day, it must have looked awesome and threatening to anyone thinking of attacking it. Ringrone Castle figured prominently in all the battles and sieges of Kinsale down to the days of James II in the year 1689 when it was defended in vain by O'Driscoll against the Duke of Marlborough. In 1690, disaster struck: three barrels of powder caught fire at the gate to the castle and blew it

The remains of de Courcey's castle at Ringrone. Like a finger pointing to the sky, it saw many a battle between the clans. In one such battle, near where the castle stands, numerous of the McCarthy followers were beaten, driven into the Bandon river and drowned.

up with about forty soldiers. The governor of the castle, Colonel O'Driscoll, and 200 of his garrison were killed; the rest surrendered.

On 1 October 1690, the Earl of Marlborough went towards Charles Fort and posted his men at various points. The following morning, he crossed the river in a fleet of small boats, and by foot and horse made Innishannon with nearly a thousand men at his disposal. When he had blown up the castle at Ringrone, he stormed the old fort, which was defended by about 400 men, 200 of whom were blown up or slain. Some surrendered while others tried to escape by water to the new fort but were killed from the shore. The governor and several officers were killed on the ramparts.

Later, the garrison of 1,200 at Charles Fort, after several skirmishes, surrendered and was allowed out with baggage and arms and conducted to Limerick. In the fort itself was found a considerable magazine and provisions sufficient to support 1,000 men for a year. There were a thousand barrels of wheat, a thousand barrels of beef, forty tons of claret (red wine from Bordeaux), great quantities of sack (dry white wine from Spain and Portugal), large amounts of brandy and strong beer. Around 1 November, a French ship laden with brandy and salt sailed into Kinsale and anchored under the old fort believing it was held by the Irish. It was soon boarded and its prize was taken by the English.

Some years later, the stones of Ringrone Castle were used to build a wall around the local graveyard. All that remains of this once fine bastion of Norman power is one portion, eighteen-foot wide; like a finger, it points to the sky to remind us that the past has a story to tell. It's ironic that one of the tombs of the de Courcey family is now within the confines of that same graveyard.

The same graveyard at Ringrone is the burial place of another family to have left its mark on this region – the Bullens. Their name was first recorded in the Kinsale area during the seventeenth century; they occupied lands north of Ballinspittle village and Roughwood House, which overlooked the Bandon river. Another branch of the family had a house – named Doras Brack – and a tract of land at the Old Head of Kinsale. Overlooking the bay, it gave the name as we know it today: Bullen's Bay.

Joseph Bullen and family are buried in St Multose churchyard in Kinsale, but their main tomb is in Ringrone graveyard. Their memorial is on the outside of the south wall of the disused church.

> This is the burying place of the family of the Bullens in the Barony of Courceys and erected by Mr Edward, John and Joseph Bullen this the seventeenth Day of December 1726. Here lieth the body of Jane Bullen, wife of Joseph Bullen of Ballyaidown, Gert n and Eldest Daughter of Travers Hodder of Hoddersfield Esq. r who departed this life the 27th day of May 1726 in the 29th year of her age.

Their arms are a chevron between three bulls' heads, similar to those of Thomas Boleyn, Earl of Wiltshire and Osmond and father of Queen Anne Boleyn; there could be a connection between the two families.

Rise of the Eóghanacht

The Irish antiquarians allow but eight families of royal extraction in Munster, of which they place four in Carbery which encompassed all the south-west part of this county. These were besides the MacCarthys, O'Mahons, or Mahowns, O'Donovans and O'Driscolls.

Those Mahowns derive their pedigree from Kean Mac Moyle Mór, who married Sarah, daughter to Brian Boruma, king of Munster, by whom he had Mahowns, the ancestor of all that sept. For in that king's reign, surnames were given to the Irish and were commonly deduced from the name of their principal ancestor, with Ó or Mac annexed. It is from this Kean that the village of Enniskean in west Cork derived its name, and also from this sept that Bandon was sometimes called Droghid Mahon, and the nearby castle, Castlemahon.

From the beginning of the eleventh century, there had arisen around Cashel two Eóghanacht families. These were destined to play a leading part in the history of Desmond and, most of all, in west Cork. These were the McCarthys and the O'Sullivans. The McCarthy family took its name from an ancestor, Carthach, a petty king of the Eóghanacht Cashel, whose great-grandfather, Ceallachan, had been king of Munster. The first king of Desmond was Tadhg, grandson of Carthach. He had been raised from obscurity to that honour in 1118 by Turlough O'Connor, king of Connacht. Turlough was taking advantage of the rivalry between the McCarthys and the O'Briens. Turlough did not want a strong Munster and so divided that province into two kingdoms, later to become known as Deas Mumhan (Desmond) and Tuadh Mumhan (Thomond). This is the true beginning of the kingdom of Desmond and the power of the McCarthy family.

Tadhg's brother, Cormac, succeeded him in 1124 and, at the Rock of Cashel, can be seen the Hiberno-Romanesque architecture of Cormac's chapel, heavily influenced by the English Romanesque style. Its context is the twelfth-century reform of the Irish Church and the growing closeness between Ireland and the Anglo-Norman England.

The old rivalry between the McCarthys and the O'Briens continued until the struggle ended with the partition of Munster between them and when the O'Briens suffered a major defeat at the Battle of Moin Mhor in 1151. O'Connor had come south to aid the McCarthys, and Dermot McCarthy was established as king of Desmond. He was known as Dermot na Cille Baine (Killbancy), and when Henry II of England landed in Waterford in 1172, he went to the monarch of his own accord, kissed his ring and payed him homage.

In 1177, Dermot McCarthy's son, Cormac, rebelled against his father and, having taken him prisoner, used him barbarously. The old king appealed for the assistance of Raymond le Gros, who was then at Limerick. Le Gros marched to his relief, vanquished the rebellious son and delivered him up to his father. McCarthy had his son beheaded and, for his services, Raymond was granted a large territory in Kerry.

Several years later – in 1261 – the McCarthys took up arms and surprised John Fitzgerald and his son, Maurice, whom they killed along with several of their knights and other gentlemen of that family. The Fitzgeralds became so oppressed by the McCarthys that they did not put a plough in the ground for twelve years. Soon after this, some differences arose between the Irish of the territories of Carbery and Muskerry. Headed by the McCarthys, Donovans, Driscolls, Mahoneys and Swineys, they weakened and destroyed each other, whereupon the Fitzgeralds began again to recover their power and authority.

With the division between the houses of York and Lancaster in 1450, most of the great English lords went to assist their friends in England, while those left behind began to quarrel among themselves for the lands the others had forsaken. The Irish, who had been banished to the mountains, saw the country weakened and came down. At first, they involved themselves in these disputes, but finding the English too weak to oppose them, the Irish soon repossessed much of the country and brought several of their former masters under their control. McCarthy Reagh drove de Courcey out of his castle at Kilbrittain, and Lord Arundel of the strand, near Clonakilty, was humiliated and forced to become a tenant to Barry Óg (Barryroe).

The Butlers were Yorkists, the Fitzgeralds were Lancastrians, and the chief men of those two families left Ireland to take part in the English civil wars, leaving their estates to be overrun by the Irish. The Irish at that time were so powerful in Co. Cork that the English paid McCarthy of Muskerry a large sum of money each year for protecting them from the insults of his countrymen.

The McCarthy clan never forgot what happened at Ringrone near Kinsale in 1261 – the slaying of their kinsmen by the Anglo-French Normans under de Courcey. Between the fourteenth and sixteenth centuries, the Courcey lordship gradually shrank in the face of continued encroachment by the McCarthys of Carbery. By the late fifteenth century, the Courcey territory had become restricted to the area enshrined in the pre-1837 barony of that name, and in 1542, MacPatrick Courcey, like his neighbour, Lord Barry Roe, was always of the retinue and company of McCarthy Reagh whenever summoned by the latter to join him on an expedition.

By the late sixteenth century, Lord Courcey was paying an annual tribute of five marks and a penny (£3/6s./9d.) to the Earl of Desmond as protection money to keep his powerful neighbour, McCarthy, at bay. But McCarthy's penetration continued and, by 1588, Sir Owen McCarthy – then lord of Carbery – had enlarged his possessions by getting the Lord Courcey's country and other lands. This was a result of the actions of Gerald – who succeeded his father, John, as Lord Courcey some time after 1538 – in first mortgaging and then disposing outright of all his lands. Much of this was to Kinsale merchants and lesser local men, but in 1558, he mortgaged Ringrone itself to Donnchadh McCarthy for £50 and forty milch cows. There followed a series of other mortgages to Donnchadh (who became McCarthy Reagh in 1566), and finally – on 9 March 1583 – Gerald released all the mortgaged lands to Sir Donnchadh's son, the famous Florence McCarthy. In December 1584, he mortgaged his other manor, Downmacpatrick or Old Head (the earlier Oldernes), to Sir Donnchadh's brother and successor, Sir Eóghan, reserving a life tenancy for himself and his wife. In August 1594, he conveyed the fee simple of these lands also to Florence.

In May 1581, Gerald had entailed his lands on his cousin, Edmond Óg of Kilnacloona, and on Gerald's death in 1599, Edmond's son, John, succeeded to the title of Lord Courcey and what little if any was left of the inheritance. The Courceys (as former tenants-in-chief) had been recognised, like the Barrys and the Roches, as peers of parliament when the latter dignity had become defined in the fifteenth century. Therefore, the king and the Dublin administration were not prepared to allow the heir to fall into destitution. That the new Lord Courcey was successful in recovering much or most of the lands alienated by his predecessor, in spite of the opposition of Florence McCarthy – indeed, the deep disfavour with which the latter, a prisoner in the Tower of London, was regarded by the government – may also have played a part in the outcome. Whatever the reasons, the Courcey family – having sunk almost to extinction – regained their position, and their landed estate descended intact until the late nineteenth century.

With the coming of the Anglo-French Normans, who were to become very dominant in south Munster, this was the age of church building in Europe – a time of learning and culture. It was a time of the friars in Timoleague, monastic settlements and Abbymahon. But there was continuing aggression between the Norman and old Gaelic Church. Things were very unbalanced at this time; the pope and the king of France were at loggerheads, resulting in the pope spending several years a prisoner in France.

There was a slight recovery in the Irish position around 1300. The pope tried to bring law and order to the Church after his return to Rome, but the cardinals turned on him and he was sacked. A great schism occurred in the Church; a special council was called and elected Pope Martin V on 11 November 1417; he reigned until 1431.

When Martin was cardinal under Pope Innocent, he supported the Council of Pisa during the great schism. His election ended the schism, but the two anti-popes, Benedict XIII and Clement VIII – with their supporters in Spain – tried to prolong the schism; by 1429, they had run out of steam. Pope Martin eventually brought law and order back to the Church.

The Normans wanted the pope to unite Cork and Cloyne, and eventually a man by the name of Purcell from Limerick was made bishop of Cork and Cloyne; he lived to be a very old man.

A canon in Kilbrittain squandered the funds of the parish and was replaced by a man from Templetrine in Co. Cork by the name of Cronin, who also proved unsuitable. More trouble lay in store. Two rivals – Roche and Fitzgerald – were jockeying for position to be the next bishop of Cork. Thady

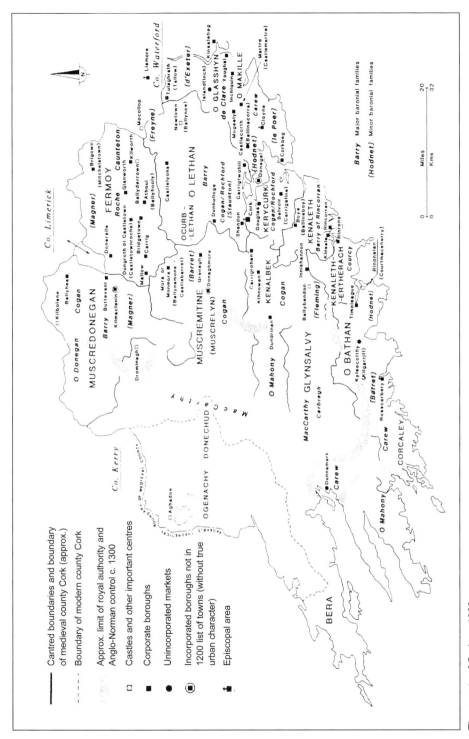

The county of Cork, c. 1300.

McCarthy was canon of Rathclaren and district. His understudy was a young man by the name of Thaddeus McCarthy. A bloody row erupted between the McCarthy Reagh and the Barrys who lost the western part of Innishannon parish. The castle at Dundaniel, at the edge of the Bandon river, was built sometime before 1515 by McCarthy Reagh. A rival McCarthy, Cormac Mac Donnchadah, unsuccessfully petitioned the pope for his lands west of Innishannon parish to be declared a separate parish on account of the obstruction by fortifications of the road between them and the parish church. The pope stubbornly set up the parish of Ballymountain, south of Innishannon, and put a man by the name of Murphy in charge. Later, Murphy had a row with the bishop and was excommunicated by the pope. Some time later, he returned and was put in charge of Rathclaren and subsequently made bishop of Ross. But O'Driscoll was already bishop in that area. Rome were confused or ill-advised and had made a mistake. Then, around 1488, the McCarthys were attacked by the O'Driscolls – a row that lasted for months. When the old bishop of Cork died, Thaddeus McCarthy was made bishop of Cork and Cloyne.

Thaddeus was a very learned and political fellow; in the fifteenth century, this gave him an important status, but the enemies of Church and state attacked him from all sides. The pope forgot that there were two assistant bishops already in Cork – Roche and Fitzgerald – so poor Thaddeus was driven out of Cork and Cloyne. This did not deter Bishop Thaddeus and, being a proud member of the McCarthy clans in south Munster, he said that no Norman planter – referring to Roche and Fitzgerald – would take the job from him. So he decided he would walk to Rome to meet the pope and put his case to him. He sailed for France and struck out on the long road to the Eternal City – a trek of several months' duration. On the way, he gathered quite a group of followers. He succeeded in meeting the pope, and the bold Thaddeus produced his papers and won his case. He headed back the long road to Ireland to claim his rightful place as bishop of Cork but, alas, he died of a fever in Piedmont, Italy. Thaddeus McCarthy's once weary bones now rest in this little town on the western border between Italy and France, not far from Monaco. In 1895, his beatification occurred and he is still called blessed Thaddeus. He should have been made a saint many years ago; many a saint achieved far less and, after the ordeal Thaddeus must have gone through, it's about time we had a saint in the McCarthy Clan.

Two other great rival groups were now coming into play – the Anglo-French Norman family de Courcey and the Irish McCarthy clan – and they would leave their mark forever. Dermot's McCarthy's son, Dónal Mór Na Curra, died in 1205 leaving three sons: Dermot of Dundrinan (died in 1230), Cormac Fionn (died in 1242) and Dónal God (died 1251). Dónal God attacked the O'Mahoneys in 1232, becoming the possessor of much of the territory. He settled in Kilbrittain, taking the castle built by the O'Mahoneys and which came to be known as Dónal Cairbeach. He was slain by the Normans in 1251 – about the time that the invading families of Norman stock, the Geraldines or the Fitzgeralds, were becoming dominant in south-west Munster and who were determined to break the power of the Irish chiefs. They were aided by none other than Dónal Rua McCarthy, son of Cormac Fionn, who claimed the kingship of the family held at that time by the sons of Dónal God. However, Dónal God's son Finghin (of Rinn Ron) rallied many of the Desmond clans to his side and inflicted a crushing defeat at the Battle of Callen near Kilgarven in Co. Kerry in 1261. Here, John FitzThomas of Desmond and his heir were defeated and killed by McCarthy. Later that year, Finghin himself was killed by de Courcey when he attacked his stronghold at Rinn Ron near Kinsale. In the following year, 1262, the Normans – under MacWilliam Burke – renewed their attack on the Desmonds and the McCarthys and, in the Battle of Toureen, Cormac, son of Dónal God and brother of Finghin (Rinn Ron), was slain.

In the year 1294, Dónal Maol McCarthy defeated and killed the brothers John and Patrick de Courcey at Inchydoney island near Clonakilty, Co. Cork. From Dónal Rua, who died in 1302, the rule over Desmond passed for two centuries from father to son without a break. Tadhg na Mainstreach (of the Monastery), great-great-grandson of Dónal Rua, was the last of the line to be given the title of king of Desmond by the annalists.

In 1300, a strip of Anglo-French territory extended from Bantry, south-east-wards through the Ilen valley to the coast, and eastwards as far as Ibane. The political geography of west Cork and south Munster was totally changed, not only by the Anglo-French invasion and the establishment of the McCarthy princes, but also by the arrival of other Gaelic ruling families who had been driven out of regions taken over by the colonists – families such as the O'Sullivans and O'Donovans. By 1201, they were already present in the O'Mahoney territory, to which they were to transfer the name of their former territory in Co. Limerick, Uí Cairbre or Carbery. In the early thirteenth century, the western part of this region was in the hands of Diarmuid McCarthy, and by 1232, Domhnall Got McCarthy, ancestor of McCarthy Reagh, was moving in to drive out and split the O'Mahoney territory.

In 1283, the Crowleys began to arrive from Connacht and, by the fourteenth and fifteenth centuries, the McCarthys and their descendants had almost wiped out the Anglo-French presence in west Cork.

Tadhg McCarthy, according to the *Annals of Innisfallen*, was the greatest wine drinker of the English or the Irish of his time. He was a contemporary of Richard II of England, to whom he made submissions. His son, Dónal McCarthy Mór, founded the famous monastery of Muckross in Killarney, Co. Kerry for the Franciscans in 1448, one of the finest examples we can see today.

Three sons of Domhnall Riabbach succeeded as lords in turn, but after the death of the second Donnchadh, in 1453, the rule of his brother, Diarmuid an Duna, came to be disputed by Donnchadh's son, Cormac. In the struggle for the earldom of Desmond between Sir Gerald and his nephew, James, in 1469–70, Cormac, then tánaiste to his uncle, was a close ally of Gerrot and succeeded with his help in deposing his uncle Diarmuid, taking prisoner two of his sons and capturing the castles of Coolmain, Kilgobbin and Monteen. In 1473, Cormac is described as ruling Carbery, while Diarmuid was nominally McCarthy Cairbreach. In 1477, however, Cormac was defeated and captured at Knocknalurgan near Carrigaline by Diarmuid's sons and their maternal uncle, Cormac Mac Taidhg of Muskerry. With the aid of their imported MacSweeney galloglass (medieval mercenary soldier), they made sure that

Cormac's lineage would come to an end; the poor man was tied upon a table, castrated and blinded before being released as no longer a danger. Evidently, Diarmuid was already dead; his eldest son, Finghin, was now installed as lord, and ruled until 1505.

Dónal Mac Fineen McCarthy Reagh (Riabhach) of Kilbrittain had married a daughter of the Earl of Desmond. Their son, Domhnall, who had been given as a hostage to Kildare in 1497, succeeded after a brief reign of an uncle. He married Kildare's daughter, Eleanor. (Kildare was lord lieutenant of Ireland in 1496).

The four sons of Domhnall and Eleanor, Cormac (na b-aine), Finghin, Donnchadh and Eóghan, all knighted in their time, were to rule over Carbery between 1531 and 1593. Cormac had to contend with his rival cousin, namesake and adversary; brother slew brother, nephews killed uncles, the rival McCarthy clans of Muskerry and Kilbrittain were at each other's throats. The earlier Cormac's brother, Eóghan, who was to slay his brother in 1495 and rule as lord for three years, was himself slain by his nephew, Cormac Óg, in alliance with Sir Thomas of Desmond. Along with Eóghan was slain Edmond Mac Dubhdara MacSweeney, a galloglass leader invited from Tir Conaill by Cormac Mac Taidhg, and when McCarthy Reagh was at war in Cork city in 1538 against King Henry VIII, his mother, Eleanor, who was now married to Maghnus O'Donnell of Tir Conaill, was the principle organiser. The citizens of Cork provided boats to ferry the rival Cormac and his men to an attack upon Carbery and Ibane. The last two of his brothers, Sir Donnchadh (died 1576) and Sir Eóghan, almost succeeded in annexing to Carbery what remained of the Courcey lordship. The last ruling McCarthy Reagh was his nephew, Domhnall (na piopal), son of Cormac, who outlived the end of the old order, surviving until 1612.

The head of McCarthy Reagh carved in relief on the gable wall of their lodge house near Kilbrittain.

In 1535, the young Earl of Kildare, who was about thirteen years of age and the only remaining heir to that illustrious family, took shelter at Kilbrittain in Co. Cork at the house of Ellen Fitzgerald, his aunt, who was widow to McCarthy Reagh. Later, she married one of the O'Donnells and made it one of the marriage articles that he should protect her nephew. When he betrayed him, she left her husband, and the young earl was obliged to fly for protection into a foreign kingdom.

On 20 February 1537, four ships with cargoes of wine from Portugal, destined for the merchants of Waterford, were being driven close to the shore in west Cork by a great storm. One of the ships, *La Sancta Maria de Soci*, laden with 100 tons of wine, was driven into the bay near the entrance of Baltimore Harbour. Fineen O'Driscoll and his son went on board the vessel and agreed with the merchants to pilot the ship to the harbour and safety for three pipes of wine (a pipe equalled four barrels or 105 gallons). Having tasted the liquor, they invited the merchants on shore to dine with them in their castle. As soon as they got them inside, they clapped them in irons, plundered seventy-two tons of wine from the ship and divided it among their neighbours. The news of this action reached the merchants of Waterford on 3 March. They fitted out a ship, well armed and manned, under the command of Pierce Dobbyn and struck off for Baltimore to teach O'Driscoll a lesson. When they arrived at Baltimore, Gilly Duff (Dubh), who was the base son of O'Driscoll, was still on board the captured ship with twenty-four of his men. Surprised, they fled down one side of the ship while Dobbyn boarded her on the other side and freed the captive crew. They pounded O'Driscoll's castle with cannon for several hours and then struck off to Waterford with the remaining twenty-five tons of wine. But they were not finished yet – O'Driscoll would pay for hijacking their ship and drinking their wine.

Towards the end of March the same year, the mayor of Waterford fitted out three ships with artillery and 400 men. Under the command of Captain Woodlock, they arrived at Baltimore Harbour on 1 April in the middle of the night, and anchored under the castle. They opened fire on the castle and sustained it throughout the night. By morning, O'Driscoll and his garrison fled, the Waterford men landed and took the castle, marched over the drawbridge and set up St George's standard. They held the castle for five days during which time they ravaged the island, destroyed the village and the Franciscan friary which stood near the castle, and a mill close by. They found a considerable amount of malt, barley and salt which they loaded up and carted off. They then burned and knocked down two more castles belonging to O'Driscoll, and Baltimore was burned.

William Grant, one of the seamen, was on top of one of the castles as it burned. With no way down, he cried for assistance and a fellow by the name of Butler tied a small cord around an arrow and fired it to Grant who in turn used it to pull up a rope. Having left himself down to safety, they all left and went back to Waterford. Such destruction, and all over a shipload of liquor.

Several years later, in 1601, Sir Fineen O'Driscoll would back the Spaniards and deliver all his castles to them. Following the Spanish defeat, they were retaken by the English. In order to ingratiate himself with Queen Elizabeth, the same Sir Fineen O'Driscoll replenished and supplied a great number of English ships of war, and entertained the captains and other officers in his castles. When the queen heard of this, she pardoned him for joining the Spaniards and called him to court, but before he arrived she died. While O'Driscoll was absent, his lands and castles were taken over by Sir Walter Coppinger, and this caused this ancient family to fall into decay.

When James, the fifteenth Earl of Desmond, died, he had four wives. His first was daughter to Lord Roche but this marriage was called into question on the pretence of consanguinity. His second wife was daughter to O'Carroll, his third was Catherine, daughter to Pierce, Earl of Ormond, and his fourth was Ellen, daughter to McCarthy Mór. Thomas, his eldest son by Lord Roche's daughter, was reputed a bastard, and did not inherit. Another son by the second wife went to Spain where he became known as an earl, and another son, John, became a bloody rebel and also fled to Spain.

In 1500, David Barry, Archdeacon of Cork and Cloyne, murdered his own brother, William Lord Barry. He himself met the same fate by Thomas Barry and, by the command of the Earl of Desmond, his body was taken out of the grave and burned.

Thirty-five years before the Battle of Kinsale, the break up of the Irish clan system was well underway. These clans were not interested in achieving one unified nation but in gaining control of as much territory as possible. O'Neill was very disappointed with the ennobling of McCarthy, and asserted that his blood and power was better than those of the best, that his ancestors were kings of Ulster, and that as they had won it by the sword he meant to keep it by the sword.

Sir Maurice of Desmond – commonly called the murderer for having killed his nephew, James – being eighty years old, assembled his followers and marched from his estate in Kerrycurihy, near Carrigaline, to prey upon the McCarthys of Muskerry. But as he was carrying off his booty, he was pursued by Sir Dermot Mac-Tiege Carthy (his son-in-law). Sir Maurice was taken prisoner and was left guarded by three horsemen while Mac-Tiege and his party pursued the rest of the bandits. In the meantime, those guarding Sir Maurice killed him and thus avenged the innocent blood of James, his nephew.

In 1565, McCarthy Mór was created Earl of Clancare (Glencare). He went over to England and made a surrender of his estate to Queen Elizabeth which she re-granted to him by letters patent and, after he had sworn fealty, conferred on him his title; she even paid the cost of his journey. He was at the same time made Lord Baron of Valentia. O'Sullivan Bear also took out a patent for his estate wherein was a proviso that he should pay all such rents and services as were due to the said Earl of Clancare. These services were as follows:

1. Upon proper notice given, he was to aid him with all his strength, and to be marshal of his forces.
2. He was to raise five kerns (light infantryman) for each arable ploughland or instead pay McCarthy Mór a beef or 6s./8d., of which he was to have his choice.
3. For every ship that came to fish or trade in O'Sullivan's harbours,

he was to pay McCarthy Mór half-a-crown.

4. He was to furnish McCarthy with all the goods and merchandise at the same rates he paid for them himself.

5. Every time McCarthy Mór thought proper to go to Bearhaven, O'Sullivan was obliged to give him and his followers entertainment for two days and two nights – wine women and drink – in his castle of Dunboy, *gratis*. And also to quarter as many as he brought with him in the adjacent country.

6. He was to send horsemeat for McCarthy Mór's horses, which he kept for his own riding; and to pay his groom 3s./4d. out of every arable plough land.

7. Whenever McCarthy's hounds, greyhounds, spaniels came that way, he must subsist them and pay 1s./8d. yearly out of every arable ploughland to his huntsman.

In 1567, Daniel McCarthy Mór, being encouraged by O'Neill's rebellion in the north and despising his new title of Earl of Clancare, assumed that of king of Munster, and made a deal with O'Sullivan Mór, MacSwiney and others. With banners flying, they marched over the Blackwater and invaded Lord Roche's country, killed several of his men, women and children, destroyed his corn, and carried off 1,500 cows and 700 sheep. In 1568, James Fitz-Maurice – son to Sir Maurice of Desmond – went into rebellion and joined the Earl of Clancare – the chief of the McCarthys – and the Fitzgerald on the pretext of religion; the true cause was the loss of their Irish extortions and other unjust exorbitances which they imposed in a tyrannical manner upon their clans.

Sir Donough McCarthy, father of Florence McCarthy Mór of Carbery, fought with the English against the Desmonds in 1575. Considered by many as one of the outstanding figures of all the McCarthys, he died in 1576. The death of Sir Owen McCarthy in 1592 created a succession problem. It was agreed by members of the Kilbrittain family that Dónal na bPiopai should succeed in accordance with the laws of the territory (his name was derived from an incident involving a shipwreck in Courtmacsherry Harbour which was carrying a cargo of pipes of wine; a wreck in olden times was deemed God's goods and the cargo was claimed by Dónal). He, in turn, was succeeded by Florence in 1592. Florence became tánaiste of Carbery at a time when the affairs of Dónal Mór of Killarney, the first Earl of Glencar, were going very badly. He had lived a profligate life and before he died in 1596, much of his property was mortgaged; this chief was the main line down and was the great-great-grandson of the founder of Muckross Abbey, Dónal Mór. Under English law, his one daughter, Lady Ellen, aged just sixteen, could not succeed him; neither could his illegitimate son. When created an earl in 1565, he had agreed to the English law whereby Ellen's future husband would inherit all of her father's property. But being under-age, she was made a ward of court which meant the queen herself held the right to give her hand in marriage. Ellen had many proposals but her secret marriage to Florence McCarthy in Muckross Abbey – in defiance of the queen's wishes– alarmed the English; the marriage would unite the McCarthy branches and render Florence as powerful in Munster as O'Neill was in Ulster.

Florence was a man of great charm and ability, not to mention diplomacy. Despite enemies at home as well as in England, he established a good relationship with the queen and her ministers, although suspicion was on him for being friendly with Spain. The fact that he had fought against the Desmonds with his father, Sir Donough, helped not a little as did the fact that his brother-in-law, Dónal (the base son of the Earl of Glencar), who later acquired the title, the Sugan Earl, had been for some time creating havoc in the Killarney area. He became known as the Robin Hood of Munster, and these two men posed a problem for the English Court – the problem as to who should succeed the Earl of Glencar. Florence was chosen as the lesser of two evils and became the master of vast estates in Kerry.

By now, Gerald, the Earl of Desmond, was restored to his estate by Queen Elizabeth after having spent seven years confined in the Tower of London. After being taken prisoner by Thomas, Earl of Ormond, in a battle in Waterford, he had assembled his forces to plunder the place. Soon after his return home from London, James Fitz-Maurice – who had also obtained the queen's pardon – informed the earl that his entering into rebellion was upon his account, in order to procure his enlargement; and to prevent his elder brother, Thomas Roe, from encroaching on his estate. He requested the earl to assign him some lands to live upon, which the earl refused, being prevented by his wife who was mother to the Earl of Ormond. James Fitz-Maurice, disappointed and desperate, plotted revenge. He confided in Edmond Fitz-Gibbon, commonly known as the White Knight, and also in John Fitz-Gerald of Imokilly and a gentleman from Kinsale by the name of Philip Roche who advised him to apply to the kings of France and Spain for assistance.

The chief cause of discord between the Earls of Ormond and Desmond was the mutual taking of preys and frequent disputes concerning the bounds of their territories. It finally came to a head when the earls appointed a day to end their differences by the sword. The place for the battle was the bounds of Cork, Limerick and Tipperary. The Earl of Desmond brought with him 4,000 foot soldiers and 750 horse, the greater number being his followers and the chief men in Munster. The Earl of Ormond came with equal forces and also brought some artillery pieces. They confronted each other in an open field for fourteen days but, contrary to their desires, did not go to battle – other great lords in the army mediated. The person that saved the day and stopped the would-be senseless blood-letting was the Countess of Desmond, mother to the Earl of Ormond. They were reconciled and made friends for the time being.

In 1578, James Fitz-Maurice made an address to Henry IV of France, complaining of the severity of the English government in Ireland and the persecution carried out against the natives on grounds of religion, but Henry took little notice of him. (Henry of Navarre (1553–1610), prior to becoming king was leader of the French Huguenots and, although going over to the Catholics on being crowned, remained in sympathy with the Protestants and protected them by the famous Edict of Nantes.) Fitz-Maurice left the French court and proceeded to Spain to make the same complaint to King Philip, and offered his country to him in the name of all the Catholics of Ireland. But Philip was not interested as a peace had been concluded between Spain and England just prior to this, and he considered it too soon to break the agreement. However, Philip packed Fitz-Maurice off to Rome and wrote letters in his favour to Gregory XIII. The pope received Fitz-Maurice and an English rebel named Stukeley whom Fitz-Maurice had met in Spain. The pope bestowed all manner of titles upon the men – knight, baron and marquis – and appointed each of them generals of the army which he and the king of Spain would furnish. He also immediately ordered 2,000 Italians to be raised for service in this army.

Fitz-Maurice, in order to prepare their reception in Ireland, took leave of the pope and headed home, leaving the newly created Marquis Stukeley to bring over the forces after him. Fitz-Maurice landed in Kerry on 1 July 1578 with Dr Nicholas Saunders, whom the pope had appointed as his legate. He gave Fitz-Maurice a consecrated standard and blessed the ground when they got ashore.

In the meantime, Stukeley set sail from Civita Vecchia with his Italians and arrived in Lisbon at the very time that Don Sebastian, king of Portugal, was fitting out an army to invade Morocco. The king persuaded Stukeley to join him in the expedition, but neither Stukeley, Don Sebastian or the Italian troops were ever again heard of, for they were slaughtered in a bloody battle with the Moors. Perhaps the pope had more interest in pushing back the Moors than helping the Irish cause.

The Spaniards were well versed in Irish affairs long before the Battle of Kinsale. In 1579, King Philip sent over 800 Spaniards, who landed in Kerry. They brought with them arms for 5,000 more and also a large sum for the papal nuncio, Saunders. The Spaniards assisted the Irish but the effort soon failed. Fitz-Maurice was later killed when being pursued by the sheriff, and Theobald Bourke was also killed. After Fitz-Maurice's death, his cousin – Maurice Fitz-John – had his head cut off. It was wrapped in a blanket under an oak tree, and his headless body was taken to Kilmallock where it was hung on another tree.

In January 1600, the crafty Florence McCarthy faced a dilemma. O'Neill marched south to Kinsale to join the Spaniards, setting up his camp at Inniscarra by the River Lee with the purpose of enlisting the help of the Munster clans. Florence had to choose between Queen Elizabeth and O'Neill, so he went to O'Neill's camp where he met his brother-in-law, Dónal, the Sugan Earl, and many of the Irish chiefs but not Dónal na bPiopai. O'Neill recognised him as the McCarthy Mór even though he had already conferred this honour on Dónal. To get out of this situation for his discussions with O'Neill, Florence pretended to the lord deputy that his action was dictated by his loyalty to the queen, but McCarthy's land from Kinsale west to Leap and Ross was being plundered by the English forces. The lord deputy did not believe him but he still got off with a stiff warning and a promise of future loyalty when he met the new president of Munster, a George Carew, on 24 April 1600.

George Carew saw through Florence McCarthy and considered him and the Sugan Earl the most dangerous men of the Munster Irish and the most likely to support the Spaniards in the event of a landing. The Sugan Earl was betrayed to Carew with a £1,000 bribe. Florence, after being promised safe conduct by Carew, was arrested in Cork and both he and the Sugan Earl were taken to the Tower of London in August 1600. Carew had plotted to poison McCarthy but the plan backfired.

When the Spaniards landed at Kinsale in September, their first enquiry was for Florence. The Battle of Kinsale might have had a different outcome had Florence, the Sugan Earl and their followers from Cork and Kerry been present to join forces with the Spaniards. Some of the McCarthy clan fought with Carew at Kinsale, as did so many other Irish clans, thus sealing the fate of the Battle of Kinsale.

The Sugan Earl was held captive until his death in 1607, but Florence was confined for forty long years and, in 1640, when he was eighty-five, death came as a final release. He was a remarkable man but prone to political somersaults and prevarication. The attempt to poison him and his arrest was proof that he was a menace to English rule in Carbery and, like O'Neill himself, unpredictable. It is quite possible that Florence McCarthy might not have lived to such a ripe old age if he had not been in exile in London because of his stance on the Battle of Kinsale.

The lands in Carbery were taken over by de Courcey, Sir Richard Boyle and others. Back in Kerry, Florence's wife, Ellen, had ingratiated herself with Carew and got back some of her father's lands. Dónal, her half-brother, in spite of many acts of treason, was returned several ploughlands and a castle as reward for presenting the English commander in Kerry, Sir C. Wilmot, with 5,000 cattle which he had stolen from the O'Sullivans, his former allies.

Florence's brother, Dermod Maol, lost his life on 13 April 1602 in a fray with his relatives when seizing cattle, and was buried in Timoleague Abbey. In 1641, his relatives backed King Charles I against the republican Cromwellians.

In January 1641, the Irish were again assembling in Carbery. Lord Muskerry, McCarthy Reagh, O'Donovan and O'Sullivan held several meetings, wrecked and burned Enniskean, Castletown and Newcestown, causing so much havoc, the English were forced to flee Clonakilty and find safe haven behind the walls of Bandon. Vast herds of cattle were taken from the English and driven to safer Irish countryside. Lord Clancarty ordered the Irish to return the cattle. They did so and were well paid for doing so; a few nights later they would again steal them.

The English were now beginning to suffer as the Irish gained the upper hand. Some hit-and-run attacks were made by the English from the town of Bandon, where several Irish were caught and hanged at the gates of the town. But still they assembled in great numbers on the outskirts of the walled town. Lord Muskerry also executed several of the common Irish within his ranks for thieving. Bandon was filled to capacity as people from the western part of the county flocked to its relative safety; one such influx was of a thousand women and children. The townsmen began to fortify the walls and towers as best they could, and some cannon were mounted upon its walls.

The assault on Bandon took place on 18 February 1641, headed by none other than McCarthy Reagh. As they approached the town walls, about 200 foot soldiers and sixty horse, under Lord Kinalmeaky, charged them and a severe conflict ensued. The foot charged from the front while the horse attacked from the rear. Of the Irish, 105 were killed – five of them gentlemen and leaders – and dozens were wounded. Fourteen prisoners were taken and executed under martial law at the main gate. Remarkably, no Englishman was killed in this battle and only a few were wounded.

This account was taken from a copy of a letter from Lord Cork to the Earl of Warwick, who adds:

> and now the boy has blooded himself upon them: I hope that God will bless him and His Majesty's forces, that as I now write but of the killing of a hundred, I shall shortly write of the killing of thousands. For their unexampled cruelty hath bred such desires of revenge in us, that every man hath laid aside all compassion, and is as bloody in his desires against them, as they have been in their execution against us.

His words nearly came true. The English Lord Forbes and his regiment landed in Kinsale and marched to Bandon; here, they were joined by three Bandon companies and some horses. On 18 October 1642, they marched west to Clonakilty where they left two Scottish and one Bandon company to secure the town while the main body headed for Rathbarry, near Rosscarbery. No sooner had they departed when the town was attacked from all sides by hoards of Irish who had been hiding in the hills close by. Captain Robert Grove, who commanded the Bandon company, advised retreat to about four miles west of their main body, but the Scottish companies refused and were soon cut to pieces by the Irish. Grove made his escape with his company to an old Danish fort close to Rosscarbery where he held out until the rest of his forces came to his relief. The reinforced English then turned on the Irish and pushed them towards the island of Inchydoney; the tide was in and upwards of 600 were drowned. In 1688, the walls of Bandon town were demolished and were never again rebuilt.

Dónal McCarthy Reagh of Kilbrittain, and many other members of the clan from Carbery, Muskerry and Kerry, backed another English king, James II, in 1689–91, and at the Battle of the Boyne in 1690, another McCarthy, from Kilgarvan, Co. Kerry, left 300 of his brave followers dead. He himself fell at Aughrim in 1691. The Boyne and Aughrim were the death knell of this great family – a more noble Irish family never existed.

Tadhg McCarthy, the next head of the family, settled in France and married Helene Shee of Kilkenny in 1701. He and many of his descendants were officers in the French navy. His son, Charles, was a captain and a knight of the Military Order of St Louis, and took part in a number of naval engagements. In August 1759, he signed an appeal to Admiral Conflans to invade Ireland. In it he suggested that if a force of 15,000 French troops landed at Kinsale, they would soon dominate the country with the help of the natives. Some three months later, a French expeditionary force was mobilised off the coast of Brittany for the invasion of England and Ireland. Part of this force included several regiments of the Irish Brigade under Lord Clare; the plan was to land in Munster, but on the eve of setting out, the French were attacked by the English and that ended the project.

The document bearing the signature of Captain McCarthy is still preserved

Kilbrittain Castle: Built by the O'Mahoneys and wrested from them by the McCarthys.

in the French naval archives. In June 1760, he was commodore of a squadron of frigates in the French West Indies. His own ship was *La Surenne*. On his way home, he was attacked and engaged by Rear-Admiral Holmes, and two of his ships were captured and one sunk. Commodore Tadhg McCarthy died in 1765, and his son, Timothy, who was also a naval officer, died at sea on board the warship *La Bayonnaise*. His second son, Denis, who was born in La Rochelle in 1716, was also a naval officer and spent many years in the French West Indian island of St Domingo. He married in 1767 and acquired quite an amount of property known as La Martiere on the island of Oleron near La Rochelle. Seven Irish gentlemen signed a document certifying that he belonged to an ancient and noble family, and the king ennobled him as Vicomte de la Martierein in 1769. By his will of 1783, he left La Martiere and £30,000 to his son, Charles Denis Jean Marie, a captain in the king's regiment of dragoons, who was admitted to the honours of the court in 1786 as Vicomte McCarthy. Charles spent five years as a member of the Chamber of Deputies and died in La Rochelle in 1831.

Another prominent member of this clan was Justin McCarthy (born in Cork in 1830, died in 1912). He became a politician, novelist and historian. His journalistic career was first in Liverpool and then in London, and from 1879–96, he was a prominent member of the Irish Party in parliament, succeeding Charles Parnell in 1890 as leader of the party.

Cormac McCarthy, Lord Muskerry, who lived at Blarney Castle, married Mary, daughter of Lord Cahir, and died in 1616 leaving two sons and one daughter. The eldest son became the first Viscount Muskerry, whilst the daughter married the eleventh Earl of Ormonde. The second son, Donald

McCarthy, built Carrignavar Castle and married Catherine, daughter of Stephen Meade.

These two had a son – Charles McCarthy – who married Catherine Roche, granddaughter of the seventh Lord Roche of Fermoy. In 1755, the owners of Carrignavar Castle were Daniel McCarthy and his wife, Elizabeth de Courcey, daughter of the twenty-fifth Baron of Kinsale.

Old Lord Kingsale was the head of the de Courcey family. He was born in 1700 and succeeded his cousin in the barony in 1720. In 1725, he married Margaretta, daughter of John Essington from Herts, England. They had one son, who died as an infant, and three daughters. The daughters were Mary, who married John O'Grady of Limerick in 1751, Elizabeth, married in 1751 to Daniel McCarthy of Carrignavar Castle, and Eleanor, who died unmarried.

In 1751, these three daughters were the co-heirs to the barony of Kingsale and to their father's fortune and estates. O'Grady and McCarthy both believed they had married heiresses, but the unexpected happened: John de Courcey landed at Portsmouth, England – all the way from Newport, Rhode Island in the American colonies. It was not long before he arrived in Ireland and presented himself to Lord Kingsale, proving to him that he was his third cousin once removed, and his male heir in the barony. This was shock indeed, but worse was to follow: the old man was satisfied with John's credentials, accepted him as heir and made a new will leaving him all his estates and money.

The families of O'Grady and McCarthy were stunned and took legal advice. Gerald, Lord Kingsale, died on 1 December 1759 and the two sons-in-law, O'Grady and McCarthy, were advised to challenge the credentials of John de Courcey. If that failed, they should claim that the old baron was out of his mind when he changed his will in favour of John. Following his death, advertisements appeared in Irish newspapers, including one from the daughters, claiming that their father was insane and ridiculing the claims of his successor to the title. However, John de Courcey was confirmed in his title and proceeded to take possession of his inheritance. This proved too much for O'Grady and McCarthy – on the night of 4 March 1760, they launched an attack on Lord Kingsale's house in Kinsale, firing guns at him. He escaped by dropping from a back window. The assailants took possession of the house and turned the new Lady Kingsale and her children out into the rain. Their conduct brought no punishment upon their heads – they were merely ejected by the sheriff the next day. Daniel McCarthy died in September 1763.

The Bandon Bridge district was represented in parliament in 1689 by Charles McCarthy Balleagh and Daniel McCarthy Reagh. This McCarthy Reagh finally settled in France. His descendent, Count McCarthy Reagh, set up one of the finest libraries in Europe, but it was later destroyed during the revolution.

Arrival of John de Courcey

The de Courceys held onto the barony until near the end of the sixteenth century. In 1587, they gave it the name of Dún Mhic Phádraig and we find mention of the manor of Downe Mc Patricke, alias the 'Oldehedd of Kynsale'.

The newly arrived John de Courcey was in 1177 created Earl of Ulster by King Henry II, but by the contrivances of Hugh de Lacy lost the king's favour. Whilst a prisoner in the Tower of London, he was sent for by King John. He was in dispute with King Philip about a town in Normandy, and they intended to resolve their dispute by single combat, as was the custom of those times. When the king's message was delivered to him, the Earl of Ulster answered,

De Courcey family arms.

'That not for the king, but for the honour of his country, he was willing to undertake the matter.' A contemporary description goes as follows:

> The day came, the place and lists were appointed, and the scaffolds were set up. The princes with their nobility on both sides.
>
> The French Champion first sallied forth, gave a turn and rested himself in his tent. De Courcey was sent for he soon came forth, gave a turn and went into his tent. When the trumpets sounded the charge, the champions came out, and viewed each other. De Courcey eyed his adversary with a wonderful stern countenance and passed by.
>
> The Frenchman, not liking his grim look, and the strong proportion of his person, so when the trumpets sounded to battle a second time, de Courcey drew his sword; upon which, the Frenchman clapped spurs to his horse, broke through the barrier, and fled into Spain. King Philip asked King John that de Courcey might be called before him, to show some proof of his strength. A stake was set in the ground, and a shirt of mail and a helmet, placed thereon; de Courcey drew his sword, looked wonderfully stern upon the princes and cleft the helmet, shirt of mail and stake so far, that none could pull out the weapon but himself.

The princes then asked him, why he looked so sour upon them? He said if he had missed his blow, he would have cut off both their heads but all was taken in good part. King John gave him great gifts and restored him to his former possessions. Around the year 1185 a halfpenny struck at Downpatrick bears the name of St Patrick on one side and de Courcey's on the other.

Kilbrittain anciently belonged to the barony of Courceys. The castle was formerly a seat of Lord Courcey and afterwards fell into the hands of McCarthy Reagh. The story goes that Lord Courcey pawned his castle and lands at Kilbrittain to McCarthy to secure the return of a white weasel that he had borrowed from him. As it happened, the weasel died. This accident gave title and McCarthy was able to keep possession.

The first Lord Courcey was William de Courcey. He was created Baron of Kinsale in the year 1397 and the privileges he enjoyed had been granted by King John to Sir John de Courcey, Earl of Ulster and his heirs forever. Next came Patrick de Courcey (1221), followed by Miles in 1286 and John de Courcey who was killed by Dónal McCarthy in the year 1294 at the island of Inchydoney, near Clonakilty. A furious feud broke out with the southern lords in 1358 – Miles de Courcey, William de Barry Óg and Richard Óg Barrett. They were contesting a parcel of land in Kinalmeaky, of which Barry was lord and where de Courcey held lands, and where Barrett was moving in. Of the de Courceys, William assumed the title in 1396, followed by Nicholas de Courcey, Patrick (1419) and Nicholas (1474), who married the daughter of the O'Mahoneys.

On 27 June 1488, Sir Richard Edgecomb arrived at Kinsale with five ships carrying 500 men to take new oaths of allegiance from the great men of Ireland. The Lord Thomas Barry (Barry Óg) went on board his ship and there did homage for his barony: but the next day, Sir Richard (at the request of James, Lord Courcey and the inhabitants of Kinsale) came into the town where, in the church of St Multosia, Lord Courcey did homage and the townsmen swore allegiance to King Henry VII.

In the years 1490 through to 1497, the whole of Ireland was swept by famine. The wet and dismal summer's corn was so scarce that a peck of wheat in the heartland of the country (Meath) was sold at five lesser ounces of silver; a gallon of ale cost 6d. and a barrel of oats in Ulster was worth a cow. Many hundreds of people perished.

After James de Courcey's death in 1499, the lordship was taken over by his younger brother, David, who was archdeacon of Cork. There was a bit of turmoil in the family again at this time, and David is supposed to have deposed his idiot nephew, Edmund. Another account says that Nicholas succeeded the idiot nephew and was then disposed by his brother.

We see in 1591 that John Fitz-John Fitz Nicholas Courcey joined Lord Courcey in a conveyance of Coolbane and Garrylucas, which is near the Old Head.

Edmund de Courcey, who was bishop of Ross, died in 1518 and is buried in the Franciscan Abbey at Timoleague. There are several other tombs for

The remains of the Anglo-French Norman castle at the Old Head Of Kinsale which belonged to the de Courcey family. Built in the thirteenth century, its inside walls were graced with fur skins.

Norman and Irish families in this abbey, including that of the McCarthy's.

In the churchyard at Ballinadee, Co. Cork, a small headstone reads: 'This is erected by Edw-de Courcey in memory of his beloved father Richard de Courcey and his family, who died in April 1802 aged 80 years.'

The powerful McCarthy Reagh of Kilbrittain had a daughter, Ellen, married to the twenty-first Lord de Courcey of Kinsale. Alliances of this kind between Anglo-Norman colonists and daughters of Irish clansmen were by no means uncommon in those days.

Almericus de Courcey was among the first to greet King James when he landed at Kinsale. He had good reason to be there as he was left a minor when his father, John, died. Under English law, all minors became wards of the court. Almericus was stubborn and his teachers could do nothing with him, so they left him go back to his estates and castles in the Old Head still a Catholic. Almericus became a member of the Irish House of Lords in Dublin, and served under Patrick Sarsfield as colonel in the horse regiment.

Miles de Courcey represented Kinsale and district in 1689 and was afterwards Lord Kingsale. From old feudal records we learn that Alemeric de Courcey held Kilkerrin just north of Ballinspittle in the year 1372 and that John Fitzgarrett held the district we now know as Garrettstown (Ballygarrett).

In 1627, Sir Dominick Sarsfield took the title of Baron of Kinsale off de Courcey. In the same year, Lord de Courcey and his son, Gerald, petitioned the king and lords of the council of England to get their title back. Sarsfield had to hand back his title. On 13 June 1720, Lord Gerald de Courcey had the privilege of kissing the hand of King George I.

Gerald, the twenty-fourth lord, married an English woman and lived and died at the Old Head; he was buried at Ringrone. He was succeeded by his cousin, John, who sat in the Irish House of Lords in 1771. That was about the end of the long residence of the de Courcey's as Catholics in the Old Head, as John's four sons became Protestants. Overlooking the now disused castle at Ringrone stands the tomb of the Norman family de Courcey, erected in the year 1819. These were the once proud people after whom the barony is today known.

One of the most historic districts in Ireland lies within what may be termed the environs of Kinsale, where ancient races played their valiant parts in mighty dramas, now lost in the mists of antiquity; and in that storied past the hinterland of the Old Head was a conspicuous stage of life and action, as grim reminders of those immemorial times we may still behold.

> Chiefless castles breathing stern farewells,
> From grey but leafy walls where ruin greenly dwells
> And here they stand, as stands a lofty mind
> Worn but unstooping to the baser crowd
> All tenantless save to the crannying wind
> Or beholding dark communion with the cloud
> There was a day when they were young and proud
> Banners on high as battles passed below
> But they who fought are in the bloody shroud
> And those that wavered are shredless dust ere now
> And the black battlements shall bear no future blow.

Skirting the beautiful wooded sloops of the Bandon river, for many miles this varied parish of Ballinspittle, in the Cuirseaca, stretches its mighty beaconed headland defiantly into the seething billows of the vast, immeasurable, uncontrollable sea.

Hang By the Neck Until You Are Dead

In Kilanetig, a small townland just north-west of Ballinspittle, worship ceased at a little church, or Mass house, when it was desecrated by Donncha Dubh McCarthy (Denis the Black), who thought it a suitable place to stable his horses. Donncha McCarthy was the leader of a famous bunch of highway robbers whose territory was the Kilbrittain–Bandon area in Co. Cork. He was born and grew up in Rockfort, situated between Brinny and Innishannon, and had two brothers, Daniel and Michael. Though all three worked for a local farmer, they were always involved in criminal activity, encouraged by their mother. Eventually, they were outlawed and became a much feared band of robbers. Donncha was the eldest, the cleverest and most notorious.

This was the time of poor roads – in most cases they were only muddy tracks – and Donncha used to get the shoes fitted to his horse in reverse fashion, so as to confuse the authorities, an age-old trick used several hundred years before by smugglers. Donncha was the terror of travellers between Bandon and Kinsale – his favourite lurking place was Shipool wood, where he would lie in wait. The authorities eventually caught up with him and his brothers. Daniel and Michael were the first to be captured, in the autumn of 1772; they had attacked the house of a Mr Holland who worked as a dairyman and caretaker for Mr Alcock at Roughgrove, near Newcestown. Mr Holland had returned from Cork late in the evening after delivering butter to the market. Amongst the items he had purchased in Cork was an iron bar which was needed for shoeing cartwheels – that is, fitting the iron band around the timber rims of the wheels. At about 1 a.m., he was awakened by the smashing in of the front door. Dan and Michael McCarthy rushed into the house and were followed by another local man, also named McCarthy. They knew that Holland would more than likely have quite a sum of money on him from his previous day's trip to Cork.

The staircase to Holland's room was very narrow and only one person could go up at a time. First up the stairs was the local McCarthy man followed by Dan Dubh carrying a loaded blunderbuss. Holland was on the top of the stairs holding the iron bar. It's more than likely that he took it upstairs when he retired for the night because in the back of his mind was the possibility that he might be robbed before he had time to lodge the sum of money the following day in the bank in Bandon. He confronted and threatened McCarthy, and told him to retreat. But the local McCarthy kept coming forward. Holland raised the bar and, with one blow to the head, killed McCarthy. Using the dead body as a shield, Holland pushed him down the stairs, knocking Dan Dubh before him to the bottom of the stairs before he had time to use his blunderbuss, which fell from his hand. A fierce struggle ensued and Holland overpowered him. Finding the blunderbuss, he took control of the situation. In the meantime, the raiders dragged the body of the local McCarthy man outside and again returned to the house, only to find that two servants in the household had come to the aid of Holland.

The gang tried to retreat but as they did so, Holland grabbed Michael Dubh and, with the aid of the servants, overpowered and secured him. Next, Holland and his employees barricaded the windows and doors, and successfully resisted the attackers who drifted away into the darkness. The neighbours had been alerted and kept guard with pikes, reaping hooks and all sorts of offensive weapons. The police were notified and within a few hours, a sergeant and a couple of guards arrived. Michael and Dan were arrested, handcuffed and led away to the police station in Bandon. News of the arrests spread like wildfire and, as the prisoners and their escorts were approaching the town, the roadside was lined with hundreds of people trying to get a glimpse of the feared outlaws.

Donncha Dubh was still at large but it would not be for long. The place of his arrest was a house at Geara in the parish of Kilmeen in west Cork. Donncha and others had kidnapped a young woman by the name of Taylor with the intention of marrying her off to one of his buddies. The Rev. Emanuel Moore, who lived in the area, heard of the outrage and assembled a posse consisting of his brothers and some neighbours. They rushed to the house and forcibly entered it. In the mêlée and struggle that followed, the Rev. Moore was killed by Donncha, who then made a dash for freedom. He was met by the guard outside the house but put up fierce resistance until eventually overpowered, disarmed and secured.

In the spring of 1773, Donncha was charged in the Cork Assizes with the murder of the Rev. Moore. The judge directed the jury to acquit him as a proper warrant for his arrest had not been issued. However, Donncha was immediately put on trial for having stolen the blunderbuss with which he had committed the murder, and for this he was found guilty and sentenced to death. In the meantime, his two brothers were found guilty of the outrage at Roughgrove and were also condemned to death.

There was a custom at the time that executions should take place in the town nearest to where the crimes were committed, so Daniel and Michael were to be executed in Bandon, and for Donncha it was Clonakilty.

In April 1773, the three prisoners arrived in Bandon. Daniel and Michael were held in the local barracks, while Donncha was taken to Clonakilty. When the prisoner and escort arrived, they found everything ready for carrying out the hanging. A huge crowd had assembled around the scaffold. As Donncha climbed the steps, he showed no fear and gave the odd wink and nod to some of his friends in the crowd. The crafty Donncha had in mind to cheat the hangman for, around his neck, he had a steel collar fitted with supports that came down around his chest and under his armpits. The brace around his neck was covered with a large neckerchief – a common article of clothing in those days. The steel collar was to prevent the noose of the rope from choking him. It is said that a blacksmith by the name of Lane from Ballincurra, who used to shoe his horses, made it for him – most likely under duress. The law stated that if you cheated the hangman once, you could not be hanged a second time for the same crime. The steel portion around his chest was probably to protect him from pistol shots when he was on the run. (Years later, another outlaw by the name of Ned Kelly, on the run in Australia, used a similar device.) However, the plan failed when a man attending the hanging – by the name of Hastings Moore, a brother of the man murdered at Geara – noticed that the scarf around Donncha's neck was very large. More than likely, he was tipped off. He asked the hangman to investigate and the search revealed the collar; it was removed and the rope readjusted. Donncha's mood changed and, as he gazed at the crowd, the trapdoor was sprung.

Meanwhile, in Bandon, preparations were well on the way at Gallows Hill, near Hill Terrace at the west end of the town. A great crowd had assembled to see the final act and were in festive mood. The two brothers were marched out, handcuffed to each other, and asked if they had anything to say. Michael replied that he could not deny the justice of his sentence and asked the crowd to pray for his soul. It is said that when he leaned down from the gallows to give his mother her last kiss, he bit off her ear, blaming her for the position in which he now found himself. Daniel told them to get on with it and get it over as soon as possible, and in seconds another two ruffians went to eternity. They were left hanging for some time and when they were later cut down, no-one came forward to claim the bodies. A local man, George Kingston – the owner of a timber yard close by – removed the bodies and had them buried in his premises. It's said his reason for burying them in his timber yard was because he suffered from pilfering – timber being stolen from his yard – and that this would be a deterrent to the superstitious Irish. I do not have any evidence to back up that theory. It is interesting to note that on 24 September 1774, just one and a half years later, Denis McCarthy – otherwise Dubh – was also hanged at Gallows Green in Cork for the same crime his father had paid the penalty for.

The point at the Old Head of Kinsale where the present lighthouse stands was known as hangman's point. Hanging and removing a person's head with a swift swipe of a sword were the order of the day. The choice of such a prominent place for a gallows was as a deterrent to local fishermen and passing ships – there for all to see and to bring back the tale.

For warring Irish clans and Anglo-Irish Normans, trying to hold onto their head was a problem. In 1583, the Earl of Desmond and the Ormonds were at each other's throats. Daniel Kelly cut the head off the old Earl of Desmond and was rewarded by Queen Elizabeth. The earl's head was sent over to the queen in England by the Earl of Ormond. Elizabeth ordered his head to be fixed upon London Bridge. His body was hidden for eight weeks and later buried in Kerry, Kelly himself was later hanged at Tyburn.

Most towns and cities had hanging squares in a prominent position and with plenty of space for people to congregate. In most cases, it was a day of great festivities and the taverns would be packed to capacity. Cork city's gallows were on Daunts Square. On 10 September 1766, a man by the name of Patrick Redmond – a tailor by trade – was to be executed for robbing a dwelling house. All the procedures were carried out and the hangman did his business – or so he thought. He left the scene leaving the poor misfortunate individual dangling in mid-air. After Redmond had been hanging for nine minutes, he was cut down by his friends who were joined by a visiting actor by the name of Glover who was very interested in the day's happenings. Glover, who was playing at a theatre in the city, felt Redmond's pulse and found that he was still alive and that he had cheated the hangman. Redmond quickly recovered, making his escape as quickly as he could. He then went to the nearest tavern and got drunk. If you escaped the hangman the first time, the law stated, you could not be hanged a second time for the same crime.

Later that night – well inebriated – Redmond sought out the man who helped in getting the hangman's noose off his neck. He found Glover at the playhouse and went on stage to thank him personally for the good deed. Upon his appearance, the whole audience was put in terror and consternation, and scattered to the four corners of the city. The sight of the man hanged earlier in the day staggering around the stage was beyond their comprehension.

On 10 April 1773, Owen McCarthy was hanged at Gallows Green in Cork for stealing a cow. For young or old, it was all the same. Thomas Carroll, aged seventy, was hanged at Gallows Green on 25 April 1767 for the theft of four cows from his neighbour, Charles McCarthy. You would think the poor man would have learned a lesson ten years earlier when transported for cow theft.

Laurence Kennedy was hanged at Gallows Green on 29 April 1775. His head was cut off and attached to the south end of the goal. He confessed to the murder of his father. He also robbed his father of £30 and in court declared that the love of money had influenced him.

Denis Long was hanged on 24 September 1785 for raping Catherine Brien. After Long had been hanging for several minutes, the rope slipped and he seized the upper part of it. It was some time before he could be disengaged from his grip and the execution completed.

Denis Daly was hung in the county goal on 5 September 1829 for the abduction of Anne Gallagher at Glanworth the previous year. The day was very bad weather wise and a small crowd attended – mainly relatives who came to claim the body for burial. At about 12 p.m., he was brought out onto the platform. Aged about thirty-six, he looked wretched. After spending a short time in prayer, the platform gave way and he was launched into eternity. Daly's body was taken back to Glanworth but his relatives took revenge and dumped his body at the prosecutor's door. A riot ensued, the police intervened, stones were thrown, the Riot Act was read and a man named Jeremiah Noonan was shot in the confusion.

Brothers, Thomas and William Fitzgerald were hanged in Cork on 4 April 1752 for highway robbery of 6 shillings. While William Fitzgerald was on trial in the city court, his brother Thomas – who was accused of the robbery, but not arrested – conscious of his own innocence, carried a quart of ale into the court and passed it to his brother in the dock. He was immediately seized, tried by the same jury, found guilty and executed with his brother.

William Leary met the same fate at Gallows Green on 11 April 1822 for the murder of his master, Davis Stanley, at Oldcourt near Kinsale. While the arrangements for the execution were in the making, the wretched criminal prayed with much fervency and apparent contrition. As he mounted the platform, there was not a sound from the immense crowd. He was launched into eternity to the accompaniment of one solitary scream from a relative. After hanging for the usual time, the body was cut down and conveyed under guard to the county infirmary for dissection.

In another case, a seventy-year-old woman was hanged in the county goal in Cork on 10 May 1851 for a murder committed in Dunmanway. The wretched woman stood on the platform, the bolt was withdrawn, the poor woman struggled for a while and then died. A large crowd in attendance were singing and dancing and in most cases drunk.

Michael Lynch was executed on the platform over the front gate of the county goal on 20 April 1865 for having murdered his father at Droumduffe, Bantry on 15 September 1864. His agonies gratified the morbid curiosity of thousands who assembled to see him die – the prevailing feeling was one of indifference. The crowd simply went to see an unusual spectacle and, when it was over, the majority of them seemed to think nothing more of it. This was the last public hanging in Cork.

The Spanish Attempts
and the Kinsale Fiasco

Spain had been enriched by its South American colonies, first plundered by Columbus in 1492. The country could extract all the gold and silver it wanted but thousands of miles and a harsh Atlantic crossing of several weeks separated the motherland from its colonies. Spain needed fertile lands close to home – within a couple of days' sailing – yet the islands of England and Ireland had eluded its grasp.

The first attempt to gain a foothold in the western isles of Europe was in the summer of 1380, during the reign of Richard II. A Spanish fleet arrived off Kinsale and was decimated. Driven by a fleet of English ships, they had been forced to take refuge in the safe haven of Kinsale. It was here that the Irish and the English attacked them; at least 400 were slain and their chief captains taken hostage, including Gonzales de Vorza and his brother, Martin de Montriga. Five ships were captured.

The great English admiral, Sir Francis Drake (b. 1540) was chased around the coast of Cork by the Spanish navy and sailed into Cork Harbour and hid his fleet up by Crosshaven in a little cove. The Spanish failed to find him and he lived to fight another day. The area is known as Drake's Pool to this day.

The next attempt was the disastrous armada expedition to England in 1588. Several factors came into play: bad planning, poor communications and the adverse weather of the North Atlantic scattering the fleet. Several of the ships were wrecked around the coast of Scotland and the west of Ireland. Some Spaniards escaped and made it to the safety of the rocky shores only to be attacked, stripped and killed – in most cases by the natives although some were taken captive by the authorities. In total, seventeen ships and 5,394 men were lost off the Irish coast.

In Bearhaven, west Cork – home to the O'Sullivan clan which had flirted with the Spaniards for years – vast quantities of munitions were constantly shipped from Spain to beef up the firepower of O'Sullivan, Gunpowder by the barrel was stored in the vaults of the castles in the year 1549. Dermot O'Sullivan was accidentally blown up in his castle when a barrel of gunpowder exploded, and his brother, Amlavus – who succeeded him – was killed soon after in a skirmish.

By 1599, the break-up of the Irish clans was in full swing. O'Neill made the journey into Munster under the pretence of a pilgrimage to the Abbey of Holy Cross, in Tipperary. When he arrived in Co. Cork, he had with him 2,500 foot soldiers and 200 horses, and he deposed Daniel Mac McCarthy Mór. Florence McCarthy replaced him as head of the family. He burned and destroyed Lord Barry's lands and those of other clans that refused to join him. He also took hostages from the Sugan Earl of Desmond and took several of Lord Barry's people prisoner.

On 21 April 1600, Lord Carew marched to Cork with 900 foot and 100 horses. He had come from Dungarvan where he had received intelligence that Florence McCarthy and others were in rebellion in Carbery, west Cork. Carew sent towards Kinsale 1,200 foot and 100 horses under the command of a Captain Flower. Florence McCarthy had assembled about 2,000 Irish and lay in ambush about midway between Cork and Kinsale, but the English – aware of his position – drew up and stood to their arms. The Irish, finding that they were discovered, resolutely attacked the English who retreated eastward, under the walls of an old castle. During the retreat, Flower ordered a party of musketeers to conceal themselves behind a high ditch where they fired upon the Irish. This caused much confusion and they quit their pursuit; in turn, they were charged by the English horse and routed. In the attack, ninety-eight Irish were killed and as many more wounded. The English lost one officer and eight private soldiers. Flower himself received several wounds and had two horses killed under him. The Irish dispersed.

The third and major attempt on Ireland was at Kinsale on 23 September 1601 when the Spanish fleet of fifty ships was spotted off the mouth of Cork Harbour. The armada of ships consisted of six men-of-war and transports carrying at least 6,000 troops, horses and all the requirements of an invading force. The admiral of the fleet was the Marquis of Santa Cruz; the vice-admiral was Don Siberio, alias Seriago; the commander of the land forces was Don Juan del Aquila, who landed with his troops and took over the town of Kinsale. They met no opposition as the garrison of only one company of English was withdrawn. The Spanish had with them a large group of Spanish women, suggesting that colonisation had been on their minds. The Spaniards' cattle and horses were farmed on the headland of Castlepark.

Very soon, the Spanish found themselves surrounded by the English forces, commanded by Lord Mountjoy. The creek at Oysterhaven – a couple of miles east of Kinsale – was not defended and it was here that the English, several days later, landed men and supplies from Dublin and made the short hike to Kinsale.

On 21 October 1601, Cormac Mac-Dermot Carty, chief of Muskerry, with the Irish under his command, attacked the Spanish trenches and drove the Spaniards back towards the town. The Spanish sent out more troops and he was obliged to give way. Sir William Godolphin and Captain Berkley came to his aid, and with their combined forces drove the Spanish back in behind the walls of Kinsale. William Godolphin, who had come over from Essex in 1599, was in command of Lord Mountjoy's brigade of horse at the Battle of Kinsale, and it was he who repelled the skirmishes of the Spaniards and the attacks of the Irish. Wounded, he fought on, and when del Aquila offered a parley, he wanted someone of special trust so Godolphin became a negotiator.

Del Aquila sent urgent messengers for help to the Lords O'Neill and

O'Donnell in the north of Ireland. The northern chiefs assembled their forces and began their long march south. When they arrived at the village of Innishannon, they were joined by approximately 500 Spaniards who had landed at Castlehaven in west Cork. They were also joined by smaller forces of the Munster chiefs. A battle plan was drawn up whereby the Irish would attack from the rear and the Spanish forces would sally forth from Kinsale town at dawn on the morning of Christmas day 1601. They would make their attack at the most unlikely time the English would expect a Catholic army to attack.

The Irish moved down the river from Innishannon and, on passing the castle at Shipool, O'Neill asked the question as to who was in residence there. The reply came that an Englishman named Barrett was the proprietor and that he had come over several hundred years earlier and had adopted the Irish way of life. O'Neill replied, 'I hate the churl' (ill-bred person). He trusted no-one and this would later backfire on him – the northern chief was slowly digging his own grave. The Irish set up camp about a mile to the rear of the English camp and effectively cut off all supplies and support from Cork. So Mountjoy, who was besieging Don Juan del Aquila in Kinsale, found himself besieged by the combined forces of O'Neill and O'Donnell.

Things went sadly wrong on Christmas eve; there was a blizzard, thunder and lightning, and to compound the situation, several of the major Irish clans in Munster who were pro-English – among them the McCarthys, O'Briens and Burkes – failed to join the forces of O'Neill and O'Donnell. These southern clans did not trust O'Neill, the northern chieftain, which is probably why the Spaniards looked for O'Neill's help in the first place as they could not rely on the support of the local clans. O'Neill had marched 300 miles in the most appalling weather, and his troops – in poor footwear and inappropriate cloth-ing – suffered several casualties. When they reached the outskirts of the battle front, morale was low. Worse still, Mountjoy had advance warning of the impending attack from an informer, the curse of Irish history down through the years.

Dawn broke, and the Irish expected to come upon a sleeping foe. Instead, they found that the English were already under arms and drawn up in battle array. The Irish forces were outnumbered and out-gunned, and they were slaughtered like sheep. The slopes leading down the hills towards Dunderrow were littered with dead horses, many of them with their intestines blown out, thus entangling some of the fleeing troops. There was much confusion as many of the smaller forces of Munster had joined the attack. At least 1,200 were killed as they fled the field of battle and many more would later perish from their wounds. The Spanish army took no major part in the Battle of Kinsale.

Don Juan del Aquila – the Spaniard who had been so eager to help the Irish cause as long as it looked profitable to him – lost his will to fight. The Irish had the English outnumbered at Kinsale and they could have won the battle if his Spanish army had joined in. Instead, he stayed safe behind the walled town of Kinsale.

Don Juan del Aquila surrendered his army on 2 January 1602 after several conferences and articles of composition were finally agreed to. These were signed on 12 January and stipulated that del Aquila quit Kinsale and the other places he held in Ireland – namely Castlehaven and Bearhaven – and that he and his troops – along with artillery, munitions and shipping victuals – would be granted safe passage to Spain. Don Juan del Aquila marched out of Kinsale with his arms, drums beating, colours flying and convoys carrying his sick and wounded, and headed for Castlehaven. It would be here in 1628 that several more skirmishes between the Spanish and the English would erupt.

Victuals supplied to del Aquila's army on quitting Kinsale consisted of 186,052 pounds of biscuit costing £2,067/4s./8d., 6,204 pounds of butter at a cost of £157/12s./3d., 47,394 pounds of meat to the tune of £789/18s./0d., 18,339 pounds of fish costing £305/13s./0d., and 1,235 pounds of rice priced at £30/17s./6d. In all, to supply the troops for their return journey to Spain cost a grand total of £3,351/5s./5d.

On hearing of del Aquila's surrender to the English at Kinsale, the Spaniards garrisoned at Dunboy Castle in west Cork flew the English colours. Dónal O'Sullivan, who had returned after the sickening defeat at Kinsale, found the gates of his castle barred against him. He was disgusted and, after a brief encounter where the Spaniards killed three of his best men, re-took his castle. He did not execute the Spaniards who had betrayed him because they were 'allies'.

The fighting at Dunboy was fierce. For several hours, the Irish defended the castle and killed a great number of the English with gunshot and stones fired from a huge catapult. About forty of the Irish tried to escape by sea but were caught and put to death by the sword. Eight escaped by jumping overboard and swam for their lives. When the English entered the castle and planted their colours, the fight for the cellars was bloody as they made their way down the narrow stone stairway in the vault where the gunpowder was stored. One of the Irish leaders – a man by the name of Taylor – was close to nine barrels of gunpowder and said that he would blow the castle and all within to pieces if they were not given free passage. But the English commander ordered another battery to attack the vault and bury them all in their castle. Eventually, Taylor and forty-eight others were forced to surrender. When the English entered the vault, they found Richard Mac-Geoghegan lying mortally wounded. On their approach, he staggered with a lighted candle towards an open barrel of gunpowder. A Captain Power grabbed and held him until he was killed.

Fifty-eight of the Irish were executed the next day. Taylor, Turlough-Roe Mac Swiney and a friar from Youghal by the name of Dominic Collins were spared in the hope that they might be of some future use. But several days later, all twelve of them were hanged – Taylor in Cork and Collins, the friar in his native Youghal.

Dunboy was in ruins. Lemcon Castle also fell to the English as did other smaller castles near Rosscarbery. The Irish forces of Tyrrell, William Bourke and O'Connor Kerry fled the county and, as they passed Muskerry, were attacked by Tiege Mac-Owen Carthy who killed several of them. On their way through Liscaroll, in north Cork, Viscount Barry attacked and killed many more. But worse was to come: when they reached the Shannon, there were no boats to make the crossing. So they killed several of their horses and made boats out of their skin to transport men and baggage, pulled across the Shannon by some of their horses. The sheriff of Tipperary and his men intercepted them and put some of them to the sword. They were attacked again in Connacht but this time, their backs to the wall, they put up a fight and killed several of the English.

In December 1602, a Captain Taaf was sent to Carbery to put down the remains of the rebels who had assembled under some of the McCarthys, and Owen Mac-Egan, the pope's apostolical vicar, was slain. He had brought considerable sums of silver to the Irish chiefs. He fought in this battle at the head of 100 Irish with a sword in one hand and his beads in the other. His chaplain was taken prisoner and executed in Cork. Thus ended the bloody aftermath of the Kinsale fiasco.

Around the end of February 1601, many pardons were granted in Munster by Queen Elizabeth. McCarthy Reagh and his followers received 210 pardons; O'Sullivan Bear and his followers received 528; O'Sullivan Mór and his followers received 481; the inhabitants of Mogeely were granted 151, and the inhabitants of Muskerry, 542. In all, about 4,000 were granted in the province.

O'Donnell fled to Spain to seek further help. O'Neill returned to Ulster where he remained until 1607 when he and his kinsman were forced through continuous English harassment to flee Ireland for Spain. Thus began the flight of the earls. This opened up the northern counties of Ulster to the Plantation. Nearly 200 years later, in the Peninsular War, on 26 October 1808, a relative of O'Neill commanded the army of Aragon in Spain where 7,000 men fought and held Sor, Lumbar and Sanguessa. Later, in February 1809, after the Battle of Tudela which stands on the river Ebro, all of O'Neill's troops fled towards Saragossa (Zaragoza) and its bloody aftermath.

In the six months the Spaniards were in Kinsale, they left their mark on the town: narrow streets, lanes, high buildings – some with balconies built in the Spanish fashion – and so many Spanish names. The little village of Scilly is typical of the Spanish style. In August 1667, a great fire broke out in the village and destroyed a large part of it.

In July of the same year, a squadron of sailing ships was sighted off the Old Head. The English inhabitants of Kinsale thought that they were coming under attack but it proved to be an English fleet under the command of Sir Jeremy Smith who sailed into the harbour with eight men-of-war, two bomb-ketches, two fire ships and a Dutch East-Indiaman of 800 tons with a rich cargo and thirteen chests of silver. Two other Dutch prizes were taken by Captain O'Brien, son of the Earl of Inchiquin.

In autumn of that year, a general peace was proclaimed between England, France, Denmark and Holland, and all was quiet again in the port of Kinsale.

After the Spaniards left, the village was colonised by a group of English fishermen who never much ventured out and always married in the village. All were in some way related to one another. Today, their descendants reside there and are more Irish than the Irish themselves.

After the defeat of the Spaniards, an important lesson was learned – the harbour had to be defended. So a large star-shaped fort was constructed at the mouth of the harbour, the first stone being laid in the year 1670 during the reign of King Charles II. It contained 100 pieces of brass cannon with twenty-four and forty-two-pound shot, mainly to cover the entrances to the harbour. The seabed approximately half a mile out to sea is littered with cannon shot, in most cases used for target practice.

On 22 August 1681, the Duke of Ormond – who at the time was the lord lieutenant – paid a visit to Kinsale and visited the new fort where his party stayed. Next morning, he was rowed up and down the harbour to observe its defences and later his party dined at Sir Robert Southwell's house. They then went to see some trials of the pilchard fishing where various groups entertained him. He dined the next day at the old fort with Sir Richard Booth, and rode around the hills of Ringcurran. His bed and breakfast was at the house of Sir Nicholas Armorer. On 25 August, he again visited the new fort where he toasted to His Majesty King Charles II and, after a discharge of artillery, he changed the name of the fort from Ringcurran to Charles Fort, and then departed for Cork well satisfied with the fortification.

On Wednesday 12 March 1688, King James landed in Kinsale. He was received and entertained by Donough, Earl of Clancarty. On his landing, the king made him one of the lords of his bedchamber and his regiment a royal regiment of guards.

The king later visited Cork, and on Sunday he heard Mass in a new chapel erected near the Franciscan friary. On his passage through the streets of Cork, he was supported by two members of that order, and many others followed, dressed in their habits.

At the same time, 5,000 French landed at Kinsale under Count Lauzun and the Marquis de Lary. The French ships at Cork and Bantry during 1688–89 are listed in table 1. Thirty-seven were men-of-war and the fleet consisted of 1,958 cannon and 11,495 men; when including four fire-ships, six floats and three other ships, a grand total of 2,223 cannon is arrived at. Its firepower alone was awesome, and the logistics for transporting so many men and their armour would have been complex. The English would not have held onto Ireland but for the continuing bickering of the Irish clans toward each other. Much help was available from Spain and France who each wanted to gain a foothold in Ireland as a launching pad for strikes at their long-standing enemy.

The importance of the port of Kinsale to the English was never more apparent than in the summer of 1691. A most glorious spectacle appeared off the coast: the English and Dutch Smyrna fleets in the port of Kinsale. The grand fleets of both nations stretched from the Old Head of Kinsale to Youghal, and if the French fleet came, it would have a hard time getting into any port close to Cork. If that city fell into enemy hands, a big portion of Munster could be controlled using Cork as a base.

On 20 December 1718, war against Spain was again proclaimed in Cork, and in 1722, Lord Shannon – a lord justice of Ireland – came to Cork. He was entertained by the corporation at very great expense, and the freedom of the city was presented to him in a gold box.

Such were the entertainment and treats held in the green of Dunderrow for one such party, in 1716, that it took six horses to carry victuals and liquor – there were thirty-six bottles of claret and twenty-four bottles of white wine.

Table 1: *French Ships at Bantry and Cork, 1688–89.*

Commander	Ship's Name	Guns	Men
Lieutenant general le Marq de Antreville, chefs d'escadres ?		62	420
Le Chevalier de Flaiour	Le Glorieux	50	380
Le Marq de Relinguess	Le Serieux	60	370
Le Marq de Nesmond	Le Constant	54	370

Captain	Ship's name	Guns	Men
D'Amblement	Le Henry	64	400
D'Hannault	Le Furieux	60	250
De Septeme	L'Ardent	62	370
De Machard	Le Burbon	62	370
De Belisle	Le Marquis	56	330
De Belfontaine	Le Prince	58	350
De Reald	Le Courageux	60	350
De Mobrane	L'Exellent	60	350
De la Hatteloire	Le Fort	58	350
De Septeville	L'Entrepenant	60	350
De Bidaw	L'Aquillon	58	330
De Chaseur	Le Vermondois	58	350
Du Palaise	Le Bon	54	300
De Gallisonviare	Le Maure	54	270
Colebert	Le Sage	50	300
D'Allis	Le Francois	46	250
De France	Le Trident	52	375
De Champigny	Le Brave	56	350
De Renault Huet	Le Termeraire	54	330
De Seguinge	Le Diamant	54	300
De Florin	Le Neptune	48	330
De St Maure	L'Arc en Ciel	54	250
Chefs D'Escadre	L'Arogant	58	250
De Genlis	L'Impersait	44	250
De Chateau Morant	Le St Michael	50	230
Baron Des Ardess	Le Faulcon	36	200
De Pontis	La Courtizane	64	370
Des Augere	Le Joli	36	200
Des Hainault	Le Moderne	50	300
De la Rougere	Le sans Pareil	58	250
De la Guiche	Le Palmier	36	200
Baron	Le Alcion	36	200
Europin	L'Opiniatre	36	200

Five labourers were employed to make seats and benches on the green, while a couple of women cut rushes and cleaned the green after the party. The total cost was £6/18s./7d. In 1722, another party held at Dunderrow required eleven horses to transport the sovereign's requirements to the green. In 1726, the cost of twelve men and horses, the building of a tent on the green, the finding of rushes for benches, sergeant's horses and two trumpeters was £2/5s./6d.

If you wanted a real feast you went to the courthouse or to Mr Southwell's house. The treat held for Lord Shannon, the lord lieutenant, on his visit to Kinsale in 1722, as mentioned above, was listed as follows:

> 4 doz. claret and 4 quarts of white wine, 6 doz. long end-pipes, 8oz. tobacco, Crame and Oyle, Cabbish and Collifflurrs, Lobstirs, Harshorn, Hurts, Mushweed Sugar and Spice, Oringes and Limmons, Frute for Puddins, Almons and Currans for Chese Caykes, Chikkins and Turkees, Peeze and Hartychoakes, 12lbs of Beakon, Gowsberrys and Red Currans, Rose Water and Bread, Pint of Sack for the Jelly, White Wine and Claret for the silly bobs, Bottle of Wine for same, Tarts and Pipes, 8 doz. Silly bobs tumblers broake or crakt etc.
>
> Finally 1s 3d to Mrs Howe for her trouble; 5s to Ed Vanmore for attending the Courthouse, and 5s to Phil Townshend beating drum for Troops. And as a deoch an doruis, 2 gals Rum for farewell entertainment to my Lord Shannon all coming to a grand total £17 16s 6d.

Things were hotting up again in 1728. Food was scarce and on 26 February, there was a great rising of the population of Cork. They marched and threatened to demolish the mayor's office – prevented only by the army. At the beginning of June the same year, riots broke out between the weavers and the butchers at the fair in the city.

In the late eighteenth and nineteenth century, Kinsale was a peaceful fishing port with a large fishing fleet bringing its catch back to the harbour. On the wharfs, a booming business was carried on of salting and packing into barrels herring and mackerel for export to England and the Continent. A poem of the time depicts the town.

> And on the broken pavement, here and there,
> Doth many a stinking sprat and herring lie
> A brandy and tobacco shop is near,
> And hens and dogs, and hogs are feeding by,
> And here a sailor's jacket hangs to dry.
> At every door, are sun-burnt matrons seen
> Mending old nets, to catch the scaly fry,
> Now singing shrill, and scolding oft between,
> Scolds answer foul-mouthed scolds, bad neighbourhood
> I ween.

Dr Milner Barry

Dr John Milner Barry was the founder of Cork Fever Hospital and House of Recovery, one of the most beneficial institutions in Cork city. He was also its first physician. Sadly, though the citizens of that city should remember his name, it is forgotten.

John Milner Barry was the eldest son of James and Elizabeth Barry. He was born in 1768 in the house of his grandmother, Mrs Milner, which was attached to Kilgobbin Castle near the village of Ballinadee, Co. Cork. Dr Barry's family had associations with another castle, at Togher, near Dunmanway. He had only one brother, a lieutenant in the army, who served all through the Peninsular War in Europe and died in Cork in 1832.

John Milner Barry went to school in Bandon and studied medicine in Edinburgh. He graduated with an MD in 1792. After a short stay in Scotland, he returned to Ireland and practised medicine in Cork until his death in 1822. He was married in 1808 to Mary, the eldest daughter of Mr William Phair of Brooklodge, near Cork. When Barry died, he left eight children. He was buried at Balinaltig, near Rathcormac. Dr Barry's second son, Dr John O'Brien Milner Barry, was born in 1815 and studied medicine at Paris from 1833–36. Like his father, he graduated at Edinburgh, in 1837. He died in Tunbridge Wells, England in 1881.

Dr Barry held for many years the lectureship on agriculture in the Royal Cork Institution, of which he was a founder. He was also president of the Cork Philosophical Society which was broken up in 1820 and later revived as the Cork Literary and Scientific Society.

In 1800, Dr Barry introduced vaccination into Cork and he also contributed many papers on vaccination, fever and similar subjects to the *London Medical and Physical Journal*. He published several pamphlets and wrote many annual reports of the Cork Fever Hospital. In some of his essays, he described forcibly the physical dangers of drunkenness and upheld the necessity of coercing habitual drunkards by law.

Around the same time, Dr Barry published an account of the nature and effects of cowpox, illustrated with cases and communications on the subject. It was addressed principally to parents with a view to promoting the extirpation of smallpox. Dr Barry also appears to have approved of effusion of water in cases of fever and of influenza, cases of which with symptoms of the most violent kind occurred in 1803.

An annual report published in 1818 in Cork by Edwards and Savage, Castle Street quotes the early history of Dr Barry's great work at the Cork Fever Hospital. Some of it is very gruesome, depicting the sanitary and social conditions in Cork city during that era.

In 1801, Dr Barry published an address to the inhabitants of the city of Cork entitled 'Report on the Infectious Diseases of Cork city'. The object of this address, which was widely circulated, was the establishment of a house of recovery for the prevention and cure of fever in Cork, according to the successful example of Waterford, Chester and Manchester, the only towns, now cities, in which such hospitals or institutions existed. His proposal received great attention from the benevolent inhabitants of Cork who had always supported every effort for the relief or advantage of the lower classes in the city. Several wealthy individuals, who at that period of time were distinguished for their extraordinary liberality towards the poor, subscribed large sums of money. Donations were in the region of £3–400. Some of the children of the wealthy put on plays which were well supported and brought in quite a substantial sum, which was used for preparing and furnishing the building. Not long after its establishment, Dr Barry was elected its physician – a post he continued to hold until his premature death.

The benefits and utility of this new Cork Fever Hospital and House of Recovery were very quick to be seen, and to its conducting committee two Acts of Parliament were passed authorising financial support to provide for its continuation. This applied also to other similar institutions in other parts of Ireland. The grand juries of the cities and towns were empowered to levy the sum of £100 at each assizes for the support of fever hospitals. This was later raised to £250 and was extended to the counties at large.

From 1803, the number of patients admitted to the Fever Hospital was 254, of which 241 were discharged – deaths only amounted to nine. In 1817, the figure for admittance had increased to 2,707 of whom 2,053 were discharged; the number of deaths was ten.

The extraordinary spread of fever in a malignant form in Cork in the year 1817 was to such an extent as to produce a marked sensation throughout the British Empire, compelling vessels from Cork to carry out quarantine in Lisbon to the great detriment of the Cork shipping trade with Portugal. This led to the suggestion that all communication should be cut off between Dublin and Cork.

Dr Barry ascribed to various causes. One of these was the neglect of sanitary safeguards; another was the prevailing poverty after the cessation of the wars with France and Napoleon's defeat – no city in the empire was affected more than Cork. This was because it had little or no industry. Cork supplied the goods and services when ships had to be stocked up, as the harbour was used extensively for transport of men, goods and horses for the war effort. With Napoleon's final defeat at Waterloo in 1815, when peace was made, there was a vast decrease in trade with prices greatly reduced. The consequence was empty stores and unattended shops. To compound this misfortune, the crops of 1816 failed, and besides its own poor in the city, hoards of people crowded in from the countryside to seek employment and to take advantage of the numerous soup kitchens that were set up at the expense of the richer inhabitants.

The suburbs and lanes were crowded beyond measure by a needy population, and the city was overburdened and the general distress augmented.

Another major cause of disease at this time was defective ventilation. Dr
Barry noted that a window tax in force at the time resulted in windows being
built up to avoid payment of the tax. To this day in the older parts of the city,
this is still evident.

With swarms of beggars infesting the streets, another cause of the propaga-
tion of disease was drunkenness. 'When this evil becomes habitual,' Dr Barry
observed, 'there is no remedy.' He adds: 'the greatest proportion of the fatal ter-
minations which occurred in the hospital originated in intoxication.'

Poor clothing was another contributory factor to the spread of fever. Dr
Barry states that nine out of ten of the labouring classes had to pawn their
clothes and, in some cases, the bedclothes were pawned as well. Up to recent
times, Cork had quite a number of pawn shops.

Given such a terrible state of affairs, one can hardly wonder at the large
number of fever patients in Cork in the years 1816–17 – the staggering figure
of 8,227. Dr Barry noted that one area of Cork that did not suffer from attacks
of fever was the Evergreen area, whose people were mostly robust, healthy,
employed in the merchant's cellars in the winter and in their gardens in the
summer. They had good food, healthy exercise and comfortable surroundings.

Malignant fever was rampant in Ireland for years. Another doctor, Hercules
Elmore – who administered to the poor in the Ballinspittle area in the 1850s –
contracted the disease. He died, as did so many young people, like Abram Wm.
Dunscombe Lane, who died at Templetrine on 12 January 1865, aged sixteen
years. In that same church a marble tablet on the wall reads:

> In memory Hercules Elmore Esq. M.D. who died 14th April 1853 aged 40
> years of malignant fever caught in the faithful and zealous discharge of
> his duties as medical officer of the Ballinspittle district. The poor lost a
> skillful and kind friend.

In Townshend's *Statistical Survey of Cork* can be found an agricultural
paper by Dr John Milner Barry, dedicated to Henry B. Evanson MB, Cork 1821
who had written 'Observations on Some Points of Medical Ethics'.

That Dr Milner Barry's philanthropic designs were meant by him not to end
with his own life may be seen by the notable injunctions he left behind him,
which will still be read with interest:

> I see no reason why the education of women, particularly in literary
> attainments, should not be conducted in the same manner with that of
> the male sex. I request that my girls may be instructed by their brothers,
> or others, in the classical languages of antiquity, *viz.*, Latin and Greek,
> especially the first, which may be taught them with the modern lan-
> guages, when they show a disposition or talents for learning them.
>
> I earnestly advise and request my children to promote by all the means
> in their power the instruction of the poor and that for this purpose they will
> not withhold their own personal assistance. To my daughters I especially

direct myself, as I well know that from the neglect of literary, religious and moral education the lower classes of their sex are not only quite unfitted for doing their respective duties in the humbler stations of life, but that numberless females are actually brought to ruin.

At this very time several young ladies belonging to the most respectable families in this city, Cork are bestowing their time successfully in educating the female children of the poor.

These observations are particularly applicable in this country where the education of the poor has been from various causes so entirely neglected, that they are for the most part in the state of utter ignorance and nearly barbarising. The personal exertions of those above them in rank would be of more service in rescuing them from this state than money.

Dr Barry was a man before his time. For the appalling suffering and humiliation that women had to endure both in the home and work-place continued well into the twentieth century. Thankfully, it has now almost disappeared and their quality of life is much enhanced and they play a huge part in the affairs of the countries of the civilised world.

Cenotaph erected on 1 May 1824 in the grounds of the Fever Hospital on the northside of Cork city to commemorate Dr John Milner Barry.

Such was the status of the poor in Cork in the nineteenth century, especially for women. In 1876, there was an infamous colony of prostitutes and wretched women of various ages – it numbered close to 130. Twenty houses were in use for the purpose of this illicit human trading as the laws of the time were ineffective in dealing with the situation. The red-light district in Cork city was in the parish of St Finbarr's, in an area south of Barrack Street, Phoenix Street and Cuthbert's Lane. On a fine summer evening in June, a Fr Michael Shinkwin, dressed in clerical garb and armed with the Bible, went into this foul and miserable district. After a week had passed. he had visited every corner of this area. Eventually, he had them kneeling and praying where before you only heard the voices of blasphemy and obscenity. Now the power of God had won, most besought pardon for their sins, and this infamous colony was disestablished – all to the credit of the courageous curate, Michael Shinkwin.

The Cork Fever Hospital was situated in the northside of the city and it closed down in the 1930s. This beneficial institution in the first fifty-seven years of operation attended to just over 97,000 patients of which 4,857 died. We should not forget its founder whose zeal, intelligence and devotion helped it to flourish and helped the poor masses in the city of Cork in the early part of the nineteenth century.

Dr John Milner Barry died from apoplexy in his house in Patrick's Hill on Ascension Day, 16 May 1822, at the young age of fifty-four. Cork had lost a skillful physician, an esteemed citizen and an eminent public benefactor.

On 1 May 1824, in the grounds of the Fever Hospital on the northside of Cork city, a cenotaph was erected to the brilliant physician born at Kilgobbin, near Ballinadee, Co. Cork. It carried the following inscription:

> In Respectful and affectionate remembrance of
> Doctor John Milner Barry
> By whose earnest exertions was founded
> By whose unwearied attention was established
> This Fever Hospital
> An Institution
> Which under God has been repeatedly
> The means of preventing
> The pernicious contagion of Typhus Fever
> From diffusing itself widely
> In the populous City of Cork
> Erected by voluntary subscriptions
> May 1st Anno Domini 1824.

Peninsular War

For six years the Iberian peninsula was devastated by a war of independence. The blood of France, Germany, England, Portugal and Spain was shed in the contest. The hostility of aristocratic Europe forced republican France to adopt a military policy that, though outrageous in appearance, was in reality one of necessity. Up until the Treaty of Tilsit, her wars were essentially defensive. Her long and bloody Continental struggle was not for pre-eminence amongst ambitious powers, not a dispute over territory, nor momentary political ascendancy, but a deadly conflict to determine whether aristocracy or democracy should predominate, equality or privilege being the principle of European civilisation.

The French Revolution was, however, pushed into existence before the hour of its natural birth. The aristocratic principle was still too vigorous, too much identified with the monarchic, to be successfully resisted by virtuous democracy. Much less could it be overthrown by a democracy, rioting in innocent blood. Napoleon had waged almost continuous war from 1803–14, inflicting crushing defeats on the major European powers. In 1812, his ambition led him to invade Russia with disastrous results. Beaten as much by the great distance involved and the cruel weather as by Russian numerical superiority, he was obliged to abandon his army and return hurriedly to Paris to raise more troops.

Russia, Austria, Prussia and Great Britain united and advanced on France. Unable to repel invasion, Napoleon was forced to abdicate in 1814 and was exiled to the island of Elba.

On 1 March 1815, he escaped and landed with less than a dozen supporters near Nice. He marched to Paris, gathering support on the way. Eighteen days later, he entered the capital and, by June, had raised a force of a 124,000 men. Napoleon then struck north-east, to seize Brussels, but between his army and the Belgian capital lay Wellington, Blucher and Waterloo.

The Peninsular War's most famous battles were Talavera, Valencia, Bailen, Saragossa, Albuera, Vittoria and Salamanca. Salamanca was the place where Fr Owen Field, the noble friar of Timoleague Abbey, was educated. This town in Spain was in the sixteenth century regarded as one of the four greatest centres of learning in Europe. Fr Field was born in 1568 and died at the grand old age of 100 years in 1668. He is buried in the abbey at Timoleague, not far from where he was born. Admiral Michael de Courcey, of the 39th Regiment and third son of John, twenty-fifth Baron of Kingsale, was killed at Vittoria

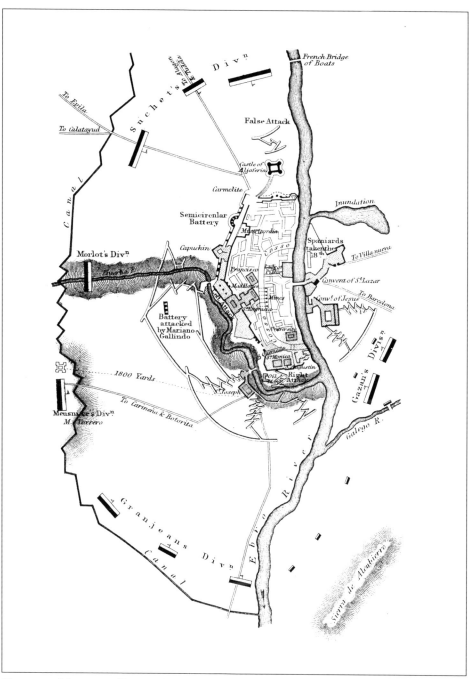

Siege map of Saragossa (Zaragoza), 1808–09. During the first siege, in the summer of 1808, Lefebvre Desnouettes failed to take the city. The second siege, in the winter of 1809, was more bloody and Saragossa fell to the French. The mortal remains of Count Charles Lefebvre Desnouettes – Napoleon's trusted general – lie in an unmarked grave in Templetrine near Garrettstown.

leaving no family. General Frederick Meade, a native of Innishannon and of the Connaught Rangers, served through the Peninsular War and was badly wounded at the Battle of Salamanca.

It is also worth noting that in Rathclaren church, Kilbrittain, a plaque reads: 'Colonel Sampson Stawell XII Royal Lancers died Aug. 21st 1849.' He fought at Vittoria, Rodrigo and Waterloo.

It was the country people, the frank Irish peasantry, who formed the backbone of the battalions which fought in the Peninsular War and were yet to fight in India. The Peninsular War was a conflict between France and Great Britain in the Iberian peninsula, and lasted from 1808–14. It grew out of the efforts of Napoleon I to control Spain and Portugal, and was sparked by a palace revolt in Madrid. In March 1808, the pro-French King Charles IV was deposed. Napoleon invaded Spain and by June had installed his brother, Joseph Bonaparte, as king of Spain.

Portugal and Spain revolted so the British sent in a force of troops under Sir Arthur Wellesley, later to become the Duke of Wellington. His mission was to aid the rebels. On 15–17 June 1808, 357 artillery troops, 349 cavalry and 8,688 infantry – a total of 9,394 troops – embarked at the port of Cork, from where they sailed on 12 July. They landed at Mondego and on 1 August proceeded to Coruna. At the same time, other troops were embarking from various parts of Britain.

By 21 August 1808, records show that under the command of Wellesley, the number of casualties were nine officers killed, fifty-five wounded and six missing. Of the lower ranks, 189 were killed, 820 wounded and 140 missing. This gave a total of 1,228 men out of action in approximately three weeks of warfare. Portugal was won over in a short space of time but the war in Spain lasted for several years. The state of the French army in Portugal on 23 May 1808 consisted of a grand total of 52,634 men and 4,454 horses.

Records show the state of the French army of Spain on 25 October 1808 – with the Emperor Napoleon commanding in person – consisted of 318,034 men on the ground and 60,740 horses, the logistics of which must have been huge. In Spain in February 1809, under the command of King Joseph, Napoleon's brother, were a total of 288,019 men and 42,726 horses. The demand for horses was great and Ireland was full of these animals. During the five years of the Peninsular War and given that the British expedition actually set out from Cork, there was a major drain on the supply of horses. Wellington's dispatches shows that he was in constant anxiety about his supply. He even discussed whether it was practical to import them from America and Brazil for his army. He spoke of paying £30–40 for good cavalry horses, and complained that England and Ireland seemed unable to supply one-twentieth of the horses that the French can command. This depletion of horses led to the introduction of the ass, or donkey, as a cheap substitute – a useful beast of burden so often mistreated. While Wellington was conquering the peninsula, the little ass was conquering Ireland; it was used mainly by the poor.

The last action of the Napoleonic Wars ended at the Battle of Waterloo on 18 June. This was fought near Brussels, Belgium. Napoleon had returned from exile and he and his army faced the allied armies of Britain, Prussia, Austria

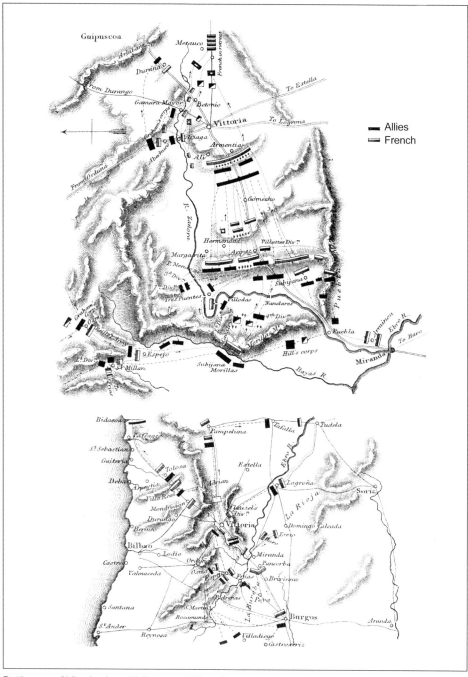

Battle map of Vittoria, June 1813. Major William Gough and Colonel Sampson Stawell of Kilbrittain both fought with distinction. Admiral Michael de Courcey of the 39th Regiment and 3rd – son of John, the twenty-fifth Baron of Kingsale – was killed at Vittoria, leaving no family. Stawell went on to fight at Rodrigo and Waterloo; he died in 1849.

and Russia. He defeated a Prussian force at Ligny and turned his forces to the British under Wellington. The British resisted successfully and were joined by another strong Prussian force under the command of Marshal Blucher. The French were routed, Napoleon abdicated and Wellington was victorious, but the cost in lives was great: the allied troops lost 22,000 men and the French as many as 30,000.

On a forty-foot-high mound overlooking the battlefield of Waterloo today can be seen a lion; this huge cast-iron monument has 226 steps leading up to its summit from where can be viewed the battlefield. This is also the place where it is believed that the Prince of Orange was wounded.

During the summer of 1815, there came a letter to a woman living in Co. Cork from her son on board HMS *Bellerophon* in Plymouth Sound. In it he describes Napoleon and the surrender. Dated Sunday 30 July 1815, it reads:

My Dear Mother,
You will be surprised at not hearing from me, but I tell you that no private letters were allowed to leave the ship before today. We have Bonaparte and suite on board; the circumstances, which led to his surrender, were his defeats in all points and were it not for the strict blockade that was kept up he would have escaped to America. We heard of his being aboard the French Frigate Saale, off Rochefort, from which moment we watched his motions. On the morning of the 14th we observed a Schooner bearing the flag of truce coming towards us we hove to for her, when Count Lascazas and General Lallemande came on board with proposals from Bonaparte.

Next morning 16th instant, at 4am we observed a man of war bearing down on us. We immediately dispatched all our small boats and Lieutenant Mott, in a barge, brought Bonaparte on board at seven am. The boats were very busily employed bringing his retinue and luggage. I never saw men exert themselves as much as ours did that day. It was decided that Admiral Hotham should take him but he was down the harbour in the ship 'Superb' and he saw him coming on board. He did everything in his power to get to our ship but it was just around eleven in the forenoon before the Admiral boarded.

Bonaparte is a fine looking man inclined to corpulency; is five feet six inches in height, his hair turning grey and a little bald on the crown of the head, no whiskers, complexion French yellow, eyes grey, Roman nose, good mouth and chin, neck short, big belly, arms stout, small white hands, and shows a good leg. He wears a cocked hat, something like our own three cornered ones, with the tri-coloured cockade in it, plain green coat, cap red and cuffs of the same, plain gold epaulets and a large star on his left breast, white waist-coat and breeches, and white silk stockings, thin shoes and buckles. Eats but two meals in the day, breakfast and dinner; these are sumptuous fish, flesh and fowl, wines, fruits, various French dishes, etc, etc. He breakfasts about eleven and dines at six, is about half an hour at each, when he generally comes on deck, or goes into the after cabin to study. We do not know what's to become of him, yet he remains on board

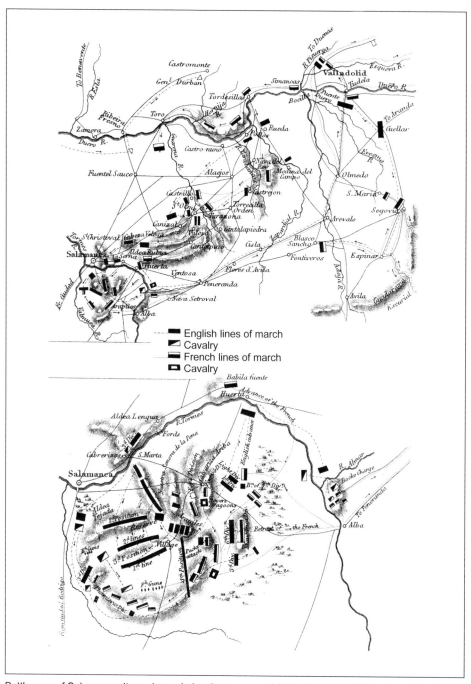

Battle map of Salamanca. It was here, during the summer of 1812, that Major William Gough fought bravely and where General Frederick Meade of Innishannon and the Connaught Rangers was badly wounded. Ten years later, Gough would lose the battle for survival, for he was drowned when the *Albion* went down on 22 April 1822.

until we hear from the Allies. P.S. I think myself lucky to belong to the old Bellerophon at this important time.

Other Corkmen were on board the *Bellerophon* at that time, too. There was Barry O'Meara, the ship's surgeon, who later accepted the emperor's invitation to remain with him in St Helena as medical adviser. There was Lieutenant William Connor RN from Ballybricken House on the shores of Cork Harbour, and there was Eames Westropp who, being the youngest officer on board, was reputed to have received Napoleon's sword.

With the Peninsular War now over, troops began to return home to Ireland and England. Having survived the battlefields of Europe and the slaughter at Waterloo, a cruel fate awaited some of the returning soldiers whose families had joined them in France. A report in a letter from Dover, England – dated 26 January – said that 'fourteen excellent transports sailed early this morning, full of troops for Ireland also two small transports for Plymouth, one for Ostend and two with troops and one hundred and sixty one horses bound for Calais.' The 59th, 82nd and 62nd regiments were returning to Ireland from France in these transports. On 30 January 1816, on the western approaches to the Old Head, near Garrettstown, the *Lord Melville* and *Boadicea* were wrecked close to the Old Head of Kinsale off Garrettstown beach. At the same time, the *Seahorse* came to grief off Tramore Bay in Co. Waterford.

The strand at Garrettstown forms a semi-circular bay at the western base of the Old Head of Kinsale and looks away in the distance to Courtmacsherry Harbour and the Seven Heads. It has proved fatal to many a ship that, in running for Kinsale or Cork Harbour, mistook their bearings and were driven upon its exposed shore and hidden rocks of which there are many. Given the prevailing south-westerly gales that blow with such ferocity during the winter months, a ship would not stand a chance of survival. If it came inside the headland, there is a long, narrow leg of rock running out between the two beaches at Garrettstown. A big portion of this ledge of rock is submerged, though exposed in low water. In general, the whole area is quite shallow and the coast of Co. Cork is quite inhospitable during the winter months.

On Tuesday evening, 30 January 1816, two huge transports were sighted trying to round the Old Head for Cork Harbour. The masters of the ships tried to run their vessels into Kinsale Harbour but to no avail – there was a severe gale from a south-easterly direction. The sailors on board tried everything within their skills to get her safely ashore. The lookout in the crow's nest spotted the beach at Garrettstown bearing down on them and, presuming the entrance to the beach was friendly, the captain decided to run his ship onto the beach in the hope that when the tide ebbed he could save as many souls as possible. By late evening, the *Lord Melville* was blown onto the shore but, alas, she got stuck on a submerged reef of rocks between the two beaches at Garrettstown. The *Boadicea* dropped anchor further out in the bay hoping to ride out the storm.

Several rescue attempts were organised by John Meade, collector of customs, John Spratt, Kinsale port surveyor, and Spiller Newman, revenue officer. They were assisted by militia from Kinsale. They had all crossed over on the ferry at Castlepark and came cross-country to the Old Head. Also on the scene from an early stage was Lt. Joseph Harty, with his sea fencibles from the Old Head signal tower.

A line was got ashore from the ship by means of a harpoon, and her fore and main masts were cut away to ease the shock of the battering of the ship against the rocks. By now, her bottom was driven in and there was several feet of water in the cabins; as it was three in the afternoon, the tide was still incoming. The situation on board was becoming most critical – a violent sea breaking into the cabin and over the stern, a howling wind and the dashing off the rocks – and it was decided to launch one of her lifeboats to get some of the women on board the stricken vessel ashore. Aboard the boat were two officers' wives, with their servants, the wife and child of a sergeant of the 59th Regiment, six of the crew and Captain Radford of the 62nd Regiment, who was in a weak state of health. The boat made for the shore but was swamped about halfway to safety. Twelve of those on board perished – only one sailor was saved.

These heart-rending scenes were witnessed by a large group of helpless people on the shore. Bodies were being washed up on the rocks and at their very feet. On board the ship, there was mayhem: women and children were screaming. The crew remained on the ship, including the troops of the 59th and 62nd Regiments, bound for Cork. There was nothing more for them to do only wait for the falling tide and hope, for the luck of providence, that the little brig would hold together. Low water was around midnight. With the help of Lt. Joseph Harty, a long spar was lashed from the nearest dry rock to the *Lord Melville*'s bow. The intention was to pass everyone on board along this long spar. At 11 p.m., this was carried out with everyone getting off safely. Lt. Harty, who was in charge of a group of men in the signal station at the Old Head, guided them all to safety with lighted sticks along the reef of rocks that extended out from the shore on this dark and stormy night. The rest of the terrified passengers and crew got safely to dry land.

Accommodation was arranged in the local cabins that dotted the shoreline. In a report filed the day after the disaster, John Meade, revenue collector of Kinsale stated how 'how happy he was to have it in his power to tell you, that the country people have behaved in the most exemplary manner and afforded every assistance in their power to the unfortunate sufferers.' Meade called on every surgeon in Kinsale and surrounding district to render assistance to those who had the misfortune to suffer broken limbs. The next day, several soldiers returned to try and salvage as much arms and baggage as was feasible. They reported total destruction and pillaging had taken place on board during the night while they slept.

The master of the *Lord Melville*, Captain Arman, suffered several broken limbs and was taken to Barry Gibbon's house at Ballinspittle, where he received a kind reception. Several weeks later, in a letter to the *Cork Southern Reporter*, he was pleased to be able to state that he was recovering well and acknowledged the kindness afforded to him by Mr Gibbons. This letter was published in the *Freeman's Journal*, Dublin, on Friday 9 February 1816. The reef that appears at low water off Garrettstown is today known as the Melville reef.

On that terrible night of 30 January 1816, the final outcome for the

Boadicea was utter disaster. Anchored offshore, she could be identified with a light burning on her mast. Shortly after midnight, the gale grew worse and the light on her mast was extinguished. With the howling wind and the driving rain, the pitiful screams for mercy of those on board were drowned out. When daylight broke, no sign of the ship could be found. The vessel had broken to pieces between the two beaches, and the most heart-rending scene of misery, desolation and death presented itself to view. The vessel seemed to be a confused mass of timber, planks and boards broken to pieces and intermixed with piles of dead bodies, men, women and children.

The bodies had to be guarded by the yeomanry to stop the pilfering of any personnel possessions; quite a number of the women had their jewels and beads attached to their dresses.

Looking out to sea on the long elevated rock that protrudes above high water, at least eighty terrified human beings were still clinging for their life. Repeated warnings were shouted from the shore telling them to stay where they were until low water. Alas, some did not heed the warning and at least thirty jumped from the rock, most of who were powerful swimmers and were intent on swimming ashore. They all perished. In most cases, not from drowning but from choking, as the sea, a mass of boiling froth, caused the clogging of lungs; others were dashed off the jagged rocks.

The remainder, approximately fifty, heeded the warning and stayed on the rock and were saved at low water when they were taken safely ashore. The bodies, strewn all round the shore, were taken to the local boathouse and were laid out for identification. This boathouse was nearby at the end of the western beach. When a final count was made, it was discovered that 255 were lost on the *Boadicea*, including the crew, and twelve from the *Lord Melville*. A sad and tragic night of terror and fear for the little coastal community with its landmark the Old Head.

A letter written in Kinsale and dated 15 January 1822 complains of stolen arms and was addressed to the Right Honourable Chief Secretary, Dublin Castle, it reads:

> We the undersigned Magistrates of the County of Cork beg leave to inform you for the information of his Excellency the Lord Lieutenant that we have cause to suspect that several persons in the Town and Barony of Kinsale, in the Barony of Courcey and in the Barony of Kinnalea not authorised by law to have or keep arms, have within their possession a quantity of Muskets and Bayonets and we beg to state the grounds and reasons of our suspicions. To be that about five years ago the inhabitants in the Barony of Courcey which adjoins Kinsale and Kinnalea became possessed of upwards of two hundred units of the arms of the unfortunate sufferers of the 82nd and 62nd Regiments who were drowned at that time on the wreck of the 'Lord Melville' and the 'Boadicea' Transports off Garrettstown strand, many of which arms have got into the hands of several of the inhabitants in Kinsale and Kinnalea.

The *Seahorse*, which was lost the same night in the bay of Tramore in Co.

Waterford, lost 277 non-commissioned officers and privates of the 2nd Battalion of the same ill-fated 59th Regiment, along with fifteen sailors and seventy-one women and children. The *Seahorse* had ran aground in the sand off Tramore. The fore-topmast fell, killed the mate and broke the leg of one of the seamen. Two anchors were then thrown out but these were dragged by the violence of the storm. The vessel was within a half-mile from the shore, in the presence of many hundreds of people on land who could give no aid to those unfortunate people on board. The *Seahorse* bottomed out and, with a huge sea breaking over the stricken vessel, it was impossible to escape. In minutes, she was smashed to pieces. However, by the grace of the Almighty, thirty-one did survive to tell the tale. As well as bodies, several chests and boxes were washed up on the beach and were robbed with the most criminal ferocity. Quite a number of the dead men, women and at least fourteen children were buried in the local churchyard at Duncannon.

In St Multose church, Kinsale, Co. Cork, a mural tablet on the north wall records the loss of the *Boadicea*. Inscribed upon it is the following: 'Sacred to the memory of Lieut. Edmund Davenport, Edwin Harding, Assistant Surgeon, Henry Randolph Scott and his wife, eight sergeants, nine corporals, one hundred and forty privates, thirteen women and sixteen children, of the 82nd Regiment, who perished on board the "Boadicea" transport, wrecked on Garrettstown Strand on the night of the 30th January, 1816. (Erected by the Officers of the Regiment).'

Many more would have been added to the death toll of the *Lord Melville* but for the heroic conduct of Lt. Joseph Harty, the gallant Corkman from Woodville in Rochestown. The lords of the Admiralty presented to Lt. Harty RN, for commanding the signal tower at the Old Head with his sea fencibles, an oval silver salver richly bordered with a gadroon edge with six shell projections; from both ends sprang two massive handles embedded with oak leaves. In the centre are the family arms: Or, on a fess sable, three doves Volant of the field, and the following inscription in acknowledgment of his services at the wrecks of the *Lord Melville* and *Boadicea* transports 'in approbation in saving the lives of four hundred persons, officers and men, of H.M. 59th and 62nd Regiments when wrecked near Kinsale'.

Joseph Harty, born in 1775, was the great-grandfather of Miss Sheila Acton of Kinsale, and she once held a photograph of Lt. Harty with his salver. I believe it is now in South Africa.

The survivors were taken to Kinsale where they stayed for three months. In April, they were taken to Dublin. The bodies of the 145 soldiers from the *Boadicea* were buried between the two beaches in a sand mound, or barrow. Here they lay for eighty-four years. In July 1900, Robert Day of Cork was visiting Garrettstown. During his visit, he learned that the sea had washed some of the dune away and more had been removed for agricultural purposes. On inspection, he found that some of the buried remains had been exposed to view and that vertebrae, thighs, arms, fingers and toe bones had fallen from the mound and lay uncovered at its feet. His mind cast back to the battlefield at Lundy's Lane at Niagara at which he had seen the spot where the 89th Royal Irish Fusiliers had been buried in the very trenches in which they fell and

how, shortly before he had arrived, they had been removed and buried in consecrated ground in a local graveyard.

This inspired Robert Day and he resolved to do the same for the 82nd
Regiment in which were many brave Irishmen, both officers and rank and file.
He wrote to a Lt. Col. A. Richardson, commanding the 2nd South Lancashire,
formerly the 82nd Regiment, who agreed to pay the expense of having the
bodies buried in consecrated ground. Day himself also made a financial contribution. Day communicated with the Rev. Ed Gibbings, rector of St Multose,
Kinsale and with Rev. J. Wood, rector of Templetrine who, with the consent of
their Select Vestry, 'most kindly gave a free grant of ground to the regiment in
the graveyard at Oldcourt which commands a view of the ocean-bound cliffs
and bays at the Old Head of Kinsale'.

A local contractor by the name of Robert Buttimore, of Kilmore mill,
Garrettstown was awarded the contract for the re-burial. On the last day of
1900, a mass grave was dug at Oldcourt. Robert Buttimore's staff of seven
men, with horses and carts, recovered the bodies of the gallant regiment and
removed them to the quiet grave. Although eighty-four years had passed since
the bodies were placed in the barrow close to the beach, their skeletons were
perfect and well preserved, lying upon their sides with their backs to the sea
as if they were asleep. Their teeth, without exception, were white and perfect.
There was no imperfection or appearance of decay.

They were laid to rest, comrades-in-death, just as they had been comrades-
in-arms in many a stricken field of battle and until the trumpet will sound the
last and great assembly. The covering stone was set in a bed of mortar and
bears the following leaded inscription:

> Sacred to the memory of 145 men of the 82nd Regt, who perished in the
> 'Boadicea' transport at Garrettstown January 30th 1816. On 31
> December 1900, they were disinterred and placed here in consecrated
> ground by Lieut. Colonel Richardson and Officers of the Regt and Robert
> Day of Cork.

Now they lie overlooking the headland that they tried in vain to sail around
during that terrible storm in January 1816. In the graveyard, a leaded marble
plaque was erected over their grave – the only reminder of those brave soldiers
who survived the wars in Europe and the slaughter of Waterloo, but who died
at another little peninsula with their women and children. Their fate this time
was not in the hands of man but in the hands of God. That peninsula is the Old
Head of Kinsale.

St James' church in Oldcourt replaced the church in Ringrone which had
become disused. St James' was completed and consecrated on 9 May 1844 by
Bishop Kyle. It was destined to have a short life – services were held there up
to 1902 when it was de-consecrated. It was dismantled in 1912. A few years
later, some of the stone from Oldcourt church was used to reconstruct the
present Ballinspittle church bell tower. It is ironic that the craftsmen who
demolished Oldcourt and constructed the bell tower at Ballinspittle were led
by none other than William Buttimore, the son of the man who had the contract

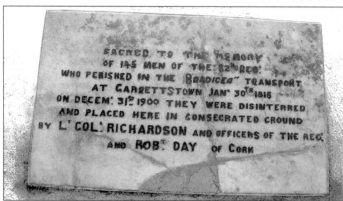

Above: Robert Buttimore of Garrettstown Mills at Kilmore with cart-load of skulls from the Peninsular War shipwreck *Boadicea* (1816) which were removed from the dunes at Garrettstown in 1900 and re-interred at Oldcourt graveyard near Ballinspittle.
Photo: Buttimore family

Centre: Headstone to those who perished on the *Boadicea* off Garrettstown, prior to being repaired and again placed over the mass grave at Oldcourt in 2001.

Bottom: On Saturday 3 November 2001, the repaired plaque was replaced over the grave of those brave men who perished so close to the shore.

Oldcourt church, closed down in 1912 and later demolished (note the padlock on the door). Some of the cut stone was used to erect the bell tower of Ballinspittle church which was constructed by William (Sonny) Buttimore in 1919. The bell tower is the oldest feature of Ballinspittle church, which was reconstructed in 1991. *Photo: Buttimore family*

to remove the bodies from the edge of Garrettstown beach and have them re-buried at Oldcourt.

Remarkable as it may seem, a photo of Oldcourt church survives. It was retrieved from the grand old lady known as Marie (Polly) Buttimore, the daughter of Robert. She kindly handed it to me and I presented a copy to Canon Thomas Kelleher PP after the renovation of his church at Ballinspittle in 1991.

During the twentieth century, Oldcourt graveyard became disused and over-grown and almost lost from memory. I remember making a visit to the site in the early 1970s and saw the plaque. It had been broken by the passing of time and quite an amount of the lead lettering had fallen out. The last century passed with speed and the dawn of the new millennium approached. One fine summer's day in the year 2001, my friend and good neighbour, Philip McCarthy, from Kilgobbin, Ballinadee, were on a historical visit around the parish, as so often we had done in the past. This time, our visit took us to the graveyard at Oldcourt. We could not locate any headstone because of the over-grown state of the site. Later, in the autumn of the same year, another such visit would reveal the outline of grave mounds and headstones, including one railed grave. Several more visits and some back-breaking work revealed the grave, but no plaque to the soldiers from the Peninsular War could be found. In August 2001, a more meticulous search was made and the little plaque was located, buried under the earth at the side of the mass grave. It was carefully removed and repaired, and kept as original as possible.

On Saturday 3 November 2001, just over a hundred years since it was first erected, the plaque was replaced over the grave of those brave men who per-ished so close to the shore. Their weary bones now rest in this little graveyard, some of them far from their native land, the plaque over their heads to com-memorate them forever.

Count Charles Lefebvre Desnouettes

Lefebvre Desnouettes' portrait, which hangs in the Museum de Armee, Paris.

General Charles Lefebvre Desnouettes was a talented and brave light-cavalry commander who loyally and gallantly served the Emperor Napoleon throughout his reign on battlefields across the Continent of Europe. He was to die off Garrettstown when the ill-fated *Albion* came to grief on its shore.

He was born in Paris on 14 September 1773, and was the son of Jean-Claude Lefebvre and his wife Madame A. Leduc. Jean-Claude was a cloth merchant in the Pont-Neuf area of Paris and was a supplier to the French army. There was at least one other son of the marriage.

Though Charles received a good education at the collège of Grassins – which had some connection with the Sorbonne – he was not a willing student. Three times he absconded to join the army and three times his parents purchased his release. His first experience of military life was soon after his sixteen birthday when he enlisted as a chasseur in the bataillon de l'Oratoire de la Garde Nationale. His persistence paid off at the young age of twenty when he was commissioned as a sous lieutenant in the 5e régiment des dragons in February 1793.

Lefebvre successively saw service with l'armee du Nord, l'armee de Sambre et Meuse, l'armee du Rhin et Moselle and l'armee d'Italie where he performed with distinction. It was during this last posting that Lefebvre first made the acquaintance of General Napoleon Bonaparte.

Lefebvre was disappointed that his unit was not selected for service with l'armee d'Orient in Egypt, but was instead sent to Belgium to quell unrest in that country.

He returned to the service of Napoleon in 1800 and was present at the Battle of Marengo on 14 June when the hero of the hour, General Louis Antoine Desaix, having received a mortal wound, died in the young soldier's arms.

He received rapid promotion and by 30 December 1802, following an appointment as adjoint à l'état-major with le Garde Consulaire, he was a chef de brigade de la 18e régiment des dragons.

During 1803–05, Lefebvre Desnouettes served with Jean de Dieu Soult in l'Armée des Côtes de l'Océan. During this period, he so impressed Napoleon that he made him honourary Écuyer Cavalcadoure de l'Empereur.

August 1805 saw him in 4e division de dragons de la cavalerie de réserve, at that time commanded by the stern forty-five-year-old equestrian expert, General Francois-Antoine-Louis Bourcier.

Displaying great courage at Elchingen on 14 October 1805, and then on the glorious field of Austerlitz, Lefebvre was made a Commandant de la Legion d'Honneur. He also took part in the campaigns of 1806 and 1807 in Austria, Prussia and Poland, and while in Prussia, in September 1806, received further promotion to Generale de Brigade.

He was, for a period, also transferred to the service of Jerome Bonaparte who had been made king of Westphalia by his brother, the emperor. He then took some well-deserved leave and briefly returned to Paris where he married a distant relative of the emperor, Mlle. Stéphanie Rolier, a pretty girl who had been brought up in the company of Napoleon's brothers and sisters. As a wedding gift, the emperor gave the newly weds the house in the rue de la Victoire where he and Josephine had spent so much time together.

Charles Lefebvre Desnouettes was around five-foot-ten-inches tall, was of slim build, with a handsome, well-defined face and a mass of black wavy hair. He was at this time clean-shaven.

After the Peace of Tillsit, Lefebvre was decorated with l'Ordre du Lion de Bavière and was then given command of the Chasseurs à cheval de la garde Impériale. Just eight weeks later, on 19 March, he was created a comte de l'Empire. His regiment was ordered to Spain with the corps d'observation des Pyrénées Occidentales under the command of le Marechal Jean Baptiste Bessieres to whom he was also appointed an ADC. On 28 August, he received further promotion to Generale de Division and saw service at Pampeluna, Tudela, Alagon and Epila before being present at the bloody siege of Saragossa. He then returned to France but it was not long before he was ordered back to Spain to accompany the emperor. He was present at the incident at Somo Sierra. In June 1808, when the insurrection commenced, Marshall Bessieres was ordered to put Burgos in a state of defence and to detach 4–5,000 men, under Lefebvre Desnouettes, against Saragossa to destroy the manufactory of arms at Placencia in Guipuscoa. While Bessieres broke the northern insurrection, Lefebvre Desnouettes' march brought on the first siege of Saragossa.

Lefebvre commenced his march on 7 June, having 2,000 infantry, some field batteries and a regiment of Polish cavalry. On 9 June, he forced a passage of the Ebro and barbarously put the leaders of the insurrection to death.

Saragossa contained 50,000 inhabitants: the city was to the right of the Ebro river, the suburb on the left and connected by a stone bridge. Lefebvre confined his operations to the right bank of the Ebro and established posts close to the gates and waited for reinforcements. The Saragosans put up fierce resistance and the battle was bloody. Lefebvre Desnouettes – active and bold – defeated the insurgents in the open country but failed to take Saragossa.

On 29 December 1808, during the Peninsular War campaign in Spain, he was commanding his chasseurs in pursuit of General Sir John Moore's retreating British army who were attempting to make their escape to the port of La Coruna. On the morning of 29 December, Lefebvre was leading a detachment of his chasseurs across the Esla river, close to the town of Benevente located on the opposite bank. He was totally unaware that elements of the British cavalry, some 2,400 strong – including squadrons of the 10th Hussars under the command of General Henry William Paget – had remained undetected behind the cover of some houses in the town. Paget

Lefebvre Desnouettes' gold ring, given to him by Napoleon as a gift. Issued on the occasion of Napoleon's coronation in Paris on 2 December 1804, it depicts the emperor's head on the inside. Desnouettes pawned the ring to make his escape from Cheltenham, England in May 1812. It is now held in Cheltenham Museum.
Photo: Cheltenham Museum

gave the signal and the 10th Hussars charged. Taken completely by surprise, the French put up a stout resistance in the face of significant numerical superiority. Quickly, the scene changed as the French fled at full speed towards the river, the British in pursuit, using their sabres on the hindmost until the French squadrons, without breaking their ranks, plunged into the stream and gained the opposite heights. There, like experienced soldiers, they wheeled and seemed inclined to come forward a second time, but when two guns opened up on them they retired.

During the battle, an officer was observed to separate from the main body and make towards another part of the river. He was followed by two men and, refusing to stop, the officer took three sabre wounds, had his horse killed under him and was taken prisoner along with some sixty of his chasseurs. He was none other than Lefebvre Desnouettes.

In this skirmish, the British lost fifty men whilst the French had fifty-five killed and wounded, and seventy taken prisoner besides their general and other officers.

The second siege of Saragossa – in January and February 1809 – was bloodier. For fifty days, the Spaniards held out. The spirit of the French army was exhausted; 20,000 were besieging 50,000 Spaniards behind the walled city. The French had crumbled the walls with their bullets, burst the convents with their mines, made several breeches with their bayonets and engaged in fierce fighting. So close was the combat that the only way to withdraw bayonets plunged into fellow human beings was to fire a musket shot into the dead or wounded. Above and in the tunnels below, where they had spared neither fire nor sword, their bravest men were falling. Famine was ripe and Saragossa still held out.

The bombardment, unceasing from 10 January, had forced the women and children to take refuge in vaults with which the city abounded. There was a constant combustion of oil, and the closeness of the atmosphere, unusual diet, fear and restlessness of mind combined to produce a pestilence which soon spread to the garrison. The strong and the weak, the daring soldier and the shrinking child, fell before it alike; and such was the predisposition to disease that the slightest wound gangrened and became incurable. In some cases, surgeons using meat-saws removed limbs. In the beginning of February, the daily deaths were from 4–500; the living were unable to bury the dead, and thousands of rotting corpses were scattered about the streets and courtyards or piled in heaps at the doors of the churches, left to dissolve in their own corruption, some partially eaten by dogs, others to be licked up by the flames of burning houses as the defence became contracted.

The suburbs, the greatest part of the walls and one-fourth of the houses were in the hands of the French. Sixteen thousand shells were thrown during the bombardment, 45,000 pounds of powder had shaken the city to its foundations and the bones of more than 40,000 persons of every age and sex bore the dreadful testimony to the constancy of the besieged.

On 20 February, Saragossa would negotiate capitulation, the Spanish garrison would march out with the honours of war, and those constituted to be prisoners would be sent to France. The officers were to retain their swords, baggage and horses, the men their knapsacks, the peasants to be sent to their homes. Property and religion was to be guaranteed. Thus ended the second and bloody siege of Saragossa.

Charles Lefebvre Desnouettes

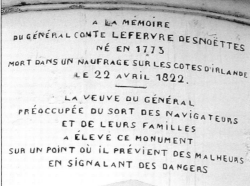

Top: Lefebvre monument at Le Harve erected by his wife as a warning to mariners of the dangers of the sea. Below: Close-up of the plaque on the monument.

was spared the horrors of Saragossa. In February 1811, he was escorted to England and detained at Cheltenham. He gave his parole and lived in a house with two other captured French generals. (That house, which exists today, is now Boots the Chemists at 131 High Street.) Numerous attempts were made to secure his release through exchange but these all failed. For the next fifteen months, the French generals were allowed the freedom of the town on condition that they not stray more than three miles from its centre.

Another prominent French general was at this time being detained at Ashby-de-la-Zouch, namely Louis-Francois Lejeune. He was successfully exchanged and, on his return to Paris, suggested to the emperor that it might be of some benefit if Lefebvre's wife were allowed to journey to England to be with her husband. Napoleon agreed to this and promptly granted Madame Lefebvre a passport. The couple were soon accepted into the social circles and became very popular and much sought-after guests. A party was even given in their honour by Albina, Countess of Buckinghamshire – this lady also lived in the town.

Around the beginning of May 1812, Lefebvre broke his parole. Disguised as a German count, his wife disguised as a young boy, the couple made their escape from Cheltenham using a signet ring as a bribe. Public opinion in Cheltenham was outraged and the remaining prisoners were transferred to Abergavenny. Meanwhile, Lefebvre rejoined Napoleon's army and saw action in a series of battles between 1813 and 1815. Following the defeat of Napoleon at Waterloo in 1815, Lefebvre fled to the United States, where he lived until 1822.

The superb gold ring that Emperor Napoleon gave to Desnouettes had on the inside a small chamber containing a portrait medallion of Napoleon crowned with laurels, such as the emperor wore at his coronation in Paris on 2 December 1804. This fact tends to support a tradition that this was one of a number of rings given as gifts by Napoleon at the time of his coronation. The ring eventually became the property of a Cheltenham solicitor by the name of John Bubb, who presented it to the museum in 1947 where it can be seen today. Exactly how and why the general's ring remained in Cheltenham is uncertain, although there is a long-standing and highly plausible tradition that it was either pawned or sold by the general in order to finance his escape.

Napoleon welcomed Lefebvre back with open arms and restored him almost immediately to his command of the Chasseurs à cheval de la garde Impériale, just in time for the ill-fated expedition to Russia. Having served in most of the major events of that expedition, Lefebvre was wounded at Inkovo on 18 October 1812. Following the disastrous retreat from Moscow and the difficult and dangerous crossing of the Berezina, Lefebvre was one of a very small and élite group that left the remnants of the Grande Armee at Smorgoni and travelled back to Paris with Napoleon.

Lefebvre served in Saxony and, on 3 April 1814, was decorated with le Grande Croix de l'Ordre de la R'eunion. He was with Mortier at Bautzen on 22 May of that year. He seized Rimbourg on 19 August and, one month later, defeated Thielmann at Mersebourg. He was then defeated at Altenbourg and served at Hanau before being made Commandeur de la Cavalerie de la Jeune

Garde. He later joined l'armee de Champagne and served with General Etienne-Antoine Marie Nansouty. He served at Brienne and received two wounds to his left side in January 1814, then successively served at La Rothiere, Montmirail, Chateau Thierry, Vauchamps and Arcis-sur-Aube.

Following Napoleon's first abdication, Lefebvre, in April 1814, commanded the escort of the deposed emperor as far as Roanne. When Napoleon prepared to leave for Elba, he said to his troops: 'I cannot take leave of you all, but I will embrace General Desnouettes on behalf of you all.'

On the restoration of the Bourbons to the throne of France, Louis XVIII made Lefebvre a Chevalier de Saint Louis and allowed him to retain command of the Chasseurs à cheval de la garde Impériale and return to Cambrai where his regiments were garrisoned.

On news of Napoleon's return from Elba, Lefebvre was one of a small group of officers (which included

Painting of Lefebvre Desnouettes which hangs on the wall of a house in the southern part of the United States. French colonies were set up in this region after Napoleon's defeat.

Generals Lallemand and Rigau) who led troops loyal to the emperor in an attempt to capture the garrison and arsenal at La Fere. They were foiled by the one-armed General d'Aboville and his men, who remained loyal to the Bourbon monarch. After Napoleon was restored to power, Lefebvre took his rightful place at his side as commander of the Chasseurs à cheval de la garde Impériale, and then served at Fleurus, Quatre Bras and Waterloo where he was once again wounded in the main cavalry charge.

After the defeat at Waterloo, Lefebvre feared for his life and, along with the Lallemand brothers and General Rigau, he left France for America. He was one of those officers in May 1816 who were condemned to death in their absence by a military tribunal.

He remained in America, living as a farmer in Alabama. His wife did attempt to join him but only got as far as England, having been violently seasick on that relatively short journey. She returned to France and continued to campaign for a pardon on her husband's behalf. Eventually, with the assistance of M. Hyde de Neuville, a royalist living in Washington, she achieved some progress in that Lefebvre was to travel to Holland and wait for official permission to re-enter France.

Desnouettes joined other Bonapartists to organise the French association, or Vine and Olive Colony, which in March 1817 had secured from Congress a grant for four townships (each six miles square) in what was then the Mississippi Territory. The settlers were to pay $2 per acre for their lands within fourteen years. The first of the settlers reached Mobile in June 1817 and went up the Tombigbee river to the mouth of the 'Black Warrior River', where they laid out a town on the White Bluff, which they called Demopolis.

Desnouettes erected log cabins on the site and one of them was used as a shrine to Napoleon. In it were souvenirs of the emperor's battles arranged around a bust of Napoleon on a pedestal made of cedar.

In the meantime, the land had been surveyed and the townships of the colony set apart. The location of Demopolis was not included in the colony's area, so they laid out another town about a mile east of the White Bluff, which they called Aigleville. The county in which they settled was given the name Marengo in commemoration of the Napoleonic battle.

Lefebvre Desnouettes opened a general store at Aigleville, selling grain and flour, which was successful for a time. Several letters written by Desnouettes in June 1818 and October 1819 to his business partner, General Bertrand Clauzel – another Bonapartist who lived near Mobile, Alabama – were concerned with joint business affairs, about supplies being shipped by river, their complicated accounts, funds, credits and their general situation. Items mentioned are rum, whiskey, corn and molasses. There is also mention of some of their fellow countrymen and their families, and in one letter he complained that his store was half-eaten by rats.

Nicholas Raoul was another of the colony's leaders, and Marshal Grouchy was one of the associates who formed the company, though he himself did not go to Alabama. His son, Victor Bertrand Clausel, did not occupy his grant on the Tombigbee, but settled near Mobile where he produced vegetables for the town market. In 1835, he was allowed to return to France and attained a prominent position under Louis Phillipe. Henry L'allemand went for a time to Alabama and later led an unsuccessful colonising expedition into Texas.

The colony in Alabama was not successful in growing vines and olive trees, and in the course of time, many of the leaders were allowed to return to France. The actual settlements did not survive though many of the French remained in Alabama. Lefebvre Desnouettes tried his hand at shipping rum from Jamaica and even teaching French at night classes. Lefebvre Desnouettes, whose wife was the sister of the French banker, La Fit, seems to have been one of the wealthiest of the settlers and was the leader of the colony. His wife ultimately secured permission for him to live in Belgium.

On 1 April 1822, a group of first-class passengers was about to take passage on the packet ship *Albion* of the Black Ball Line, which had begun a semi-monthly schedule from New York to Liverpool. Of this cosmopolitan group of passengers, the most interesting to board the Black Baller from the little steamer that bore them down the bay to where she lay moored was a Charles Lefebvre Desnouettes. Travelling in the company of three other French gentlemen, Desnouettes assumed the name of M. Gravez of Paris. He was wearing a beard and whiskers in an attempt to conceal his identity. He would have little to say to his fellow passengers, and the French officers accompanying him on board were also trying to conceal their identities. Their attempt at secrecy came to nothing; on board were two senior British army officers, both of whom had served in the Peninsular War, and they were well informed about the French general who had broken his parole. For that general to find himself a fellow passenger with two such senior British officers must have been intensely embarrassing to him.

As the vessel approached the south coast of Ireland, it encountered a severe storm and, on the night of 22 April, the *Albion* foundered on the rocks off western Garrettstown. Of the fifty-four passengers and crew on board the vessel, only nine survived.

The first huge wave struck the ship as she approached the rocks. Count Lefebvre Desnouettes tried to get up on deck but in the process had his arm broken, thus impeding his escape. The end was near for one of Napoleon's dashing young cavalry commanders, and as the next wave broke over the doomed *Albion*, it washed the general overboard. He perished on the rocky shores of Garrettstown on his way to meet his beloved wife and daughter and ultimately, his beloved France. Lefebvre Desnouettes is buried in an unmarked grave in Templetrine churchyard, approximately one mile from where he perished.

General Charles Lefebvre Desnouettes' wife, Stéphanie, had a monument erected to her husband's memory at St Adresse, near Le Harve. Its purpose was to act as a beacon to navigators and those at sea. It still survives today.

The general's name is inscribed on the west face of l'Arc de Triomphe Etoile in Paris and the Musee de l'armee has a portrait of him by Weygandt painted in 1807; it shows him wearing the decorations of Bavaria and Westphalia. The Army Museum in London has his sabretache, taken from him when he was captured at Benevente in 1808.

The emperor held Lefebvre Desnouettes in very high esteem and in his will left the general the sum of 50,000 francs.

The general had only one child – a daughter, Charlotte Llavinie. She was born in 1816 and must have been conceived just prior to the Battle of Waterloo. In 1836, the daughter married a M. de Sancy Parabere.

At Easter 2001, close to the anniversary of his death and 179 years on, during a visit to France accompanied by a friend whose grand-uncle died in the killing fields of Europe in the Great War of 1914–18, I visited Le Harve and, as we approached – driving cautiously through the streets of Le Harve – we could see in the distance the white beacon that Lefebvre's distraught wife had paid for and erected to his memory on learning of his death. Overlooking the harbour in the district of St Address, it is known as 'Le Pain du Sucre'. The inscription translates as follows: 'In memory of General Count Charles Lefebvre Desnouettes, born in 1773, died in a shipwreck on the Irish coast on the 22nd of April 1822.' The general's widow, anxious about seafarers and their families, erected this monument at a point to signal the dangers and avoid tragedies.

Next, our journey took us to Paris where we studied the west face of l'Arc de Triomphe and saw the name of Charles Lefebvre Desnouettes – his name etched forever. Our search took us to the Musee de Armee where I admired the portrait of Napoleon's dashing young cavalry officer, painted by Weygandt in

1807. The portrait now hangs on the Wall of Honour in Paris, the capital city that was once the centre of Napoleon's empire – a portrait of a man whose bones lie in an unmarked grave in the remote graveyard at Templetrine near Kinsale in Ireland.

We left the Le Musee de L'Armee and, as I stumbled into the thousands that walked passed us on our way to the Champs Élysées, an eerie silence came over me. Here was I, on a quest in search of these memorials to the Frenchman, the great friend of Napoleon who perished on the rocky shore at the Old Head of Kinsale in 1822 and who engaged in the bloody slaughter of Europe, and aware that the man who accompanied me on my journey had lost his grand-uncle in the Great War and that his name is also etched in stone – on le Memorial de Thiepval for the 73,000 soldiers who have no known grave. I had seen the painting of Count Charles Lefebvre Desnouettes and my friend had seen the monument at Thiepval. We both went home to Ireland at peace.

Alexander Metcalf Fisher

esides the French and British cabin passengers on board the *Albion*, there were eight Americans, one of whom was Alexander Metcalf Fisher MA, a professor of mathematics and natural philosophy at Yale, from where he had graduated with Phi Beta Kappa honours only nine years before (an honourary society of American college and university students showing high academic achievement).

Alexander Metcalf Fisher was the eldest child of Deacon Caleb and Sally Fisher of Franklin, Massachusetts, and grandson of Hezekiah and Abigail (Daniels) Fisher of North Franklin. Born on 22 July 1794, his mother was a woman of uncommon mathematical talent. One of his sisters married Dr John W Tenney (Brown University, 1823). He was prepared for college at Leicester Academy by Luther Wilson (Williams College, 1807). He was of small and very slender physique, and had a remarkable mental quickness. At his graduation, he delivered the Salutatory Oration. He then spent a year in study under the direction of his pastor, the Rev. Dr Nathaniel Emmons (Yale, 1767), and began a second year of study in mental and moral science and theology in the Andover Seminary. But in the course of the year, Alexander returned to his father's farm on account of ill health.

Professor Alexander Metcalf Fisher of Yale University, lost on the *Albion* in his twenty-eighth year. *Photo: Yale University*

At commencement in 1815, he was elected a tutor in the college and, notwithstanding the apprehensions of his friends, took up office in the autumn. Attention to his favourite studies seemed to invigorate his health and in July 1817, when Professor Day was elected president, he was made adjunct professor of mathematics and natural philosophy. He was promoted to full professorship in 1819.

In the spring of 1822, he was determined to visit Europe for the benefit of his health and to acquire the French language, and even more so to improve himself in his profession by observing the condition of foreign institutions. The young Professor Fisher took eight months absent leave and set sail on the *Albion* on 1 April 1822. While on board waiting for the ship to sail, he wrote his last letter to his family, describing the people who were to become his fellow passengers. This letter was delivered by hand to his family.

When the *Albion* foundered close to the Old Head off the coast of Co. Cork, the frail professor perished with all but one of his fellow cabin passengers. He had not yet completed his twenty-eighth year. We believe he is buried in Templetrine churchyard.

In such a brief life, there was little opportunity for great achievement but Professor Fisher's friends and colleagues have left on record unstinted praise of his character and promise. His mental endowments were unquestionably superior and his attainments in various departments of knowledge unusual.

In the judgment of his classmate, Olmsted – writing several years later – Alexander Metcalf Fisher's greatness as a mathematician was the fruit of no peculiar bias or genius for that particular field of knowledge, but resulted naturally from the application of a mind of remarkable strength and acuteness to a subject of the greatest difficulty.

Alexander Metcalf Fisher was engaged to Catherine Esther, the eldest daughter of the Rev. Dr Lyman Beecher (Yale, 1797). After his death, she never married. A portrait of Professor Fisher, painted after his death by S.F.B. Morse (Yale, 1810), is owned by the college, as is also a bust by Hezekiah Augur, presented by his classmates.

Professor James L. Kingsley, AM Professor of the Hebrew, Greek and Latin languages, delivered a eulogy on Professor Fisher in the college chapel on 26 June 1822. This was published afterwards and some reminiscences by his classmate, Professor Olmsted, appeared in the *New Englander* in 1843.

Hezekiah Augur, the sculptor, was born in New Haven, Connecticut on 21 February 1791. He was a shoemaker by trade and enjoyed few educational opportunities. He became a woodcarver and invented a woodcarving machine and a number of other ingenious devices, including a machine for weaving worsted lace. He then developed a taste for sculpture and made some wonderfully accurate copies of the head of Apollo, a bust of Washington and a statue of Sappho. His 'Jephtha and his Daughter', said to be his best work, is in the Trumbull Gallery at Yale College. The honourary degree of AM was conferred upon him by Yale College in 1833. He died in New Haven on 10 January 1858. The twenty-seven-inch bust of Professor Fisher by Hezekiah Augur can be seen to this day in Yale University art gallery.

The cosmopolitan nature of passengers travelling from the New World to

Europe and its western isles has been commented on. One such person deserves a mention because of the humorous nature of his story. He was George Robert Goodwin Hill (son of Thomas Hill, gentleman, Jamaica). Hill was an undergraduate of Oxford and matriculated at Magdalen Hall, Oxford on 24 January 1815, aged twenty. His life was short but a merry one, and he liked the tipple of the bottle. Mr Hill was the Church of England clergyman in Jamaica, and in 1818 was brought before the Ecclesiastical Court of the commissaries of the diocese, which was under the titular authority of the bishop of London, acting through his commissaries at the instance of the church wardens of the parish church of Kingston, Jamaica. Reverend Hill's antics were notorious; some of his activities are now a matter of court records kept in Spanish Town and also in Kingston. Hill was charged with failing to bury a corpse, for refusing to baptise a sick child on a Sunday, and for conducting a service and preaching a sermon in the parish church whilst showing physical evidence of having very recently taken part in a boxing match – he was sporting a black eye. Also partaking in other activities likely to bring the Church and his calling into disrepute.

The Reverend Hill was as quick with his tongue as he was with his fists. Hill took the battle into the camp of the enemy by preaching a famous sermon on the subject of keeping the Sabbath holy, and roundly accused the hierarchy of profaning the Sabbath by finding work for their coloured employees. Even the magistracy was not exempt from Hill's strictures on his white associates.

The Ecclesiastical Court upheld the dignity of its lay counterpart and decided that Hill had used his pulpit as a coward's castle to put his point of view across, and they suspended him from his clerical duties for a period of nine months. Mr Hill set sail on the *Albion* from New York to Liverpool but when the storm broke he had another fight on his hands – this time for survival. He did not succeed for he perished off Garrettstown on 22 April 1822.

Powell Families of Fame and Tragedy

In a lonely graveyard, high up on a hill called Templetrine in the parish of Courceys, Co. Cork, there is a limestone slab with a simple inscription: 'Anne Powell Spinster daughter of William Dummer and Anne Powell of York in Upper Canada. Born 1787 deceased 1822.' Inside the church, a plaque on the wall reads: 'Anne Powell spinster was a passenger in the ship "Albion" (wrecked on this coast on April 22nd 1822) and perished with many others, but her body being recovered from the sea received from the charity of strangers Christian burial in the cemetery of this church in grateful memory whereof this marble is inscribed by W.D.P.' These three initials stand for William Dummer Powell.

William Dummer Powell, at one time chief justice of Upper Canada, lived a life marred with disappointment, sorrow and tragedy. He came from an old Welsh family by the name of Howell, which had their seat in Caer Howell in Montgomeryshire. One branch of the family settled in England in the seventeenth century and their name was Anglicised to Powell. William's grandfather, John Powell, left England for Boston where he became secretary to Governor William Dummer of Massachusetts, and later married Dummer's daughter, Anne. Their son, John, became a prosperous merchant in Boston, marrying a Janet Grant of a wealthy Scottish family. William Dummer Powell, born in Boston in 1755, was the eldest son of John and Janet. At the tender age of nine, he was sent to be educated in England and Holland where he learned Dutch and French, something which would prove useful to him in later life. In 1772, at the age of seventeen, William returned to Boston and studied law.

Boston at this time was already disloyal to the Crown; the Tea Party was to take place the following year. Anticipating the coming troubles, William's mother took him to New York where the loyalists were congregating. Here, his mother contracted smallpox and died, aged just thirty-nine. Young William returned to Boston and joined the British garrison as a volunteer. In 1775, he married Anne Murray, daughter of an English doctor. As a loyalist, the estates of William's father were confiscated, and the whole family set sail for England. At Middle Temple, William continued to study law, whilst his wife, Anne, had three sons in quick succession.

Leaving his young family in England, William set sail for Quebec in 1779 where his mother's cousin was attorney general. In Montreal, he established himself as a practising lawyer, and sent for his wife and children to join him. During the voyage, however, the ship was captured by the Americans who took Anne as a prisoner to Boston. Fortunately, family influence soon had her released and returned to Montreal.

The Powell's lost an infant daughter, Anne, in 1783, much to the distress of William. In 1784, whilst he was in England with a petition from Montreal lawyers to have English law introduced into Quebec, a fourth son was born to Anne and William, christened Jeremiah.

On his return from England, William travelled to Boston with a view to regaining his father's confiscated property, but to no avail. Back in Montreal, though held in high esteem by the governor, William was constantly being accused of treason for his attempts to secure US lands for himself; he was even accused of being an American citizen.

By now, the family had increased to six, including two girls: Anne, of whom we shall hear of later, born in 1787, and Elizabeth, born in 1789. In 1792, Powell was devastated at the loss of his favourite sister, Anne, in childbirth.

At this time, William Powell was a judge in Detroit which remained under English control until 1796. However, serious problems began to develop. A traitorous letter was published, supposedly from William to the American secretary of war. To avoid danger to himself and his family, he sent Anne and the children back to England. However, the damning reports in newspapers in both America and England meant that any chances of promotion were put on

Powell's home in York, Canada. (York was the earlier name for Toronto.)

hold. He had earlier been assured that he would be made chief justice of Upper Canada when the vacancy occurred. But when another Englishman, by the name of John Elmsley, was appointed chief justice of Upper Canada, Ontario in 1796 with a salary of £1,100, William was humiliated.

To compound his problems, the first family tragedy occurred in 1794. William's youngest son, Thomas – aged ten years – drowned while in school in Kingston.

In 1798, Judge William Dummer Powell moved to York, which had been proclaimed the capital in 1793. As reward for his loyalism, he was granted a house and 100 acres. His wife and each of their children received a grant of 1,200 acres – wastelands worth a mere 2 shillings an acre. The Powells named their large country house 'Caer Howell', after their old Welsh home.

In 1810, the second family tragedy struck. William Dummer Powell jnr. was a promising young lawyer in Niagara. When he fell in love with Sarah Stephenson, only fifteen years old, his parents sternly forbade the marriage, though primarily for political reasons. Undeterred, the lovers eloped and were married in Niagara. This romantic episode caused a great stir but their young life together was cut short after just three years. William jnr. died of a fever, leaving an eighteen-year-old widow and two infant daughters. Sarah returned to her father's home whilst the babies were left in the charge of her in-laws, the Powells. It is interesting to note that at one time, there were four Anne Powells in the one house: the judge's wife, his sister – who had joined them from England in 1789 – their daughter and granddaughter.

The third Powell family tragedy concerned Jeremiah, born in 1784. Educated in England, his father placed him in a counting house in New York in 1801. Three years later, Jeremiah ventured to Haiti where he sold military ornaments, epaulettes, sword knots and gold lace. Believing the items to be gold, he submitted an invoice for $3,000 to the dictator of Haiti, Emperor Dessalines. On discovering the items were not gold, the emperor threatened Jeremiah with death. He returned to New York where he had the ornaments tested and found that they were brass gilt.

Back in Haiti, and while trying to make peace with Dessalines, Jeremiah befriended Miranda, a Venezuelan man determined to free his homeland from Spain. Jeremiah joined Miranda's rebel army as a major, but when the Spanish navy caught them, Miranda fled. Some of the captured leaders were executed at once on board the ship. Jeremiah was taken prisoner to Spain.

Anne Powell's brother, George Murray, sent word from New York that Jeremiah was sentenced to death. William Dummer Powell was heading back home to York via New York when he received word that his son's sentence had been commuted to life imprisonment. Powell was determined to free his son. He obtained leave of absence, borrowed some money and went to Boston to see the Spanish consul to plead for his son's release. From there, he went to New York where he gave letters to influential officials. Next, he travelled to London. His funds exhausted and nearly penniless, William collected back-salary to continue his pursuit, and it was in London that he met with Lord Holland who provided many letters of introduction. William next travelled to Lisbon, but was delayed for a couple of months, unable to get a pass into

Spain. When he did finally arrive, he petitioned the king for Jeremiah's release. A letter from Dr Edward Jenner, the discoverer of a vaccine with which he had vaccinated the Spanish royal family, helped to persuade the king to sign the release.

William returned to Canada via England, sending a sloop fitted out by George Murray to fetch Jeremiah. While there was great rejoicing at Jeremiah's safe return, he quickly left again to pursue his fortune in Barbados. He sailed from Halifax but found that the promise of a high position in the West Indies had evaporated. He left Curacao for England on the ship *Alexander* in December 1808, but neither the ship nor Jeremiah were ever seen again.

During Powell's ascent to the peak of his career, there were always enemies present. Following a visit to the chief justice's house, William Warren Baldwin, a doctor and lawyer from Ireland, wrote to the attorney general, William Firth, to complain about Powell's table manners. He described how Powell and his son, John, dropped their knives, and with a lump of bread in one hand and a fork in the other, heaped their fish upon their bread and pushed it into their mouths with their fingers before gobbling up the contents of their plates. Baldwin considered this poor breeding.

Such was the feasting and entertaining in the Powell household that an extension was built onto the house. Mrs Powell, with the help of several servants, was expected to give large dinner parties at least twice a week for up to sixteen people. There was so much alcohol in the household that an incident occurred in 1826. A shelf in the cellar basement collapsed under the weight of more than ten dozen bottles of brandy, and it shook the house like a clap of thunder. A man walking down the lane thought it was a cannon shot. It was no wonder that one of Mrs Powell's sons, John, died from alcoholic poisoning in 1827.

William Dummer Powell finally achieved his ambition in 1816. At the age of sixty-one, he became chief justice of Upper Canada. Often at loggerheads with top officials, there were several attempts to get him to resign, including the offer of a pension of a £1,000 a year. But Dummer Powell clung to office, and sat as chief justice for the last time in July 1825. However, by this time, a fourth family tragedy had occurred. Three years earlier, in April 1822, Anne and William Powell's daughter, Anne, was drowned off the south coast of Ireland.

Anne Powell was born in Montreal on 10 March 1787, the sixth child and second daughter to be born to the Powells. Anne's mother rejoiced when her daughter and namesake was born, but little did she know that this daughter would bring her great grief.

Anne grew up into a beautiful, talented and gifted woman. She was well travelled for the times and had lived with her mother's family in New York. In 1811, she studied in Montreal with the intention of obtaining a teacher's certificate. Before the outbreak of the war with America in 1812, she returned to York where her desire to teach led her to become the tutor of her two orphaned nieces.

Despite her expensive education, Anne's mother felt she required more knowledge and experience. After the capture of York, Toronto in April 1813,

Anne devoted herself to tending the convalescent soldiers quartered with the Powells. Anne never married, perhaps because her social sphere was so narrow – the population of York in 1822 was no more than 2,000 people, with the leading families in this region numbering no more than thirty. Most of these people were from Cork, whilst some of them had been army officers during the revolution and the 1812 Canada–US war. Peter Russell, a second-in-command, came from Kinsale, Co. Cork; William Willcocks, a merchant, had been lord mayor of Cork; the Baldwin family had been farmers in Upton and Carrigaline, Co. Cork. Also resident in the area was Francis Hincks, son of Dix Hincks, rector of a church on Princes Street in Cork city, alongside the market.

Anne's first romantic involvement had occurred in 1807 at the age of twenty. She was courted by Laurent Quetton St George, a French adventurer sixteen years her senior. This thirty-six year old French aristocrat found refuge in Canada after fleeing France following Napoleon's first defeat. Born in Verargues, France in 1771, he was christened Laurent Quet, though his family used the name Quetton. He adopted the surname St George in England in 1796 as grateful acknowledgement to the country. He arrived in Canada in 1799, and was involved in the fur trade with the Mississauga Indians. Later, in 1802, St George moved to Niagara and then to York where he operated a prosperous store.

It was not long before the young and flighty Anne Powell caught his eye, and he courted her on and off for several months until Mrs Powell dismissed his presumptuous affair. She felt her daughter was too good for him since he was in the trade business. In fact, Quetton St George eventually became one of Toronto's most successful business people. Perhaps the attitude of Anne's mother goes someway to explaining why Anne and her sister Elizabeth never married.

Later, in the words of Dr John Strachan, she became 'distracted over a charming young lawyer', John Beverley Robinson. Robinson was born on 26 July 1791 at a place called Berthier, Lower Canada. John was only seven years old when his father died suddenly. His father's friend educated him and, at the age of sixteen, John – interested in law and able to mix easily – was sent to Kingston and from there moved to York, now Toronto. Here, he was drawn into the circle of Chief Justice William Powell.

Robinson had performed creditably during the war and, at the age of twenty-one, had gained the post of acting attorney general as a result of the influence of Judge Powell. It was rumoured around York that Robinson's friendship with Powell's daughter, Anne, had secured his appointment. Indeed, it is unlikely that the ambitious Robinson would discourage familiarity with his benefactor's daughter. When Robinson decided to further himself by attending the English Inns of Court, Anne found a way to follow him. In 1816, the year her father was seeking the post of chief justice, Anne travelled with her father to England. Upon her arrival, she again took up with the young lawyer, who gallantly escorted her about London. When they were seen around London's hotels and boarding houses, it bordered on a scandal, but this did not deter Anne. However, unknown to her, John Beverley Robinson had developed a passionate interest in an English woman, Emma Walker, daughter of Charles Walker of Harlesden, Middlesex. Emma was exceedingly pretty, very pleasing and engaging in her manner and appearance. John Robinson fell in love with Emma but found himself in a very embarrassing situation. Anne Powell was a very determined woman who knew what she wanted and had always got her own way. She had known John from her childhood years and loved him very much. When she had accompanied her father to England, her sole purpose was to keep up her pursuit of her beloved John.

By the summer of 1816, John was getting desperate. He had his mind fixed on Miss Emma Walker and was sure that her mind was fixed also. Emma, who still addressed him as my dear Mr Robinson, wrote him a letter telling him to end his interest in Miss Powell. She firmly pointed out to him that it was his duty to make his feelings plain to his pursuer, and delivered an ultimatum to Robinson. 'I can scarcely expect you this morning for the interesting engagement you have had with your fair lover who must occupy much of your leisure.' She went on to say that if he wished their courtship to continue, he had best advise Miss Powell that he was no longer a free man. 'From my heart I pity her, however painful her feelings may have been for you, would not wisdom have displayed itself lately, I know that you gave encouragement to her unfortunate feelings for only your own conscience can most truly tell you.' She continued: 'I am a young and saucy lecturer, am I not and you give me so little opportunity of indulging my taste in this way.'

John Robinson met with Anne Powell to inform her that he was in love with another woman. Anne was stunned, as she had assumed that John would eventually marry her. Though his stepfather, Elisha Beman, was only a tavern-keeper, most people in York had taken for granted that John and Anne Powell would marry. Deeply hurt, and hoping he would change his mind, Anne considered a meeting with Emma. For the present, she refrained from this type of action, but set about visiting taverns in the hope of a chance meeting with her beloved John and his new lover. Anne also informed her father, Judge Powell – now chief justice – that John was engaged to another woman. The rector of York, John Strachan, a family friend of the Powells, wrote to Robinson to ascertain whether he was 'under any engagements directly or indirectly to Miss Powell'.

On 5 June 1817, John and Emma Walker were married, and in early July they left England for Upper Canada. Here, Robinson continued his work as solicitor general and was shortly after promoted to attorney general. But although Robinson's marriage to Emma may have disappointed the Powells, it did not diminish their affection for him. Anne herself hoped that nothing would ever interrupt the friendly intercourse between the families.

Anne Powell remained in England with her relatives. In 1817, she had reached her thirtieth birthday and began to realise that she was now unlikely ever to marry. Her father wanted her to return to York but she resisted. Her stubborn disposition led her to disregard the expense to which she put others, but her drawings from her father's account in London made her an unwelcome burden. On 6 September 1818, Anne wrote a letter to her mother in Canada, explaining her reasons for staying another year in England. In the letter, she discusses marriage in general and what constitutes a fine young man. 'What I call a fine young man is not often to be met with even in England; in general those who are clever are anything but good, and those who are good are anything but clever.' Anne mentions in her letter her wonderful aunt who, at the age of eighty-six, was sitting by the fire sewing a gusset into her corset. 'I do not know how she can see. The room is so dark that I can hardly write myself.' She also tells her mother that her aunt told her of the happenings back home in York involving one of the two servant girls who had a baby. 'I believe it is Matty, poor thing. No finer servants would you ever find again and there should be no suspicion as to who is the father of the infant (because I have mine). I hope no-one will be too hard upon her. Her mind was once delicate as ours and that she conceals the name of the father is a proof that there is still some principle remaining. There is one man in York whom I feel certain had no share in it.' She asked her mother to thank Papa for his kind letter – 'perhaps it is as good as I deserve. I now tremble at every shilling that I spend and Papa can afford it and if he was by me with the money in his pocket, he would indulge me much more than I ever indulge myself. I hope that Papa will excuse me if I have taken more than he intended I should have, and I recollect that ten or twenty pounds will not ruin him. With dutiful love to Papa and yourself and love to the rest of the family, I am my dear Mama, your dutiful and affectionate daughter, Anne Powell.'

It was not long after her return from England in the summer of 1819 that her parents began to question her sanity. She displayed a bitter hatred for them, a suspicion of her sisters and a tyrannical domination over her nieces. The orphans came so much under her sway that she flew into a rage when her sister merely attempted to take them for a walk. Perhaps her most embarrassing eccentricity was her continuing infatuation with John Robinson. She sent him correspondence which his brother, William Benjamin, described to Samuel Peter Jarvis – Anne's brother-in-law – 'as some of the most sexual explicit letters you ever saw'. Anne considered Emma Robinson to be possessed of a romantic history and hardly a fit companion for her beloved John. For her part, Emma was a match for Anne. She routinely burned her unopened letters, set her face like a flint, never faltered in the vigilance of her guard, called her a hussy, a whore, a prostitute and refused to admit her to the Robinson house.

Although there was tension between Anne and her mother, where her father was concerned she could do nothing right. She had no regard for expenditure and when her father met her in New York, where Anne had stopped on her way back from England, the judge was mortified. He accused her of vanity; she was parading around the streets with a short green shift and he claimed she looked like a 'whore' or a 'market girl'.

Anne felt that her parents and relatives were persecuting her. The strain began to tell and she spoke about going to England for another visit. This was about the time that John Beverley Robinson was also making plans for a return journey to England. Anne herself was so much in love with John that she was willing to give all her desire to him. It was during one such encounter, in the autumn of 1821, that he imprudently invited her to accompany him and his wife on their journey to England. It seems his sexual desire for Anne had not diminished and that these encounters had been going on over several years.

When Emma discovered that Anne had intended to travel with them, she was furious and she put John in a very embarrassing position. He had kept his invitation to Anne quiet, but York at that time was a small place and rumours abounded. John twisted the story and made it seem it was Anne's own idea.

Anne Powell was not about to give up her beloved John without a fight. She had not forgotten his promise made the last time they had made love, and she intended to keep him to his word. By now, Anne was getting more frustrated, and her most bizarre behaviour occurred during the winter of 1822. Robinson, now promoted to attorney general and leader of the government in the House of Assembly, was dispatched to England to negotiate a customs dispute with Lower Canada. Just as the Robinsons were about to leave York for their trip to England, via New York, Anne called on the attorney general and his wife at their house, and begged to be allowed to accompany him. He positively refused.

Anne's brother, Grant – who was a medical doctor – and Dr Strachan tried to reason with her. At last, her mother, although scandalised by Anne's 'wanton and indecent behaviour', sanctioned her departure in deference to the attorney general. However, Mrs Powell promised the Robinsons a forty-eight-hour head start. A distraught Anne was bound and locked into her bedroom by her brother and Dr Strachan, aided by her mother. The family had planned to arrange a journey to England for her at a later time, hoping the situation could be diffused.

Deep in the Canadian winter, the Robinson's started out in a sleigh driven by a servant and equipped with warm clothes and emergency food. Anne learned of her beloved's departure after spending the night in tears. The following morning, she asked to see her mother to whom she apologised, expressing profound sorrow for her conduct. Shortly afterwards, she escaped, without either money or luggage, and chartered a sleigh with a view to following John to New York. Travelling in wintertime, when the rivers and lakes were frozen and the roads packed with snow, horse-drawn sleigh or a cutter was commonplace. The passengers would wrap themselves up in warm furs and woollen blankets. Anne Powell must have been a woman of sheer determination and physical strength to undertake this gruelling journey of nearly 500 miles, from York to New York, in temperatures of -10–20°C and without proper winter clothes. The journey would have taken her at least ten days.

When Mrs Powell found that her wayward daughter had escaped to follow Robinson, she collapsed in despair at such scandalous behaviour. Family prestige was at stake. Mrs Powell considered her daughter's behaviour as systematic persecution of another woman and very unchristian, and felt that no sane woman would carry on with such antics. In a letter to another of her daughters, Eliza, dated 3 February, she wrote:

> My Dearest Eliza,
> To tell you the scene that has been exhibited in this house, since eleven o'clock, of connivance on my part by furnishing your worthless sister Anne with a sleigh and horses and her audacity in keeping a servant employed to watch the Attorney General's movements. This has involved us in such

disgrace that I fear it can never be conquered. We are the subject of conversation right up to Government house and the girls have acted weakly. They cancelled their feelings and did not communicate to me. I have dismissed a servant for disobeying orders.

I say to you that your sister has accomplished her design and escaped from the house, or rather, eluded the vigilance of your brother Grant who was at the house early in the morning and left with neither coat or change of clothes. Can I tell you what happened last night. Dr Strachan and Grant took her to her room, received her promise that she would not move and locked the door. At 7 a.m. in the morning the servant took her breakfast upstairs to her room and we supposed that it was there she was with her nieces.

We all stayed down in the parlour for some time. Later in the morning we were informed that she was met on the road to Kingston. We went back up and her nieces confessed that she had gone. In the midst of the disgrace with which we are overwhelmed, the screaming and tears that occurred were because Uncle Grant had locked their poor aunt's baggage in another room and now she was really gone with no coat to keep her warm. My heart sickens for not having long since separated these young people from her.

No human being has been near us today. The disgrace of a daughter of this family having fled from her father's house, gone I know not where to find a sleigh and gone without clothes or money, at the mercy of the man who drives her. Where she is God knows. My heart bleeds for the inevitable miseries she has drawn upon her head. Before she went yesterday she came in to my room, expressed sorrow at what had passed, gave assurances of future conduct that would meet my approbation.

Another factor prompting Anne's leaving home was the tyranny of her domineering mother with the help of the conservative bishop of York, John Strachan, a daily visitor to the house. This man carried great influence with the elders of the family.

When Anne's father heard of the latest development, he flew into a rage. He was infuriated by his daughter's perverse conduct. 'I will not consider coming into contact with her again,' he swore, and called her a miserable wretch, a freak, a baneful comet, a fiend, a monster in human disguise. He said that he had been advised by his brother-in-law to consider invoking the Lunacy Act.

Meanwhile, at Cobourg (Lower Ontario), the Robinsons had been obliged to halt their journey as Emma Robinson was very ill. On the second morning there, Anne Powell arrived in a hired sleigh with no companion or servant, a considerable feat for a woman. But Anne Powell was no ordinary woman – she had a heart of a lioness and her quest to be with her lover spurred her on. Having encountered the Robinsons, she followed them on their journey to New York City, stopping where they stopped and always attempting to secure the room next to or opposite them. She haunted them day and night, and her interest in the Robinson's baby, Emily, was kept at bay by the child's nurse, Abby. It is possible that Anne had ill intentions towards the baby.

At Albany, New York, Anne's brother, Grant, caught up with her and tried to persuade her to return home. His assertion that the world would suppose she had an improper regard for John Beverly Robinson prompted her to fly into a rage. If that was the opinion of the world, she said, she must clear her character by preserving her intention. Grant tried a financial ploy, telling her she was entitled to a sum of money – her share of her mother's property. But Anne would not hear of it. Before she had left home, she said, she did not care much about going to England, but so much gossip had been bandied about that now she felt it was her duty to go and nothing would stop her.

Once in New York, Robinson and his party, which included his brother, Peter, booked their passage to Liverpool. Anne Powell booked passage on the same ship. When Mrs Robinson discovered that Anne was going to be travelling with them, she began making other arrangements for travelling to Liverpool. Robinson, under severe pressure from his wife, approached the ship's captain and explained that his wife would not travel on his ship with Anne Powell, and that under no circumstances was she to be permitted to sail aboard the vessel. The captain, fearing he might lose a large sailing party, complied with the request. Anne Powell was removed with her baggage onto the quayside on a cold February morning. But as the Robinsons began their voyage, they were haunted by the thought that Anne Powell was concealed on board and would reveal herself when they were well out to sea. In fact, they were never to see her again.

In a letter dated 3 March 1822, written by Mrs Powell to her other daughter, Mrs S.P. Jarvis, she says:

> My dearest Mary,
> The systematic persecution in which she perseveres. She is convinced that she is acting the part of a Christian. However, it was the fact that she left her home never to return while my head is above the earth. Mrs Robinson was after her fatiguing journey rendered doubly so by the successful plan of your sister to stop at the same houses where she boasts she was always considered as the lady of the house.

The delayed departure of Anne Powell for England from New York gave her father time to reconsider his position towards his daughter. He decided to make some provision for her support, and explained to his wife that he had an idea to their 'mutual plague'. He talked of sending her to France where there were English boarding houses under the name of convents, a not uncommon retreat for decayed branches of good families. With this plan in mind, he resolved to make it up with his daughter, to speak to her himself to see if she would see reason. It was some consolation to him later, when he heard of her death, that he had managed to contain his resentment.

Anne Powell had been compelled to make new arrangements and considered sailed aboard the *Amity*, due to depart New York around 17 March. She had been invited to book passage on this packet by a businessman named Jacob Harvey from Cork. However, this ship would carry mainly male passengers, prompting Anne to decline his offer.

The next packet ship due to sail was the *Albion* and Anne took passage on it.

It sailed from New York on 1 April 1822 and was caught in a violent gale off the south coast of Ireland. When the ship began taking water, Anne took her turn at the pumps, her precious life to save. She fought like a tiger. She did everything that was required of her and when the end was near, her bravery was second to none.

When the *Albion* struck the rocks the first time in the grey dawn of the morning of 22 April 1822, Anne Murray Powell could be seen clinging to the broken mast, and when a second huge wave caught the stricken *Albion*, it hit her broadside and drove the vessel closer to the shore. Anne bravely held on, and with the anchors and torn rigging sweeping across the shattered deck, Anne Powell's pitiful cries for help could be heard through the shrieking wind, crying in vain as she did so many times for her lover, John Beverly Robinson. So close to the shore and safety, clinging onto the mast with one hand, and gripping in the other hand a little purse of gold given by her father at New York before she set sail, the next wave swept to her death Anne Murray Powell, the wayward daughter of Upper Canada's chief justice. As she met her end, she could be seen waving her purse of gold at the penniless masses gathered high upon the safety of the cliff-top, almost within reach and yet powerless to be of any assistance to her. When the storm abated and the tide ebbed, it was these same strangers who found and removed her shattered, half-naked body, cast among the jagged rocks off western Garrettstown, close to the Old Head of Kinsale. Poor Miss Powell – so brave and energetic – found rest at last in a watery grave.

John Purcell, the steward at Thomas Rochfort's of Garrettstown, took charge of Anne Powell's body. She was taken to Garrettstown House where her remains rested while he ordered a wooden coffin, which was made from local timber and cut at Kilmore sawmills. Her burial took place after a dignified service and she was laid to rest in the corner of Templetrine graveyard. Weary she must have been, travelling across the barren frozen lands of Canada on her way to New York, her long wait in New York, her arduous journey, only then to be cast ashore in Ireland. Now the bones and mortal remains of the daughter of the once powerful chief justice of Upper Canada, William Dummer Powell, lie alone in a corner of a graveyard thousands of miles from her home in her native Canada.

Anne's father, Judge Powell, was at this time in London on business, and had intended to be reconciled with his daughter, whom deep down he loved. Not knowing of her whereabouts and frantic with worry, he hired an agent to trawl the streets of Liverpool to see if his daughter had arrived from New York. Unknown to the judge, his daughter's fate had already been sealed. A letter arrived on 10 April 1822 at Judge Powell's boarding house in London.

> Dear Sir
> Your favour of the 3rd came duly to hand and I should have had much pleasure in paying attention to Miss Powell but at my going to the Waterloo this morning to enquire if she had stayed there with the rest of the passengers from the 'Amity' that arrived yesterday, I was informed that no such lady was a passenger by that ship.

I then went down to the Leyford and received the same answer. The enclosed came under cover to me which I read on coming to town this morning. I daresay it will explain the reason of your daughter not having taken passage by that ship.
I remain dear Sir yours
John Gordon

Anne Powell's body was identified by a brooch given to her by her father as a birthday present a few years earlier. When Judge Powell learned of the disaster, he was full of sorrow and regret, and walked the streets of London in a daze, ending up in the Houses of Parliament. Though Powell was broken-hearted, he could not show it for his job and family prestige was at stake. In a cruel stroke of fate, Powell found himself standing in the streets of London alongside John Beverley Robinson – the man his daughter had idolised and for whom she had lost her life. Robinson pretended not to notice Powell.

Later, the distraught Powell interviewed the surviving crewmen and arranged for his daughter's burial.

A letter from John Gordon to Chief Justice Powell in London, dated 4 May 1822, reads:

On the day you wrote me or certainly the following one, you worked through the lamentable account of the logs of the 'Albion' on board of which vessel was your poor unfortunate daughter. Not knowing where you were to be found and thinking it probable that you had gone in to Hampshire with our friend Harben, I made the earliest communication to him of this melancholy event with a request that he would have it conveyed to you as quickly as possible, although I have written him three times since he left London. I have not yet heard from him.

The London papers give all the particulars that we know regarding the saving and interment of the unfortunate bodies, and I have seen that poor Miss Powell has been amongst those that have been numbered and deposited in their mother earth, shall I refrain on delivering the letter you enclosed.
I remain Dear Sir,
John Gordon

Anne Powell's sister's, Eliza Powell and Mary Jarvis, communicated by letter and speak of how the tragedy affected their two nieces, Mary and Anne.

Their meals are taken in their room and when anyone enters they stop talking or whisper. They are under great strain and miss their aunt Anne. Mama desires me to give you her love. She had a letter from Papa which now makes her feel much better. He writes in good spirits that he had received the fatal news in London on the 23rd April.

She mentions to her sister that letters had arrived in Canada from John Robinson on 29 May and he did not mention a word of the shipwreck or Anne.

Papa had taken out comfortable lodgings for her in London and had done all in his power to make her happy and respectable, poor thing. Her fate is dreadful to think of. I can't but hope that we shall hear some particulars of her. I think Papa will see the Mate of the ship and the young man that was saved. It would be a comfort to know that she was aware and prepared for her fate.

I do indeed pity John Beverly Robinson. I think he ought never to make an idle or insincere speech again, for from that we date all this misery. I cannot blame him for his opposing her going with them, though I always wished he had not.

Eliza, who was writing from York, asks her sister in Richmond to procure four pairs of pretty, good-sized, black, silk stockings as the ones in York are too small for anyone. They wanted them for the mourning and 'Mama sends on $20'. The letter ends with her mentioning the *Albion* and that a Mr Wood came out on her from England last year.

She was one of the most thought-of ships that sailed and the Captain as much, as a well behaved man and a good seaman.
Ever your affectionate sister E. Powell

Anne Powell would have survived but fate was not with her as we see in this letter from Jacob Harvey.

Jacob Harvey, a businessman from Cork, presents his respects to Judge Powell and has the melancholy satisfaction of learning with his nephew for him a breast pin which he received from his uncle Reuben Harvey of Cork to whom it had been given by the mate of the 'Albion' who took it himself from the breast of Miss Powell after her body was found and who requests that it might be immediately forwarded to Judge Powell in his name. It may be information, which Judge Powell has not received before, to tell him that an official account of the melancholy shipwreck has been published by the mate, which appeared in the Cork Southern Reporter of the 6th inst. Jacob Harvey regrets that he has not that newspaper to leave with Judge Powell.

Jacob Harvey sailed from New York in the ship *Amity*, which left that city two weeks prior to the *Albion* and

most sincerely laments that Miss Powell did not pursue her original intentions of being one of his companions as they were favoured with a summer's passage of 21 days.

Jacob Harvey would have preferred leaving this breast pin until he had a personal interview with Judge Powell but was fearful, as his stay in town is limited to a few days, that such an opportunity might not arise.

Harvey's motivation for asking Anne Powell to travel with him may not have been entirely honourable, and she refused his company.

Back home in Canada, the people of the small community in York were stunned by the news of Anne's death. 'It is impossible to say what I have felt and what I continue to feel,' wrote her distraught mother. Fourteen years later, on 22 April, she wrote: 'This is a painful anniversary indeed. No day passes without a thought for her daughter that would not live to the stiff life of propriety.' Anne Powell's mother was haunted by her daughter's memory.

Charles Fothergill's *Weekly Register* reported the wreck of the *Albion* in lurid detail but tactfully mentioned only in passing Anne's presence on the ship. Nevertheless, Anne's infatuation had made the family, as Mrs Powell put it, the subject of gossip 'from the Government House to Forests Stable', and hastened the decline of its prestige. The object of her obsession was held at least partly to blame, and there was now an open rupture between the Powells and the Robinsons.

Two months after Anne's death, Chief Justice William Dummer Powell made a pilgrimage to Garrettstown. Co. Cork to organise the erection of a tombstone at Templetrine graveyard over his daughter's grave. When Thomas Rochfort of Garrettstown Estate brought him to where his daughter's mortal remains lay buried, a great weakness came over him. Powell fell to his knees and felt a propensity to tears; he was full of regret and remorse and was much disturbed by painful images. He wished that he had been more understanding of his difficult daughter who was so similar to him in temperament. He felt so much regret that he took Communion for the first time in fifty years, and was comforted by the Rev. John Rogerson Cotter, the rector of Templetrine.

One year later, on 19 June 1823, Jacob Harvey wrote to Judge Powell from New York:

> I have but just returned from Ireland, which I hope thou wilt accept as an apology for my not having sooner informed thee of the performance of the melancholy service thou confided to my care in London last summer. Agreeably to thy request I desired my Uncle in Cork to have a suitable tombstone placed over the grave of Miss Powell, with the inscription furnished by thee, and also to have the Marble Tablet placed in a proper situation inside of the Church all which he undertook most willingly, and when I was last in Cork, I had the satisfaction of learning that everything was completely done. Mr. Rochford very kindly afforded every facility the total expense, including freight and charges on the marble tablet from London. The cost of the Tombstone, transportation of both to Garrettstown and erection in the Churchyard there amounts to eleven pounds, 6 shillings, Irish or $46.33 dollars, which thou may suit thy own convenience in refunding me. I had intended transmitting this information through George Gallagher, but I find he is not in this city and likely to be absent for some time. Mr Murray, whom I met a few days ago, gave me thy direction and requested I would write to thee.
> I remain with respect,
> Thy Friend, Jacob Harvey.
> My address is Abraham Bell & Co. 61 Pine St. New York.

The reply from William Powell was as follows:

> Received 30th June and same day with bill from the Bank.
> Much Respected Friend,
> Your kind attention to the brotherly commission you undertook for me in London calls for my warmest thanks, which I beg you to accept and communicate to your friend Mr. Rochford in Ireland. I enclose the amount of the Charges incurred, reasonable almost beyond belief. I do not offend by any addition, receiving as a friendly obligation the services you offered and procured with such Christian Charity, but beg to hold myself, in all gratitude, your debtor, to serve yourself or Friends.
> W. D. P.

Anne's Powell's eccentric conduct and tragic death contributed to the declining influence and weakened mental state of William Dummer Powell, though his career was already on the wane for other reasons. William Powell and John

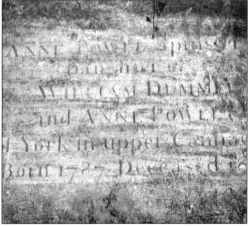

Above: Anne Powell's final resting place in Templetrine graveyard near Garrettstown, Co. Cork. Right, top: Close-up of inscription on the grave slab. Right, below: Plaque in Templetrine church in memory of Anne Powell, erected by her father.

ANNE POWELL. Spinster.
was a Passenger in the Ship ALBION (wrecked on this Coast on the 22 nd April 1822) and perished with many others: but her Body being recovered from the Sea, received from the Charity of Strangers christian Burial in the Cemetery of this Church:_in grateful Memory whereof this Marble is inscribed by
W. D. P.

Robinson became bitter political enemies but the women of the families gradually re-established social ties; none of them, however, could forget Anne. For Robinson, the incident was socially awkward, possibly even embarrassing, but little else, as by now he was well established in government. Neither the event itself nor the break with the Powells affected his career in the slightest.

On a voyage to England thirty years later, Robinson made a note in his diary as the ship passed the Old Head of Kinsale at the point where the *Albion* was lost. His thoughts went back to those days so long ago when Anne and himself were lovers, and a hidden tear was shed.

A hundred and forty-six years later – in 1968 – while looking for her grave, I found what I thought to be the spot where she was buried. The inscription was so faded and worn, it was impossible to read. I decided to repair the supports on the underside of her tomb and I lifted the slab to carry out this work. There, underneath, was the full inscription, perfectly clear to read. I concluded that the sculptor, when carving the inscription in 1823, had made a mistake, turned over the slab and carved the inscription again. Several years later, on closer examination, I found that the two inscriptions on each side are identical. It is possible that Judge Powell had instructed the sculptor to carve it on both sides so as to be sure that she would be remembered. One hundred and eighty years after her tragic death, that inscription is plain to be seen in the churchyard of Templetrine.

Chief Justice William Dummer Powell fell from grace in 1825 and was replaced a short time later by John Beverly Robinson, the man he elevated to power and who had been indirectly involved in the death of his daughter. Dummer Powell died in York in 1834, aged seventy-nine years – the same year York was renamed Toronto. Anne Murray Powell outlived her husband by fifteen years and died in Toronto in 1849 at the age of ninety-three.

John Beverley Robinson suffered a severe attack of gout in the spring of 1861 and resigned his post on 15 March 1862. Following another attack of gout, Robinson died at his home at the age of sixty-two on 31 January 1863.

The tragic life and death of Anne Powell can haunt us still – a grim reminder of the consequences of violating the social standards of correct female behaviour in the early nineteenth century. Many years later, the sad saga of Anne Murray Powell has haunted me. From a young and tender age, the name of Anne Powell was etched on my mind, and I will always remember her.

Emigration from a Poverty-stricken Land: 1820s

On Saturday 27 September 1958, an historical plaque commemorating the 1825 Robinson Settlement was unveiled in Victoria Park, Water Street, Peterborough. This was one in a series of plaques being erected throughout the province by the Department of Travel and Publicity, on the advice of the Archaeological and Historic Sites Board of Ontario. Many an Irish body lay beneath the frozen soil of Canada.

The Peterborough Historical Society sponsored the unveiling ceremony. Speakers included Professor T.F. McLlwraith of the University of Toronto, a member of the Archaeological and Historic Sites Board, His Worship J.A. Dewart, Mayor of Peterborough, Mr James Gifford, warden of Peterborough county, and representatives of the federal and provincial governments. The plaque was unveiled by a descendant of one of the Irish immigrants who arrived in 1825 with Peter Robinson. The plaque reads: 'The Robinson Settlement 1825'.

In an effort to alleviate poverty and unemployment in Ireland, the British government in 1825 sponsored a settlement of Irish immigrants in the Newcastle district of Upper Canada. Peter Robinson, later that province's commissioner of Crown lands, was appointed superintendent and, in May, 2,024 persons sailed from Cork. A few settled elsewhere and disease thinned their numbers, but by September, the remainder were gathered in temporary shelters on the site of Peterborough. Under Robinson's supervision, free rations were distributed until November 1826. Cabins were erected and 1,878 settlers successfully established on land in the Peterborough region.

Although Peterborough was established in 1820, the real beginning of the town and much of the surrounding region may be dated from the arrival of close to 2,000 Irish immigrants in 1825 under the superintendence of Peter Robinson. Born in New Brunswick in 1785, Peter was the eldest son of Christopher Robinson, an officer in the Queen's Rangers, and Esther Sayer. His parents came to Upper Canada in 1792, settling first at Kingston, then at York (now Toronto; it was renamed in 1834 after the war with America in 1812).

Peter Robinson served with distinction at the capture of Detroit, where he commanded a rifle company, and in the defence of Michilimackinac. In 1817, he was elected to the legislative assembly of Upper Canada. In 1827, he was appointed commissioner of Crown lands with a seat in both the executive and legislative councils. He was the elder brother of Sir John Beverley Robinson, a prominent lawyer, politician and judge who served as chief justice of Upper

Canada from 1830 to 1862. (It should be noted that one of John Beverley Robinson's former lovers, Anne Powell, was lost off Garrettstown on the packet ship *Albion* on 22 April 1822, and is buried at Templetrine graveyard overlooking Ballinspittle village.)

In the early 1820s, extreme poverty, bordering in many cases on famine, was the lot of the lower classes in Ireland. Violent disturbances were frequent, heightened by the struggle for Catholic emancipation. When Robert Wilmot Horton, under-secretary of state for colonial affairs, prepared a scheme for state-assisted emigration, landlords and tenants in the disturbed areas were eager to co-operate. Peter Robinson was appointed to superintend the project.

The district from which the major portion of the settlers came was the barony of Fermoy. This area, approximately twenty by forty miles, is north of the Blackwater river in the northern part of Co. Cork. Most of the communities were within forty-five miles of the city of Cork. Peter Robinson, in his search for emigrants, visited the communities of Fermoy, Ballyhooly, Mallow, Newmarket, Charleville, Kildorrery, Doneraile, Kilworth and numerous other smaller villages in the barony.

Of the great landowners from whose estates most of the Robinson settlers came, Lord Kingston had his country seat at Mitchelstown, Lord Doneraile in Doneraile, Lord Mountcasel at Kilworth, C.D Jephson held the area around Mallow, W.W. Beecher the Liscarroll district, R.D. Aldwort was the landlord in the Newmarket area and Captain Roberts in the Charleville district. A plan was devised by Wilmot-Horton to encourage British emigration to Upper Canada, believing it a way to offset the influence of predominantly American immigration, to increase the Anglophone population in Canada and to maintain the British connection with the colonies. To Wilmot-Horton, the plan, which received government approval in January 1823, would make 'the redundant labour and the curse of the mother country, the active labour and blessing of the colonies.' As they considered potential immigrants, their attention turned to Ireland as a source, and they received encouragement and help from the Irish administration. Peter Robinson was asked by the colonial secretary to supervise the migration to Upper Canada.

The plans for immigration, which Wilmot-Horton introduced, would have been dangerously theoretical without Peter Robinson. He provided the local knowledge and practical good sense missing from many nineteenth-century colonisation schemes. Robinson also brought an unusual amount of first-hand experience to the job of commissioner of Crown lands. So long as the emphasis was on opening the province by making land available to actual settlers, his priorities were right. In 1822, Peter went to England as a tourist and the following year was introduced as an expert on backwoods settlement by his friend, Robert John Wilmot-Horton, the new under-secretary of state for the colonies. An enthusiastic Malthusian, Wilmot Horton had a scheme to bring peace and prosperity to Ireland through the sponsored emigration of thousands of dispossessed tenant farmers whose continued presence blocked agricultural improvement. He had obtained the government's consent to a small-scale, experimental scheme for sending emigrants to Upper Canada, and he found his superintendent in Peter Robinson.

Wilmot-Horton deliberately introduced his scheme in the Blackwater river valley of Co. Cork, a region where there was no tradition of emigration and where the Insurrection Act was in force. He sent Robinson there in the spring of three successive years. If nothing else, Robinson proved for Wilmot-Horton what a single, personable interviewer with a few key introductions could accomplish. On his first visit to the Blackwater valley, Robinson found that there were many who were willing to equate assisted emigration with transportation. Two years later, the would-be emigrants needed sponsorship even to get on a list. Robinson was besieged by applicants at every town and wrote in terms of 50,000 applying for 2,000 places. At the completion of the difficult task of selection in 1825, he was satisfied that his candidates were 'a better description of people than those taken out in 1823 although they are wretchedly poor'. Poverty was one of Wilmot-Horton's firm preconditions.

During his trips to Ireland, Peter Robinson became a close friend of Dr Farmar, the founder of the North Infirmary Hospital in Cork city. Dr Farmar resided at Mount Oval on the Rochestown Road on the eastern outskirts of the city. Later, he moved to a house close to where the present Cork Airport is situated, which is why the airport is called Farmar's Cross. Peter Robinson used to stay at what was then known as Conroy's Hotel in Oliver Plunkett Street in Cork city.

In July 1823, about 500 emigrants were given free transportation and supplies, and were settled in the townships of Ramsay, Huntly, Parkenham and Goulbourn in the Bathurst district of Upper Canada. These emigrants sailed from Queenstown (now Cobh), Co. Cork to Quebec. Quite a few of the emigrants came from the harbour area of Cork – Passage, Monkstown, Ringaskiddy – an area with massive unemployment following the cessation of work at Spike Island, the boat-yard and docks at Haulbowlin and the munitions dump at Rocky Island.

In 1825, a second, larger movement was authorised to the Newcastle district. Most of these Irish emigrants were from the portion of Co. Cork lying north of the Blackwater river. On 8 May 1825, nine ships sailed from Cobh, Cork carrying 2,024 emigrants (710 adults, the rest children). One of these ships was *Albion II*. The original *Albion* was wrecked off Garrettstown on 22 April 1822. *Albion II* departed from Cork bound for Quebec. Under Captain John Mills, *Albion II* carried 191 souls – fifty-six males over fourteen years, thirty-nine males under fourteen years, fifty-two females over fourteen years and forty-four females under fourteen years. Surgeons were assigned to each ship and they seem to have been responsible for the general administration and discipline on board. The settlers landed at Quebec and were taken by ship to Montreal, and from there by bateaux to Prescott and Kingston.

Among those beginning a new life in Canada were James Healy and family from Buttevant, James Barry from Doneraile, Michael Fullam (twenty-eight) from Doneraile, his wife, Judith (twenty-six) and their three children, Catherine (seven), Michael (five) and Mary (two); Dónal Shea (thirty-four) also from Doneraile, his wife and four children; Daniel Connor (thirty-three) from Kanturk, his wife, Bridget (twenty-six) and complete family; John Clancy (thirty) from Rock Mills, Cork, his wife, Elma (thirty) and their four children, Ellen, William, John and Johanna; Timothy Sweeney (thirty-four) from Buttervant, his wife, Johanna (thirty), who died a few short months later on 31 December 1826, their three children, Honora (eleven), Mary (nine), and Catherine (four); William Reilly (thirty-five) from Ballyclough, his wife, Elizabeth (thirty) and their six children: Thomas (thirteen),

Joseph (eleven), John (eight), Mary (four), Jeremiah (two) and Johanna (one); John Sheehan (thirty-nine) from Churchtown, his wife, Bridget (thirty-six) and their six children: Cornelius (twenty-one), Timothy (eighteen), Patrick (fourteen), Michael (eight), John (six), Mary (sixteen); John Regan (thirty-two), also from Churchtown, his wife, Mary (thirty) and their two children.

Whole families left, leaving no-one at home. Take the case of John Collins, aged forty, from Askeaton, Co. Limerick. With him went his wife, Johanna, aged forty, and their children: Michael (twenty), twins Timothy and John (eighteen), Catherine (fourteen), Edmond (twelve), Bridget (three), Maurice (one) and another boy aged sixteen.

By September, most of the immigrants were in Cobourg. Robinson proceeded to improve the trail to Rice Lake and constructed a large scow (a barge for transporting freight) to carry the settlers and their belongings up the Otonabee river to Scott's Plains. This became the headquarters of the settlement. Most of the settlers were located on lots and by the end of the year, a total of 1,878 were settled in the area around Scott's Plains, which included the townships of Emily, Duoro, Ennismore, Otonabee, Asphodel, Smith, Ops and Marmora. Each family was allocated 100 acres of land, the exact location apparently being made by drawing numbered slips of paper from a hat. Probably lots were then traded among individuals to allow relatives and friends to settle near one another. Since few of the settlers were expert axe-men, Robinson expedited matters by having simple log cabins built under contract by experienced woodsmen on the various lots. Each family was given a cow, construction tools and cooking utensil, three bushels of seed potatoes, one peck of corn seed, and rations of flour and salt pork. A committee, which included a resident doctor and a priest, supervised the settlement for the first eighteen months. Given his circle at York, Peter appeared unusually tolerant of his Roman Catholic charges. The members of Lieutenant Governor Sir Peregrine Maitland's administration supported the settlements for Peter's sake and because of Wilmot-Horton's interest and instructions, but they held to the belief that Irish Roman Catholics were the least desirable of 'British' settlers. Robinson's 1823 immigrants were therefore watched with nervous anticipation. Although a few failed to adjust to settlement among Irish and Scot's Protestants, as a group they were involved in only one incident – in May 1824 – serious enough to attract more than local attention. Colonel James Fitzgibbon went to mediate and the government continued its support, but Robinson's 1825 settlers were to be located elsewhere by themselves.

The one-time parliamentary grants for the larger and more ambitious immigration of 1825 produced difficulty for Robinson's management of the operation. The grants were made late in the spring, so late that he arrived in Upper Canada after the settlers. It had been impossible to make the advance preparations which might have cut costs. Hindsight suggested that a depot should have been established and the work of opening a settlement begun during the previous winter, the customary season for transporting bulk supplies by sleigh and chopping a first clearing. There had been no funds and no authority for this work. For the same reason, the ships' surgeons who conducted the immigrants up the St Lawrence had to make do with existing facilities. Robinson's organisation was greatly criticised for holding the immigrants in an improvised tent city at Kingston until his arrival in August, but this action had been taken on Maitland's orders. Once at Kingston, Robinson moved his settlers forward to the Newcastle district and on to the lots he chose for them with an energy and resourcefulness that showed him at his best. In 1823, William Marshall, his second-in-command, had criticised his indulgence. In 1825, Robinson declared that he intended to be stricter at Scott's Mills, the depot for the distribution of supplies. In fact, order within the settlement depended on good will and on his personal authority over the immigrants, and he continued to seek to 'gain them by kindness'. George Hume Reade, their doctor in 1825 and a more sympathetic observer than Marshall, singled out for particular praise Robinson's 'kind manner' and 'up-right principle' in his handling of 'the lower class of the Irish'. Robinson liked his job and had no doubt in 1824 that he preferred working with Wilmot-Horton to the possibility held out by John Galt of superintending the sale of the Crown lands of Upper Canada in the future Canada Company.

In the sparsely settled townships of the Newcastle district to the north of Rice Lake, the 1,825 immigrants were certain of a welcome from the inhabitants and of a good choice of Crown land. But they faced a long, difficult journey in an unusually hot summer. The heat aggravated both the fever and ague contracted locally, and the endemic illnesses that the immigrants brought with them. Robinson himself developed a fever from which he 'never perfectly recovered from and most of his assistants were also sick over the course of the summer and fall.' At Scott's Mills, a town-site was surveyed by Richard Birdsall in 1825 and named for Robinson. The community, which grew up around the depot, contained grist and sawmills built with government funds and became the hub of a rudimentary road system. Many Upper Canadians would have spent the money differently but most could agree that the Peterborough immigration had successfully pioneered a new region. Robinson is still best remembered as the founder of Peterborough.

Robinson had left the 1823 immigrants as soon as they were located. He stayed with the 1825 settlers until March 1826, when he completed a personal inspection of all lots and a report of improvements. In all, he had located just under 2,000 immigrants in nine townships in the Newcastle district. Not all locations had been taken up and some remained temporarily vacant as families regrouped to begin work on a single lot, but still the totals of land cleared and of produce raised, which Robinson sent off to Wilmot-Horton, were signs of a flourishing settlement. Robinson's stock was high in the Colonial Office when he returned to England in 1826 and 1827 to give evidence to two select committees on emigration, called at Wilmot-Horton's instigation. Wilmot Horton's scheme, in its Irish formulation, proved too expensive to win the sponsorship of government or landlord. Although he recognised his failure in Britain, he sought to provide for the continuation of some elements of his scheme in Upper Canada after his resignation in January 1828. Before he left office, he had Robinson appointed, in July 1827, commissioner of Crown lands (Upper Canada's first surveyor general of woods). The Crown Lands Department was created to oversee the implementation of a new policy for the sale of Crown properties, including disposal by auction and payment by installment which, Wilmot-Horton believed, would allow indigent immigrants to acquire land.

Robinson's tenure in the Crown Lands Department was shaped by a dramatic rise in immigration from the British Isles, which peaked in 1832, the year of a cholera epidemic. Contemporary statistics for emigration to British North America are understated and unreliable, but they reflect reality. Figures of 12–13,000 for 1826–29 rose through 30,000 in 1830 to 58,000 in 1831 and 66,000 a year later, dropping to 28,000 in 1833. Each year, a proportion of the immigrants arriving in Upper Canada failed to fit into the province's economy. They could not find work and lacked the capital to establish themselves by their own efforts. Lieutenant Governor Sir John Colborne, who replaced Maitland in 1828, turned to Robinson to use his expertise and the resources of his department to provide for indigent immigrants. In addition to agents responsible for a port, road project, or settlement, Robinson employed others on a casual basis as particular needs arose. Agents in the lake ports directed needy immigrants to their colleagues inland who, at specified places, offered work, usually the opening of roads, and fifty-acre lots on extended terms.

Robinson and his agents were caught between these orders and the pressing needs of families who were in their care because they had no other recourse. Much depended on the experience and discretion of the agents, for Robinson issued orders requiring prior approval of new expenses only in May 1833.

The severest test came in summer 1832 when Upper Canada's first cholera victims were identified. Colborne based his strategy on a belief that the greatest danger lay in allowing large numbers of immigrants to congregate in temporary quarters. Top priority in 1832 went to moving immigrants out of York and the other towns along their route. Robinson's network held up under this pressure despite the difficulties caused by fear of infection. Charges for transportation rose and, in some communities, all doors were closed to strangers. Yet even Roswell Mount, at the distant end of the chain, got his people placed and in some shape for winter. The epidemic did not lead to civil disorder and families did not starve in the new settlements. In midsummer 1832, Robinson began to see what the cost of this achievement would be. His policy, as in the 1820s, was always to get immigrants settled and to worry about accounts only after the end of the short season in which they could be located successfully. His effort indeed proved so costly that it destroyed his operation rather that brought it credit.

Robinson was on a bad footing with the lieutenant governor when a paralytic attack on 23 June left him 'deprived of the use of his left side'. And seeing no prospect of recovery, Head demanded his early resignation from the Crown Lands Department and, in order for its business to continue, offered the position to Robert Baldwin Sullivan. Robinson closed his books as commissioner for Crown lands and for clergy reserves in August but seems to have continued as nominal surveyor general of woods until 9 May 1837. Robinson wrote his will that month on the realistic assumption that most of the land he had acquired privately would have to be sold to cover his accounts. A list of his lands in 1837 recorded more than 7,592 acres and a couple of additional properties in Toronto. Printed family records say that Peter died unmarried, but two children, lsabella and Frederick, were his main concern in his will. Peter Robinson died on 8 July 1838 at the age of fifty-three.

The *Albion*: 1822

When growing up at Garrettstown in the early 1950s, I was intrigued by the tale of the *Albion*. My father, Denis, died in 1948, leaving three of us under the age of five and our mother, who was eight months' pregnant. Not long before our father died, he sat up in his bed, which was upstairs, and said how broken hearted he was at leaving us all behind, we being so young and it being the lean time of the late 1940s. Some of the timbers in the roof over his head were made from planks that came from the wreck of the *Albion*.

With no father-figure to look up to, it was to my uncle, grandfather and some other older people who lived close by that I listened and learned the tale of that little ship which hit the cliff-face so many years before, and of the great tragedy that occurred.

About 100 yards from our house, on the sea side, lived by himself an old man whose name was Jim. All his family had long gone to live in America. On a Sunday, Jim – with his soft, ragged hat, grey, hairy head, long whiskers and wearing a pair of big hobnail boots – would be out by the edge of the dust-covered road in front of his house watching the odd straggler on their way to the beach. On one such day in the late 1940s, my aunt – who was on holidays from Cork city – took my sister and myself on a trip to the beach. Jim approached us and offered me a mug of milk which did not look at all appealing as the mug had not seen water for many a month and had a very brown colour to it. I refused to partake in the consumption of its contents, whereas Jim forced my aunt to drink. Jim died in 1949. Little was I to know then that Jim's grandfather brought one of the survivors of the *Albion* up the cliff-face on that fateful morning of 22 April 1822 – a considerable feat.

The big talking point in our area was the *Lusitania* which had sunk in view of our house in May 1915. When the great liners of the last century were passing the Old Head on their way from New York to Liverpool, and again on their return journey, our grandmother would shout from outside, where she would be hanging out the bed sheets to bleach on the bushes, 'Come out, come out, the *Mauritania* is going west,' or 'The *Queen Mary* is going east.' For we had a great view, living as we did in an elevated place at upper Garrettstown. With my brother and sister, we would stare in awe as the black smoke poured from the funnels of the big liners as they sliced through the water like a knife cutting butter and leaving in their wake a white trail. This sight lasted for at least fifteen minutes and, as a big ship started to disappear over the horizon, we would suddenly think of our other tiny young brother and would run back into the house and grab him from his timber playpen. 'Be careful with him,' would be the call from our mother. We would then scramble over the field to get a better view and try to point out to him the tiny speck in the distance, but he would only stare into space and look at the movements of our hands. Little did we know that he was to leave us forever very soon, God love him, for he was killed with our grandfather at the very tender age of three-and-a-half years. It broke our mother's heart but she kept it to herself. The year was 1952.

The little school in Ballinspittle served us well but times were hard. Our mother was great – she kept us spick-and-span and gave us plenty to eat. But part-time work after school hours was the norm in our area and it was all to make ends meet. As I got older and ventured closer to the shore, I would meet the odd old fellow gathering driftwood washed up by the storms; the song was always the same – there he would be, sheltering from the biting wind behind the ruin of an old house or pillar, looking out to sea, the drop from his nose frequently wiped with the sleeve of his coat: ''Twas a bad night, a south-east gale; the sea is mad, boiling. It was a night like that the *Albion* was lost west along.'

The next ten years passed away very quickly, and growing up can play tricks on you. One fine summer's day in the early part of the 1960s, as I walked along the cliff-tops, who did I bump into but my Uncle Dan who for many a year was the ploughman at Garrettstown. He ploughed the furrow with two big Clydesdale horses and watched the steamers and great liners ply to and fro, carrying expectant passengers to the Promised Land. Dan was now retired. 'Were you fishing over the rocks?' I asked him.

'No,' was the reply.

'Can you show me the place where the *Albion* was lost.'

'Come on,' he said to me, 'for I must go home to my dinner or Mage will kill me.'

We went over the cliffs for about a quarter of a mile, stumbling as we made our way along. We had to cross at least two small streams and gullies. I'm sure Uncle Dan had a few pints in him because he stopped to water the pony several times! Then, as we approached a small outcrop, he threw himself down on the long grass, sticking a sop of the grass in his mouth and pointed: 'It's over there – that's the Albion rock, and do you see that hole in the side of the cliff? That's called the Albion cave. Keep away from it and mind your own business. That ship was carrying gold and there was a professor lost on her with a woman holding a purse of gold in her hand; she was shouting for someone to save her. You will have no luck for poking around there,' he said.

That gold was supposed to be forbidden – I knew that part of the story to be rubbish or a fairy tale. 'Go on Uncle Dan,' said I, 'tell me more.'

'Several years ago your father and another fellow – Bill – found a gold coin over there; that was back in the 1930s. They were digging in the gravel at low tide, as so many other people did in the years gone by, all looking for the forbidden gold. They took the coin home and put it up on the window ledge for all to see but Bill had a bloody pet jackdaw who whipped it away. 'Twas never again to be seen, and there was never any luck around the place after that. Keep away boy.'

So he left me staring at the rock. The tide was in so I could do no more and I went home to my mother. When I told her what I had found out, she said 'Are you mad or what?' I kept my mouth shut after that and said no more.

I then informed a couple of friends of mine from a market town, about twelve miles inland. I got to know these two fellows a few years earlier. Like myself, they, too, were looking for the Holy Grail and we ended up most weekends digging holes in different places around the parish after listening to a tale from some old codger telling us that there was an underground tunnel or gold buried there. Talk about being daft but in those days it was easy to be entertained. I told my friends of what I had found out about the *Albion*. One fellow was going to a very prestigious college in Dublin and had plenty of time on his hands during the college holidays, so he started writing away to see what he could find out about the *Albion*. As it transpired, the other fellow followed the same path.

In the meantime, the big fad in our area was the local platform – a square of concrete made smooth from the leather of the shoes and the crystals that were scattered upon it so everyone could glide across its surface with ease. Nearly every major crossroads had one of some sort, and it was here that the young men and women would gather for a Sunday night's dancing. Young girls would come out from the local towns by bike or foot. This was great because there was a scarcity of the opposite sex in the country areas – emigration had taken its toll.

One such night in midsummer, at this spot, I met Mary, who had won several

The *Albion*, which was of the Black Ball Line, in full sail in New York Harbour.

medals for step-dancing. She kept complaining that I was walking or stepping on her toes – I was a bit clumsy and not very good at waltzing – 'twas always an old-time waltz. Little did I know then that straight out from where we used to dance, the *Albion* passed on her final fifteen minutes before being smashed to pieces on the rocks. After a few years, we got married and had two very fine, caring children.

Another few years passed and I met man who had left the area in the depression of the 1920s. We all knew him as the 'Yank', and he used to come home in the summer from America. Pad was his name and, when on holiday, he would never let a day pass without making a trip along the cliff-tops. Eventually, he was to die not in his native land but on the sidewalk in Boston in the 1980s, killed by a vehicle. He was full of history and I learned a lot from him. He told me that I would eventually find gold and this really put a fever in me. Later, one weekend, there was a very low tide and, armed with nothing other than a spade and my knowledge of the shoreline, and with the information that I got from the uncle and Pad, I started digging and scraping at the place shown to me. This work carried on most weekends – indeed, for several months – and to many a local person at the time I was looked upon as not being all there – an odd fellow. I suppose they thought I was daft!

The first thing I came across was a black stone, rounded from the pounding of the sea over the years. These stones were different from the other type in the area and they were much heavier, leading me to suspect that they must surely be the ballast off a ship. As it transpired, I was correct, but these ballast stones were scattered over a wide area so more work had to be done.

Where exactly did the ship founder? I had heard that in the latter part of the nineteenth century, divers were employed by the local customs to look for some of the gold the little ship had carried. With the cliff-face steep and the shoreline rocky, they must have used some sort of a small salvage boat or punt; so where did they moor it? I went to the outer rock and started looking for some signs of hooks. Several days passed before I found rusted marks on the rock in between the crevices. I chipped and scraped and in the end found the remains of the mooring pins. Now I was almost sure that I had located the exact spot where the *Albion* had foundered on that fateful morning of 22 April 1822. I was overjoyed but also overcome with emotion as I thought of the unfortunate people who perished in that ferocious storm, and here was I, standing in the same place, only this time the sea was calm and peaceful. This was April 1972, exactly 150 years after the disaster.

I contacted the friends of mine whom I spoke about earlier who, by now, were very much involved in maritime history and had taken up diving to explore under the sea: Patrick O'Sullivan, who years later would write the very interesting book entitled, *The* Lusitania: *Unravelling the Mysteries,* and Alan Roddie of Bandon, Co. Cork who by now had graduated from Trinity College, Dublin. Between them, they had gathered quite a lot of information on the *Albion*, and it was decided that a diving operation was the only way to locate anything from the vessel.

In those days, if you lived close by the sea you never learned to swim. On the initial diving inspection of the *Albion* wreck site, I fitted myself out with a

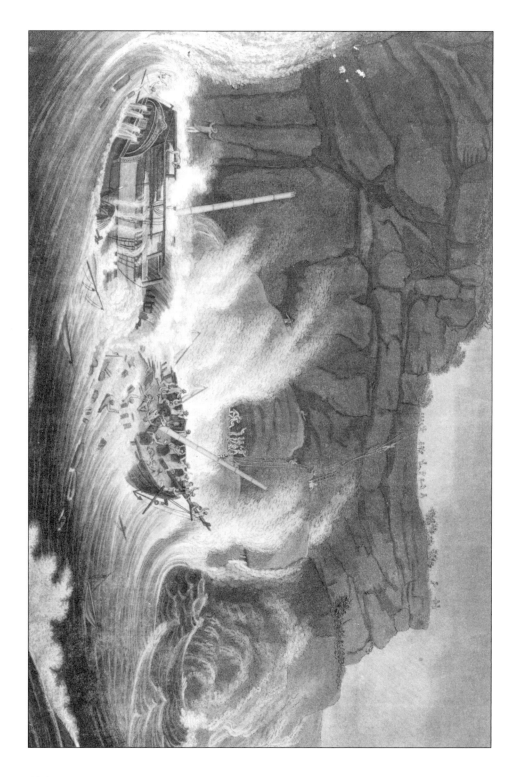

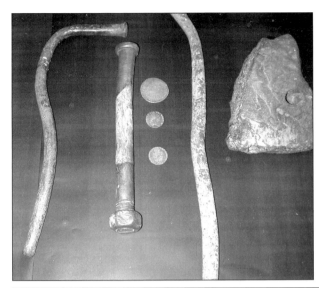

Left: All that was found at the *Albion* wreck site in 1970s – a few gold coins, some copper fastening pins, and a black ballast stone, an abundance of which was strewn on the shoreline.

Opposite: The *Albion* on the rocks off western Garrettstown. The engraving is by Thomas Birch who was guided in his work by William Everhart of Chester, Penn., the only cabin passenger to survive. It depicts the harrowing scene on that fateful morning of 22 April 1822. The lady in the centre, dressed in white, is supposed to be Anne Powell. The penniless masses gather on the cliff-tops, powerless to be of any assistance.

Photo: Mariners' Museum, Newport

ragged piece of rubber-stitched wetsuit and weighed it down with several pieces of lead. My quest for gold took control of me, forgetting I could not swim. I left the rock and jumped in only to find myself submerged and gasping for air after several minutes. I was dragged up onto the rock by my friend. Exhausted, Uncle Dan's words came back to haunt me.

During the months from May to September 1972, the following team of divers made a survey of the wreck site: Paddy O'Sullivan, Paddy Power, Alan Roddie, Ciaran Dempsey, Richard Cole and myself. I had gained confidence in my ability to traverse the water; the method we used was an air lift – a huge version of a vacuum cleaner to move the sand – and it was here, in water no more than fifteen-foot deep, that the survey revealed copper nails, brass tacks, lead sheeting, iron ingots, ballast stones and some gold and silver coins. In the autumn of that year, a cleric friend of mine, who was a great historian – Fr Gus O'Regan – gave a sermon off the altar in west Cork about the forbidden gold we had found. This must have frightened the daylights out of us because we were never again to return to do more salvage work at the site. So now I will begin to tell the tale of this nineteenth-century passenger-ship disaster.

The earliest American ships usually carried cargo belonging to the ship's owner – the owner and the captain, or the owner and the crew. Later, ships carried goods partly for the owners and partly for friendly adventurers. It has been said that the transatlantic sailing packet lines were developed in response to the demand following the end of the war of 1812 for a closer commercial relationship between the United States and the Old World. The demand for prompt, rapid and reliable transportation of passengers, mail and freight became a pressing factor among New York merchants and capitalists.

During 1817, five New York men had the vision and courage to inaugurate a transatlantic packet service, called the Black Ball Line. These Quakers and Friends were Isaac Wright and his son, William, Francis Thompson, Benjamin

Marshall and Jeremiah Thompson. Some of them were textile importers. It was decided that four ships would be built in succession: the *Amity,* under its master, John Stanton; the *Courier*, with William Browne as captain; the *Pacific*, with captain Jono Williams; and the *James Munroe*. These vessels would sail from New York on the fifth and one from Liverpool on the first of every month.

Their commanders were men of great experience and activity, and they would do all in their power to render these packets as eligible conveyances for passengers and to deliver their cargoes on time. By 23 February 1818, the Black Ball Line of packets was in full service.

A packet's crew consisted of the captain and three mates: the chief, or first mate, upheld the dignity of the quarterdeck while the second and third mates were the real handlers, driving and working the crew. Then came the carpenter, a steward, two cooks – one for the crew and one for the cabin – a cabin boy and about twenty sailors.

The *Pacific* saw only one year with the Black Ball Line before being sold off, but she had an active sea life with another shipping company until 1882. A new ship was built to replace the *Pacific* and she was to be named the *Albion* (Albion was the old Celtic name for Britain). Built by Sidney Wright (Isaac Wright's talented shipbuilding nephew), the *Albion* was launched on 25 January 1819. Her crossing from New York to Liverpool was best at twenty-seven days, her slowest forty-one days, and her average thirty-four days. But her life was to be short. Registered in New York, the *Albion*'s dimensions were as follows: weight: 434 tons; length: 113 feet; breadth: 29 feet 4 inches. She had two decks, three masts, a billet head, square stern and was white-bottomed with bright-coloured stakes on her sides and presumably was copper-fastened.

Her captain was John Williams, better known in the Black Ball sailor's shanty as 'Kicking' Jack Williams. He was more or less the commodore of the line and had kept a close eye on the *Albion* during her construction. Williams had married the daughter of Captain Stanton, who was master of another Black Baller, the *Amity*. Williams alone was one of the four original captains who had inaugurated the packet service in 1818 and who was still in command of a Black Baller.

When the last of the cargo of cotton, gold and beeswax, along with the stores and provisions, were being loaded on board the *Albion* in New York Harbour under the eagle eye of Captain Williams and supervised by his first mate, Henry Cammeyer, and the second mate, Edward Smith, little did they realise that, of the three of them, only Henry Cammeyer would survive the fatal journey that lay before them. With all the passengers safely on board, the crew were ready on the first day of April 1822. The *Albion* hoisted her sails and sailed out the harbour. The passengers waved goodbye to their friends in the town of New York and set forth into the North Atlantic for the port of Liverpool.

The journey from New York to Liverpool for twenty days was smooth and plain sailing, but on Saturday 20 April, a strong gale blew up and after several hours became a violent storm. The packet ship *Albion* had all her hatches closed and the terrified passengers were locked below the deck in wet, dark

The exact spot in western Garrettstown at which Anne Powell lost her life on the *Albion* on that fateful morning of 22 April 1822.

and dismal conditions. Most of the occupants were seasick, mingling their moans with the creaking of the ship's joints. She plunged her knightheads into the sea which flooded the main deck above them, and when she rolled, she was washed by the waves of water that broke against her bulwarks. The fierce gale shrieked through the shrouds and played upon the running rigging.

Above on deck, 'Kicking' Jack Williams had a fight on his hands trying to steer his ship and keep her afloat. The cursing of his officers and the growling of his sailors as they were being washed from the pumps made a scene that no pen can paint. Still, the little *Albion* battled the elements to stay afloat and continued on her journey.

By Sunday 21 April, the ferocity of the storm had eased somewhat. Captain Williams tried to console his terrified passengers and told them that they were off the south Irish coast, close to Cape Clear and, all going well, he hoped he would make Liverpool in twenty-four hours. Sadly, that was not to be. Suddenly, out of the blue came a violent squall and the *Albion* was hit by a freak wave which threw the ship on her beam ends. The main mast, the head of the mizzen mast and fore-topmast were toppled, and the decks swept clear of everything, including the lifeboats, caboose house, bulwarks and compasses. All the hatches were thrown open and six of the crew – including Captain Williams – and one passenger were swept overboard. All below deck, including the cabin rooms, was filled with water and the ship became unmanageable. The stricken *Albion* was driven before the gale. The crew lashed themselves to the pumps, trying to keep her afloat, and were helped in their task by a female cabin passenger: Miss Powell. A few week's later, a seaman's song on the loss of the *Albion* contained a verse in praise of Miss Powell's heroism.

The ship was a mess, with ropes and torn rigging compounded by the fact that the ship's three main axes were strapped to the roundhouse which had been swept overboard, thus making it impossible to cut away the tangle of masts and rigging hanging overboard. At about 1 a.m. on the morning of 22 April, the first mate, Henry Cammeyer, spotted the now disused old lighthouse at the Old Head of Kinsale, and must have known that the end was near for the *Albion*, her passengers and the remains of the crew. At about 3 a.m., all were summoned up on deck as the jagged cliffs of Ireland approached. Just before she entered the breakers off the cliffs of western Garrettstown in Courtmacsherry Bay in the grey light of dawn, Cammeyer shouted 'every man for himself and God for us all', and the *Albion* struck the rocks and tore her bottom asunder. The next wave threw her broadside across the rocks and there was mayhem on board. As men, women and children were washed overboard, the yards of tangled sails and ropes made escape impossible.

On the cliff-tops, the penniless cliff-dwellers – who had emerged from their mud-walled cabins – were powerless to be of any assistance and gazed in awe at what was unfolding below them. Some of them had seen many a ship founder in the past, only this was different – the crew and passengers were being pounded to pieces against the sheer cliff-face a mere twenty yards from where they stood.

The *Cork Southern Reporter* carried reports of the ship's fate:

> The 'Albion' whose loss at Garrettstown bay we first mentioned in our paper of Tuesday, was one of the finest classes of ships between Liverpool and New York and was 500 tons burthen. We have since learned some further particulars, by which it appears that her loss was attended with circumstances of a peculiarly afflicting nature. She had lived out the tremendous gale of the entire day on Sunday, and Captain Williams consoled the passengers at eight o'clock in the evening, with the hope of being able to reach Liverpool on the day but only after which cheering expectation induced almost all the passengers particularly the females to retire to rest. In some short time, however, a violent squall came on, which in a moment carried away the masts, and their being no possibility to disengaging them from the rigging, they encumbered the hull that she became unmanageable, and drifted at the mercy of the waves, till the lighthouse of the Old Head was discovered, the wreck still nearing in, when the first mate told the sad news to the passengers that there was no longer any hope, and soon after she struck. From thence forward all was distress and confusion. The vessel soon went to pieces and of the crew and passengers, only six of the former and nine of the latter were saved.
>
> The mate is among the preserved, and that preservation was almost miraculous. He was thrown on a cliff by a wave, and had succeeded in climbing to the top of it when another took him off. He was thrown back and was more fortunate but his appearance bespeaks the suffering he endured from the beating of his body against the rocks. He is dreadfully bruised.

The number of passengers, we believe, was 25. Of these, we have already stated, one only was saved: a gentleman of Boston who traded with Liverpool. He had arrived at New York almost as the 'Albion' was on the point of sailing, and had not time to get bale for a large sum in specie, which he had. It was therefore shipped and lost.

Several of the bodies have been washed ashore, and Jacob Mark, Esq. the American Consul at this port, having repaired to the scene where the wreck took place, immediately on learning the melancholy intelligence, has done everything befitting his station, and a man of humanity under the circumstances. He has provide coffins for the bodies and caused them to be interred with their respective name affixed, having first had the mate to point them out, in order that if the families of any of them should wish hereafter to have the bodies removed, they may be enabled to do so. Mr. Mark's conduct is in every respect praiseworthy and he has taken measures for the protection of everything that has been washed ashore, as well for securing any thing that may yet be recovered.

Among the property already found is a box of specie – and among the bodies washed ashore is that of a French lady. She was extremely beautiful – when first discovered by some respectable persons it was entirely naked. It was mentioned to us as a fact, which we think ought to be mentioned, that a country boy, who saw the body, took off his outside coat and covered it and it is related of others of the country people that they also took off their warm clothing and put them on the unfortunate and nearly half perished part of the crew that escaped. While there are so may to censure and condemn their crimes, let them at least have justice rendered to their good qualities. It is distressing to be obliged to add to this melancholy event that, on Wednesday, a boat from Courtmacsherry, in which were eight men, in endeavouring to save a piece of the wreck was upset, and of the eight, seven were drowned.

The bodies marked (+) have been picked up and buried. A great number of bills drawn by the British officers in America, on Greenwood and Cox, army agents in London, and on other persons in England have also been washed ashore. Mr. Mark's activity and vigilance have been successful in recovering whatever has been saved. Mr. Gibbons of Ballinspittle House, the agent for Lloyds, at Kinsale, has been unwearied in to attentions, and whatever the mansion of Mr. Rochfort, of Garrettstown could contribute for the relatives of the survivors has been bounteously administered.

Major Gough's watch and seals have been picked up, and a small gold watch was found in Col. Provost's fob. These articles Mr. Mark has in his possession. The box of specie, of which we have spoken, contains coins foreign and English, to the value of £5,000. It is addressed to T.U. & Co. care of C. Hughes, Liverpool. The bills found are to an immense amount of London, Paris, and different parts of the Continent. Mr. Mark speaks in terms of great praise of the exertions of Mr. Pratt, surveyor of Kinsale and of Mr. John Purcell, a confidential steward of Mr Rochfort.

The following letter, from a correspondent in Liverpool, gives the painful news of the wreck and total loss of the packet ship 'Albion', from this port for Liverpool, together with all the passengers but one or two and the Captain and all the crew but seven. Two other letters, published in Liverpool, and containing all the particulars that had been received of this distressing disaster, will be among our extracts.

Garrettstown, Thursday evening, April 25th, 1822

Sir – I have only time to inform you that we found, near where the wreck of the 'Albion' lay, this day, different gold coins in a small box in all by a rough calculation amounting to upwards of £3,000. The coins being many of them foreign, and of different sizes prevents me from giving the exact sum, but it has all been brought up here safe, and counted in the presence of Mr. Pratt, the officer of the customs, Mr. Lemon and myself. I haste to acquaint you of this pleasing circumstance.

I have the honour to be sir, your most obedient and humble servant, John Purcell.

Liverpool, April 27th 1822

I have to inform you of the melancholy loss of the 'Albion', Captain Williams and sad to relate, the Captain and all the passengers, except one (twenty-seven ladies and gentlemen) are said to have perished. This disastrous event happened on the morning of the 22nd, very near the head of Old Kinsale. No particulars have yet been received and we remain in the most painful anxiety to hear the names of the sufferers. It is a most extraordinary fact, that no person here that I can find out knows the names of any of them. It is said that the ship was demasted in a severe gale on the 21st, and all their efforts to keep her off the shore were rendered unavailing, as she was within fifty yards of the shore. Such is the nature of the coast there that the persons who were on the spot could render little or no assistance, only seven of the crew and one passenger having been saved. This gentleman's name is not known. He was so much exhausted that he could give no information, either about himself or the others but it is said he is from Boston. The body of Lieutenant Colonel Prevost, of the 67th Regiment, has come on shore.

Liverpool, May 1st

In addition to the particulars of the loss of the 'Albion' published on the 27th the following has been received.

Kinsale, 4th Month 26th 1822.

On my arrival here on the 22nd, I wrote you a hasty letter, apprising you of the melancholy fate of the ship 'Albion'. I went over the fatal spot and cannot describe the scene that presented itself to my view, nor am I disposed to dwell on the heart-rending scene.

I shall be as brief as possible. Henry Cammeyer, the first mate, is saved, and six of the crew. The whole company on board, including passengers, amounted to fifty-six of whom forty-five perished and nine are saved. The logbook being lost, the mate could not give me a list of the passengers but from memory, he has given me the names of eighteen, which are annexed.

As the bodies that were found lay on the shore, the mate pointed out to me their respective names, which were put on paper and placed on each body and I gave direction that the graves should be numbered and a list made out, which I expected to get this day, by which it can be ascertained where each body lies in the grave yard.

A clergyman attended this melancholy procession. This may be some consolation to the afflicted relatives of the dead. Very little of the wreck remains and the country people are carrying it off in all directions, in small pieces. I have desired the remnants to be put up at auction and sold. I inquired of the mate about the specie. There were two boxes for you, two for Professor Fisher, a passenger, besides a package of dollars belonging to the only cabin passenger saved, Mr. Everhart, of Pennsylvania, who is very ill in bed. The mate thought I had not the least chance of recovering a dollar. I, however, thought otherwise. I accordingly took aside a confidential man, John Purcell, who is in the employment and enjoys the unlimited confidence of my worthy and respectable friend, Thomas Rochford, Esq. of Garrettstown, who owns all the land in the neighbourhood. I told him to employ a few men on whose honesty he could depend and set them to work to examine the spot where I received the mate's report where the money might be and that I would give him a good commission (I think I said five per cent) if he could prevent plunder and save the property. Late last night I received the enclosed, by express and I am now on the point of returning to the wreck. The box was broken open and plunder attempted. Yours truly, Jacob Mark
Cropper, Benson & Co.

The first news of the tragedy reached New York on 28 May 1822 when the fast sailing ship *Martha*, under the command of her owner, Captain William Sketchley, arrived in New York in a passage of thirty days from Liverpool, and delivered the news that the packet ship *Albion*, commanded by Captain John Williams and bound from New York for Liverpool, had been wrecked on the south coast of Ireland with the loss of nearly all her passengers and crew. At the time of the *Martha* sailing, the only news to have reached Liverpool was contained in two letters from the scene of the wreck and was very vague. One letter came from the American consul in Cork and the other from John Purcell, the steward for Thomas Rochfort of Garrettstown estate.

The melancholy and affecting intelligence created a deep sensation in New York and the flags of all vessels in the harbour were placed at half-mast.

June 13th 1822
It is our painful duty this week to record one of the most terrible disasters, at sea, that has occurred for many years; we mean the loss of the ship Albion, on the coast of Ireland.

We have given the details at length, for there they have a sad and melancholy interest, rendered deeper and lasting, by the recollections we must all have of several of the unfortunate sufferers.

It is, indeed, a frightful calamity but we ought to regard it as one of those awful lessons which does he who rides on the whirlwind and directs the storm decree for our good. It should at least teach us to be humble, and the need we all have of a support greater, and better far, than that which poor, frail man can impart to his fellow.

The terror of the wreck was not easily forgotten; the engraving shown was made in America about four months after the tragedy occurred. The engraver's name was Thomas Birch, and William Everhart gave him guidance in this work, the only surviving cabin passenger of the *Albion*. It was placed in public exhibition in New York and Philadelphia and viewed by thousands of people.

The wreck became a byword and the possibilities of meeting the same fate was for many years to come often in the minds of those who travelled the Atlantic shuttle.

Crew saved
The first mate, Henry Cammeyer, who saw the *Albion*'s crew and passengers hit the cliff-face that fateful morning was saved and lived to tell the tale. So, too, did William Hyate, the boatswain, and John Simons, John Richards, Francis Bloom, Ebenezer Warner and Hierom Raymond.

Passengers saved
William Everhart esq. Chester, Penn., was the only cabin passenger to survive. He suffered two fractured legs and was carried up the cliff on the back of a small tenant farmer named Thomas Coveney, of Garrettstown, and was later taken to the house of George Barry Gibbons where he was nursed back to health. It was he who later gave Birch guidance in his work on the painting of the final moments of the *Albion*, as she was broadside on the rocks at Garrettstown.

Steerage passengers saved
One steerage passenger was saved: Stephen Chase of Canada.

Steerage passengers lost but whose bodies were never recovered
Mr Harrison, carpenter, M. Baldwin, cotton spinner, Yorkshire and Dr Carver, a veterinary surgeon.

Crew lost
Three bodies of the crew were found and buried in Templetrine: William Dockwood and two Negro cooks, Thomas Hill and Adam Johnson.

Crew lost but whose bodies were never recovered
Captain John Williams (swept overboard off Cape Clear; he left a wife and seven children), the second mate, Edward Smith, Alexander Adams, the ship's carpenter, Harman Nelson, Harman Richardson, Henry Whittrall, William Trisserly, James Wiley, Robert McLelland (from Ireland), Thomas Goodman, Samuel Wilson, a boy, William Snow, a boy, Lloyd Potter, a Negro steward; Samuel Penny, a Negro steward, Francis Issac, a Negro boy.

Cabin passengers lost but whose bodies were never recovered
Mr A.D. Conyers, from Troy, New York and Master Gardiner of Paris.

Cabin and steerage passengers whose bodies were found and later buried in Templetrine
Lieutenant Colonel Augustine J. Prevost, of the 67th South Hampshire Regiment, who took part in the Battle of Barrossa. Rev. George Robert Goodwin Hill, a graduate from Oxford returning from Jamaica. Nelson Ross, Troy, New York, William H. Dwight, Boston, who traded with Liverpool and had specie with him to a large amount. Mr Benyon, London, Mr William Proctor, New York, Mr Hyde Clark and Mrs Hyde Clark, Mrs Pye, Miss Anne Powell from York in Canada, Madame Gardiner of Paris, Mrs Mary Brereton, Mrs Mary Hunt, Mr Vincent Millicent, France, General Charles Lefebvre Desnouettes, three other unnamed French gentlemen and Professor Alexander Metcalf Fisher MA. professor of mathematics, New Haven (Yale) College. There is some doubt about him as it was said that his body was never recovered. On the centenary of his death in 1922, the graduates and lecturers of Yale University unveiled a bust in his memory in the college library. Four other unidentified bodies were found and interred. Finally, lost on the *Albion* and buried in Templetrine was Major William Gough, 68th Regiment, who fought with Wellington at Waterloo and was wounded at the Battle of Salamanca.

William Gough was the third son of George Gough of Woodstown, Co. Limerick. His brothers were Major George Gough (1775–1841), Thomas Bambury Gough (1777–1860), Dean of Derry, and Hugh Gough (1779–1869), who was rewarded for his military career in the field by being made the first Viscount Gough.

Major William Gough belonged to the 68th Foot; it is now called the Durham Light Infantry. Gough was severely wounded in the Battle of Vittoria during the Peninsular War and fought bravely at the Battle of Salamanca with the Duke of Wellington on 22 July 1812. Wellington's army of 48,000 suffered 5,200 casualties but inflicted nearly 14,000 casualties on Marmont's 50,000-strong French army. This was one of Wellington's most impressive military achievements.

After the Peninsular War and the Battle of Waterloo, several British officers went to Canada, among them Gough. He was returning to England when he set sail on the packet ship *Albion*. Another influential British officer, a Lt. Col. Augustine J. Prevost, who fought with distinction, accompanied him. He was attached to the 67th South Hampshire Regiment and commanded that regiment, taking it into action at the Battle of Barrossa during the Peninsular War.

As the ship approached the rocks, the first mate summoned all passengers on deck and told them it was impossible for him to save her. As the women shrieked, Major Gough declared in good army fashion, 'Death come as he would was an unwelcome messenger, but that they must meet him like men.' Let it be known that man kept them apart and on opposite sides in the battlefields of Europe, each fighting for king and emperor, but fate and God brought them together for they died side by side on the jagged rocks of Garrettstown west in the grey dawn of morning on that fateful day, 22 April 1822.

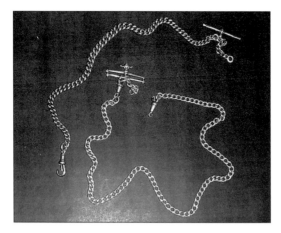

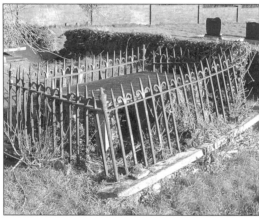

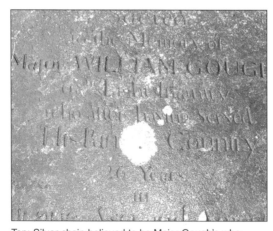

Top: Silver chain believed to be Major Gough's who perished in the *Albion*. Photo: Manning family, Garylucas
Centre: Major Gough's railed grave in Templetrine.
Bottom: Close-up of Major Gough's tomb slab.

In a railed grave at Templetrine, a headstone reads: 'Major William Gough who served his King and country in Europe, Asia and America, Salamanca, Vittoria in the 44th year of his age, shot in the left leg, wounded in India, 68th Light Infantry 1778–1822.'

After the loss of life on the *Albion*, great thought was put into the design of life-preservers. The first one submitted was like an ordinary mattress and patented by a vendor of beds and bedding – a Mr Jackson.

On 15 June 1822, the new Black Ball ship, *Liverpool*, was launched to replace the *Albion*. One month later, on 16 July 1822, the *Liverpool*, under the command of Captain William Lee jnr., sailed from New York to Liverpool on her maiden voyage. Nine days out from New York, she struck an iceberg in thick fog and sank – all her passengers and crew were saved by means of the ship's small boats. They all reached St John's, Newfoundland on 1 August.

After several days, the remains of the proud packet ship *Albion* was stripped down to its bare hull. Everything that could be manhandled was removed and accounts at the time reported that country people were running off in all directions, carrying with them anything they could lay their hands on. The remains of the wreck was sold off by auction for the sum of £40–60. The seaman's song, composed a few weeks after the sinking of the *Albion*, goes as follows:

Our main mast it broke in two
Our mizen washed away.
Our Captain was swept over board
Into the raging deep,
Which caused full many a sailor bold
For to mourn and weep
The crew lashed themselves to the pumps
And spent all that night thus
There was a lady fair on board
Anne Powell it was her name.
Whose honour ought to be inscribed
Upon the list of fame,
She asked to take her turn at the pumps
Her precious life to save.
No sooner was her quest denied
She met a watery grave.
In Templetrine Church a memorial
To her memory may be seen.
Full fifty-nine we had on board
When from New York we set sail,
And only nine escaped the wreck
To tell the dreadful tale.

In 1946, an enquiry was made by a Mr Alexander Orr Victor of Yale University library. The advertisement was carried in the local regional paper, the *Southern Star*. It was in connection with the *Albion* shipwreck and of a well-known Yale professor by the name of Alexander Metcalf Fisher, one of those who perished on the ship. A reply was received from Mr James Coveney of upper Garrettstown. Mr Coveney went to the spot where the *Albion* met her fate in 1822 and explained that his grandfather carried one of the passengers, a Mr Everhart from Philadelphia, up the cliff-face. He had suffered two broken legs and was nursed back to health in the home of George Barry Gibbons at Ballinspittle.

It's ironic that I complete this work and the story of the *Albion* on 22 April 2002, exactly 180 years since the dreadful loss of the Black Ball ship off Garrettstown on Monday 22 April 1822.

Anne Bonney: Female Pirate from the Old Head

Anne Bonney (née Cormac) was born on 8 March 1700 at the Old Head of Kinsale at what is now a disused site close to the present pier. She was the illegitimate daughter of a prominent lawyer and his wife's maid.

Anne was a pretty, vivacious child and was idolised by her father. Anne's father had a good standing in local professional circles but the ensuing scandal and a gradual decline in prestige and financial matters forced him to flee Ireland in disgrace with his lover and daughter. Shortly after arriving in Charleston, Carolina, Cormac changed from his legal profession to that of planter, and his beloved Anne grew into an attractive girl in the pleasant setting of their comfortable home.

Ruin of the house in which Anne Bonney was born, at the Old Head of Kinsale. At the bottom of the picture can be seen the old fireplace.

The first permanent settlers were a mixed company of Irish and English who arrived in 1670 from Kinsale and years later from Cork, so it can be assumed that Cormac had contacts before he left the Old Head. He became a prosperous estate owner and the old man had ambitious plans for the daughter who kept house for him until she reached the age of sixteen. But his plans were shattered when she announced that she had fallen in love with a good-looking but penniless sailor by the name of James Bonney, and that she intended to marry. One of Bonney's reasons for wanting to marry Anne was so as to steal the plantation from her father. Anne would not listen to her father's advice to give up this outrageous plan as she was very headstrong and had a violent temper. She eloped with her new-found boyfriend, and her father – who refused to sanction the match – cut off all financial aid to his daughter.

Anne became a bride with expensive tastes but with no money. Her husband had expected that his young wife would be well provided for by her father. Finding that her only fortune was her good looks and with no means to support themselves, they set sail for the island of New Providence in the Bahamas hoping that they would find some employment. It was here that Bonney turned informer and stool pigeon for Governor Woods Rogers, turning in as a pirate for a handsome reward any sailor he did not like.

Anne quickly grew to dislike her spineless husband, and spent most of her time with the pirate élite. Paramours were the order of the day and a celebrated homosexual ran a popular ladies' establishment. Anne was in great favour with the male population and her body was much sought after. A life of prostitution provided plenty of money and beer.

One of the richest men on the island caught her attentions: Chidley Bayard. In order to keep him she would have to fight his current lover, a violent Spanish beauty named Maria. One night, while they were attending a ball, Anne met up with the spiteful sister-in law of Governor Lawes of Jamaica. A row broke out and all hell broke loose, with Anne leading the mêlée. Crinoline dresses were ripped asunder, the men folk dived for cover and skin and hair was flying. Anne threw several punches and gave Maria two black eyes and knocked out several of her teeth. It was rumoured that in her youth, Anne had killed a Negro servant woman who was driving her mad. The likelihood of this story was that she was defending herself. Anne was in the process of being hauled off to jail but Bayard's power kept her free. What else could he do as he had slept with her on several occasions. She could make a disgrace of him, and this way he could be assured of her confidence and his position would be safe.

Anne enjoyed spending Bayard's money and travelled with him quite frequently, but from then on he avoided taking her on business trips in case she would embarrass him, as she was quite fond of the liquor.

With Bayard being away quite often, Anne got fed up and started playing around with the many sailors and pirates in her sights. She quickly caught the eye of one 'Calico' Jack Rackham, a handsome rogue who knew how to spend money and also how to steal it. The attraction was mutual.

Around this time – in the 1720s – this group of islands was a haven and resting place for Caribbean pirates, buccaneers and cutthroats. In this setting, you had the handsome Captain Jack Rackham, famed and feared throughout the West Indies for his daredevil acts of piracy. He had met Anne and swept her off her feet, and the stage was set where she would play out his life drama.

Anne asked her sailor husband if he would give her freedom in exchange for a liberal sum of money which her dashing new lover offered to provide. Bonney turned down the proposal and instead took the matter up with Governor Rogers who said that Anne should be flogged by Jack himself and returned to her true husband. That night, after stealing a sloop, Calico and Anne slipped out of the harbour and embarked on a life of piracy. At Rackham's suggestion, she went to sea with him disguised in men's clothing, pledging that she would never reveal the secret of her sex to her shipmates.

Anne accompanied her pirate lover on most of his buccaneering cruises and proved his equal – nay, was superior to him – with sword and pistol. Showing reckless courage, she fought, pillaged and plundered with ruthless brutality. Her only concession to her womanhood was when, on odd occasions, she was with child. These confinements were usually in Cuba where she lived in the extravagance of luxury with all the characteristics of a freebooter. Whenever these confinements were over, Anne would join Rackham again and set sail under the skull and crossbones, and acted as his trusted lieutenant.

Things changed when fate dealt a hand on board the brigantine sailed by Anne and her lover. Another woman made a dramatic entrance, also disguised in men's clothing. Her name was Mary Read. In many ways, the life of Mary Read in her early womanhood had been like that of Anne Bonney. Mary's fair skin and beardless face, her fine sparkling, blue eyes and cheerful manners gave her a boyish appearance that was a challenge to Anne. Unaware of each other's secret, Anne took a liking to the dashing young 'man' and confessed to Mary that she had fallen in love with 'him', while at the same time revealing her sex, much to the embarrassment of the latter. Mary had no choice only to divulge her womanhood and, after both had recovered from their surprise and most likely disappointment, the two girls became great friends. In the meantime, Rackham had become very disturbed by the growing intimacy between his sweetheart and the young sailor and, in a fit of jealousy and rage, threatened he would cut the young man's throat. Anne was forced to let him into the secret, which Rackham never betrayed.

For several turbulent months, Rackham sailed the seas looting merchantmen homeward bound from Jamaica. It was on one of these raids that an attractive youth was taken prisoner, and it was to him that Mary lost her heart. No doubt this was the reason Mary did not show her affection for Captain Rackham, and amicable relations were maintained between herself and Anne Bonney. They fought valiantly side by side, using sword and musketoon with terrorising effect on their victims. Mary proved her devotion to her young lover when, one day, her sweetheart had a violent quarrel with a fellow pirate who challenged him to a duel. As the sloop lay anchored off one of the islands, the men appointed an hour for the following day when they would go ashore and fight. Desperate that the man she loved might be killed, Mary picked a quarrel with the fellow and challenged him to a duel herself. He agreed to fight two hours earlier than his engagement with his other opponent. Unknown to her lover, the two antagonists slipped ashore at the appointed time, and fought with sword and pistol in true pirate fashion. Mary outwitted the ferociously attacking ruffian by taking him off guard, and she wounded him mortally.

Fortune was kind to Jack Rackham and he captured several ships, but his career was coming to an end fast. Retribution overtook him when the governor of Jamaica sent out a fast-sailing sloop manned by a detachment of marines. They sighted the pirate ship and, before the cumbersome brigantine could get its anchor, the king's men boarded the pirate ship. Most of the pirates on board, including Captain Rackham, scattered in panic and went below deck, but not Mary Read, Anne Bonney and one of the crew. The two women ran after them, cursing and swearing and calling them cowards, and forced them at pistol point to come up again and fight like men. However, the odds were against them and they surrendered. All the prisoners were taken to Jamaica where Jack and his followers were given a quick trial and sentenced to be hanged. Rackham was executed at Gallows Point, Port Royal in November 1720. His body was later cut down and hung in chains on one of the quay walls, along with eight of his crew. There is, to this day, a tiny island in the outer harbour of Kingston in Jamaica known as Rackham's Cay.

The last request of Rackham before his execution was to be allowed to visit his sweetheart. This was granted as a special favour but brought him not consolation but sneers and taunts from his outraged Anne, whose final words to him were: 'I'm sorry to see you here, Jack, but if you fought like a man you would not be hanged like a dog.'

Mary and Anne each managed to escape justice as they were found to be expectant mothers at the time of their trials, so execution was postponed. The judge asked was there any reason why they should escape being hanged and their answer was, 'My Lord, we plead with our bellies.' But Mary died in prison of a fever at the young age of twenty-seven, whilst Anne was reprieved after the birth of her child, fathered not by Jack but by a Dr Michael Radcliffe, a man whose life Anne had once saved. Radcliffe vowed to save her from the gallows, and she was granted pardon by Governor Lawes on condition that she leave the West Indies and never return. It was well known that Governor Lawes had received a letter from a pirate named Roberts telling him to let Bonney go free or feel the thunder of his guns from Port Royal to Kingston.

Michael Radcliffe and Anne were married – she now being a widow since her former husband, James Bonney, was lost when his ship capsized in a hurricane off the Bahamas. Two days after Bonney and Radcliffe were married, they boarded a sloop bound for Norfolk, Virginia and joined the pioneers heading westward. Radcliffe had taken her away from the life of prostitution. After this, she must have faded into the background as no further record can be found about her.

The house at the bottom of the Old Head, close to the sea, in which Anne Bonney was born and where she lived for a time was later occupied by the Bullens, and is known today as Bullen's Bay. In a small graveyard at Ringrone, embedded in its disused church wall overlooking Kinsale estuary, is the burial place of one branch of the Bullen family. Erected in December 1726, the crest on their tombstone carries three eagles; at the upper right and left side are two angels, and on both sides beneath is proudly displayed the skull and crossbones. In the same graveyard, another tombstone also carries the skull and crossbones; perhaps someone back home remembered Anne Bonney, the female pirate from the Old Head.

In 1970, Grenada in the West Indies issued two stamps to commemorate Anne Bonney and her fellow pirate, Mary Read.

One of Ireland's best-known pirate queens was Grace O'Malley – in Irish, Grainne Ní Mhaille. Born in Connacht, she married O'Flaherty and had three children before she took to the high seas. At the height of her career, she controlled three raiding ships and approximately 200 fighting men along the Irish coast. Her headquarters were on Clare Island, twelve miles to the north of Inishbofin off the Mayo coast. In 1588, Queen Elizabeth came to the English throne and Grainne's husband was among the Irish leaders executed in England's effort to consolidate its control of Ireland. Grainne stepped up her attacks on English ships and, in 1566, she was married again, to Sir Richard Bourke, and had one son. She was then jailed for at least two years and later returned to sea. In 1579, her brother and son were taken hostage but still she did not back down. Then, in 1588, Elizabeth granted her a pardon. Either she did not heed it or the English forces in Ireland did not care about it. A battle continued at the gates of her castle and then, in 1593, Grainne went to England and sailed up the River Thames to meet the queen herself. Grainne was a big woman and held out her hand, which was a little higher than the queen's, so Elizabeth had to raise her hand. They conversed in Latin: 'I would like to make you a countess,' Elizabeth said to her.

'Oh, but you can't do that,' said Grainne.

'Why can't I?' asked Elizabeth.

'Amn't I a queen the same as yourself!' said Grainne. The queen was very impressed with her and the two of them became great friends. The queen also ordered the English in Ireland to cease harassing her and her family, and made Grainne's son the Earl of Mayo. Nevertheless, Grainne headed back to Ireland and continued the fight until the Irish were defeated at the Battle of Kinsale in 1601.

Jim Ó Dálaigh (O'Daly) was fishing with his crew off the Old Head of Kinsale in the early part of the nineteenth century when, suddenly, off the headland in the tidal race appeared an English ship with a press gang on board. The press gangs were used to forcibly recruit men into the navy and young fishermen were terrified of them as they could pounce at any time. The ship bore down on them with great speed, and Jim O'Daly and his crew rowed through the tidal race with all their might, keeping close to the rocks that they all knew so well, and defied the efforts of the press gang to capture them. Several times, their boat was grappled with hooks but O'Daly's crew managed to fend them off and make for the shallow waters of Sandycove, near Kinsale, with the press gang in hot pursuit.

In the meantime, O'Daly's neighbours at Sandycove fishing village heard the commotion and rushed to the shore and croosted the living daylights out of the press gang (threw stones at them) while O'Daly and his hardy crew jumped into the water and eventually got ashore. The English officer in charge called off his pursuit and shouted out, 'Sorry you escaped – one of you would be worth ten of what I've got.'

There are townlands at the Old Head known as Lispatrick and Bally-mackean. The old people used to call the top of the head, the Island, and where the present lighthouse now stands was known as Hangman's Point. Close by the lighthouse, on the east and west side, steps are cut out of the solid rock leading down to the water's edge. These were to facilitate the servicing and bringing in of supplies to the lighthouse. In olden times, powder was needed for the fog guns and oil to provide light for the lamp. It was much safer to get supplies in by sea – weather permitting – than by road. Around the coast, steps and pathways were hewn out of solid rock, and some good examples can still be seen today, especially in Garrettstown West. People are often mistaken as to why they were cut there – some say by pirates in olden times, to facilitate lightning raids. In reality, the only thing the pirates did when they came ashore was cut throats, if anyone was foolish enough to hang around. The real reason for these steps being cut around the coast was to facilitate the large mass of people living close to the shore who used to fetch seaweed in twig baskets and use it as manure to fertilise crops. The steps also gave easy access to their fishing boats during the summer months. Smugglers may also have

Steps hewn from the solid rock. Some say they were used by pirates. With so many people living by the sea, they were crucial for accessing the rocky coves to fetch seaweed which was brought up in twig baskets and used to fertilise the soil.

used these steps, since smuggling was once rife. In the late eighteenth century, France and Spain were at war with England, seriously disrupting Irish trade with England and with the Continent. Tobacco and other goods were brought ashore and carried inland on horseback.

On 20 June 1631, a most terrible disaster befell the little community in the village of Baltimore, west Cork. In the dead of night, two Algerine rovers landed their men and plundered and raped throughout the village. Taking scores of the inhabitants prisoners, men, women children were carried off to Algeria. One man, by the name of William Gunter, had his wife and seven sons kidnapped. A Dungarvan fisherman, by the name of Hacket, piloted the Algerian pirates into Baltimore. They had picked him up at sea, and he was later condemned and executed for his cowardly deed.

> Thy pride is gone, thy glory is over
> Ruined and neglected Baltimore.

In 1636, the south-west coast was infested by Turks, assisted by the French. They came into Cork Harbour, took a boat with eight men on board and gave chase to two more. They escaped by driving their boats up on the rocks, with the townspeople of Cobh looking on and powerless to help them. When the Turks landed their prisoners in France, they were frog-marched in chains across the country to Marseille and then shipped to Algeria where they were sold.

Beacons were erected around remote areas of the west-Cork coast; from here, powder shots could be fired to alert the community if raiders were sited. But not all pirates came by ship; there were also land pirates, known as 'wreckers'. On a stormy night, when a ship would be seeking shelter, it would be lured onto the rocks by a very clever method using a cow with a special apparatus attached to the horns into which would be placed a lantern with a lighted candle. The poor animal would be driven along the cliff – back and forth – and on a stormy night, a passing ship on the lookout for a safe berth to ride out a storm, on seeing the rocking light on the shore-side, would think it another ship in safe anchorage. The unsuspecting ship would approach until it was too late, and would be smashed to pieces off the jagged rocks, to the delight of the perpetrators.

A very dangerous pirate by the name of Pieter Nuyt once infested the western coast of Co. Cork. The Old Head had frequent visits from Mr Nuyt, who came from a wealthy Dutch family but who'd had a scandalous career. He served on board several ships of the East India Company but was dismissed for his misconduct in Formosa and Japan (1627–30). Around 1631, legend has it that he buried his plunder in a place close to Black Head, high up on the cliffs over a cave. Some of his crew at that time were of African origin. Wrapping their loot in an old ship's canvas sail, Nuyt asked one of these sailors would he guard the treasure with his life. He replied that he would, where-upon Nuyt drew his pistol, shot him dead and buried him with the treasure before sealing up the cliff-face.

In the early 1970s, a local group of which I was a member tried in vain to

Nuyt's Cave: The pirate, Pieter Nuyt, is reputed to have concealed his plunder here.

explore the sealed cave high up on the cliff-face, the supposed burial place of the long-sought-after treasure. After several days of digging into the cliff-face, disaster struck. Our scaffold ropes gave way when a large piece of the cliff-top slipped, nearly killing the three of us. Pieter Nuyt's ill-gotten gains remain to be found another day. The inlet nearby is known as Pirates Cove.

Pieter Nuyt had not only robbed on the seas but made many attacks on the shore. In a letter from the lord president, St Leger, in 1631, he informs the government that Nuyt had three ships under his command: his own was a twenty-gun ship of 300 tons burden; a ship he took from St Malo, of 160 tons, was his vice-admiral's; the third, belonging to Dieppe, also mounted fifteen guns. At the time the letter was written – in the month of May – Nuyt lay with his fleet at Crookhaven, in west Cork, where he victualled, watered and took his wife on board. Soon after, the government sent him a pardon which he at first refused but would later accept.

Other Shipwrecks

Of the many shipwrecks in the area around the Old Head of Kinsale, the most famous is the RMS *Lusitania*– a victim of war lost within sight of the Old Head on 7 May 1915. On 7 May 1995, eighty years later, a memorial was erected at the Old Head, overlooking the wreck site, to the memory of the 1,201 men, women and children who lost their lives on that fateful day. It's ironic to note that one of the *Lusitania*'s former captains, a man by the name of Patrick Dow, lived in Garrettstown overlooking the Old Head and went to school in Ballinspittle for a time.

> She ploughed the waves the proudest of them all
> Where now above her ocean grave they crowded big and small
> And fling defiance to the knight who did this awful deed
> Where fifty fathoms deep now rests the regal queen of speed.

The Old Head and surrounding coast was a graveyard for ships, the bay often being mistaken for Kinsale Harbour. HMS *Stillorgen*, a ninety-gun warship, was wrecked off Bream rock in 1778. The *City of Chicago*, a passenger ship of some 5,000 tonnes struck the west side of the Old Head in blinding fog in July 1893, thankfully with no loss of life. This same ship, on a previous voyage, brought de Valera to Ireland as a baby (he became president of our country). Other shipwrecks include the *Pearl of Gloucester* and *Stonewall Jackson*, and there were a number of unidentified ships: lost at night, by daybreak nothing would be found but floating wreckage.

One Christmas night, a ship – the *Rob Roy* – came ashore on the white strand at the base of the Old Head. Carrying a cargo of coal, flour and meal, she got stuck fast in the sand where she stayed for two weeks. The cargo was dumped overboard to lighten the vessel, and most of the flour, coal and meal was taken away by the people of the district rather than have it become a total loss. With the help of a tugboat and a high tide, the ship was pulled off the sand and, on a cold January evening in 1909, a crowd stood on the strand to bid farewell to the sailing ship that brought the finest Christmas present the Old Head ever knew.

The most bizarre boating tragedy that befell the people of the Old Head happened on 28 August 1877. Ten local fishermen went on a day's fishing in an open, four-tonne boat with five oars and a seine net. While yards from Black

Left: *Lusitania* memorial, erected at a high point at the Old Head in 1995 to commemorate those who were lost eighty years before. Right: Headstone for Captain William Thomas Turner OBE, RNR, 'commodore of the Cunard S.S. Line, who was in command of the R.M.S. Lusitania when she was torpedoed 7th May 1915. Born 23rd Oct. 1857, died 23rd June 1933. "Faithful Unto Death"'.

Postcard depicting the loss of the *Lusitania*, issued in 1981 by the Isle of Man postal service. In the foreground is the Manx lugger, *Wanderer*, the first rescue boat to reach the stricken liner.

A boat-keeper's cottage at the edge of the sea.

Head, they struck a sunken rock. The sea was choppy, capsizing the boat and throwing the ten men in. Of the ten on board, five lost their lives: John Nagle, James Coghlan, John Collins, Timothy Quinn and Keane Connolly. The survivors, clinging to the upturned boat and holding onto the floating oars, were taken out to sea for a mile and back again by the current, until rescued by a William Manning who came on the scene with two small boats. Those that were saved were James Roche, Jeremiah Quinn, Jeremiah Forde, Patrick Minihane and Jeremiah Kingston.

A sailing ship named *Gelf of Quebec* was wrecked off Garrettstown with a cargo of timber logs so huge in size that they proved impossible to handle. However, they did not elude one man: with a high tide and a number of horses, he floated them to the mouth of the river. He pulled them upriver where he winched them up to his sawmill at Kilmore. Here, they were cut into planks and beams. Quite a number of houses in the area were roofed with timber from the *Gelf of Quebec*.

Old Head Signal Tower

At the high point of the Old Head, outside the castle's defensive walls, stands a signal tower. The prospect of invasion by Napoleon Bonaparte in 1795–96 prompted the building of these signal towers around the coasts of Britain, and the aborted invasion at Bantry Bay in 1798 led to coastal defences being beefed up around Ireland. In 1806, signal stations, or towers, were established, their function being to speed up communication on the movements of shipping and to forward information to naval and military authorities based in the main towns and cities. The tower at the Old Head was built to a standard pattern: two storeys' high over a semi-basement with a single-storey addition, and from ground level to parapet the height was about thirty-five feet. The weather-slated structure had a machicolation, or projecting gallery, over the entrance and small overhanging turrets, called bartizans.

Signal tower at the Old Head of Kinsale. They were sited on prominent headlands and islands along Ireland's east, south and west coasts to warn of any attempt at invasion by Napoleon.

The buildings were designed to be defensible against attack by a disaffected population, and were within sight of one another.

The tower at the Old Head of Kinsale is some eighteen-foot square external, the walls being about two-foot thick. The tower's main entrance door was on the second floor, and access was by means of a ladder, always in the up position. The doors were sheeted with iron for protection against fire.

Most of the towers had a flat roof with two rows of sockets for timber joists – which suggested a particularly strong structure – and were protected by a parapet incorporating the three machicolations.

The ground-floor windows are relatively small, square openings. The first-floor windows are of the same width but of taller proportions, typical of Georgian domestic architecture.

With the entrance door at first-floor level on the seaward elevation, the two flank walls contain the windows at ground and first floor, while the splayed rear wall is blank with fireplaces and chimney.

The stone and slate was quarried locally and evidence of this can be seen in the area today. The labour used consisted of both male and female, the majority from the general area. They used straw baskets, handbarrows and mules to get the slate from inaccessible quarries. Male labour was approximately 2d. per day with a female earning 1d. Most of the workers were barefoot.

The signal system was a tall mast with a gaff, a rectangular flag and a blue pendant, and black canvas-covered hoops which could be hoisted to convey different messages. The mast was about fifty-foot high and had a square bar to secure the thirty-foot flagstaff and gaff which was set at an angle from the mast so the balls could be hoisted. In some cases, when the weather did not permit the hoisting of the canvas, a fire was lit on its roof.

Local men were at that time joining what was then called Coastal Defence, the Sea Fencibles, a volunteer naval reserve. In most cases, they were seafaring men who joined up in case of a French invasion, and were trained to use pikes for defence and to man small craft. It was from these ranks that the crews were picked to man the signal stations. Each tower was under the charge of a navy lieutenant who was allotted a good midshipman and a number of others for lookouts and signal duties. The signal station also had military guards at various times. Approximately eighty-four of these towers were constructed in some of the remotest headlands off the west coast of Ireland. The Old Head tower was completed in September 1804.

From the Old Head, the line of signal posts continued westward to the Seven Heads, Galley Head, Glandore Head, Toe Head and Kedge Point. Most of the towers were situated along the south-east coast, the south and west to north coasts. The east coast was considered safe because the Irish Sea was protected by naval patrols.

The tower at the Old Head became redundant when Napoleon Bonaparte was defeated in early 1814. The threat of an invasion was over and a family which had moved into the region took up residence in the Old Head tower. It later fell into decay and its timbers were removed. Some day, perhaps, it will be restored to its former glory. It stands today as a towering reminder of a time when the French almost changed the course of Irish history.

The Ancient and Modern Lights
of the Old Head of Kinsale

The Old Head is one of the major lights on the south coast and also serves as a guide to the entrance of Kinsale Harbour. Whilst there are references to a lighted beacon at the Old Head dating back to early and pre-Christian times, the first proper lighthouse is still in existence. It was one of six erected around the Irish coast by Sir Robert Reading under letters patent granted to him by Charles II on 13 November 1665. The cottage-type lighthouse had an open coal-fire in a brazier on its roof.

The peninsula of the Old Head of Kinsale that saw many a shipwreck looks peaceful, but the inner confines of the bay are treacherous in a storm. It was here that the troopships *Lord Melville* and the *Boadicea* were wrecked in January 1816. Later, the passenger ship *Albion* came to grief here on 22 April 1822.

On 18 November 1703, a petition from the sovereign burgesses and commonalty of Kinsale was presented to the House of Commons looking for the reinstatement of the light, which has been unreasonably disconnected for upwards of twenty years. One can presume the petition was successful because of the existence of a lease between Lord Kingsale and Mr. J. Steele, collector of the port of Kinsale, covering the lighthouse and one acre of land, 'Irish plantation measure of 1.6 acre statute'. Also, in 1774, an account by Dr Smith on the county of Cork says, 'having upon the top of the headland an excellent Lighthouse'.

During 1804, the Revenue Commissioners, who were responsible for lighthouses around the Irish coast, except the Port of Dublin, instructed their contractor for lighting, Mr Thomas Rogers, to construct a temporary six-foot-diameter lantern with twelve oil lamps and reflectors to replace the coal fire on the roof.

In July 1812 (two years after the Corporation for Preserving and Improving the Port of Dublin had taken over the fourteen coastal lighthouses from the Revenue Commissioners), George Halpin, inspector of lighthouses, reported the poor state of the temporary lighthouse and stated that it required to be replaced by a more permanent building and a suitable light apparatus. Three months later, sanction was obtained to build a new light. Its design was similar to the new lighthouse under construction at Baily, Howth Head – that is, a forty-two-foot (12.8m.) high tower with a concentric keeper's dwelling around its base. The new lighthouse was designed by the inspector and built by the board's tradesmen at a cost of almost £9,500. The fixed white light was established on 16 May 1814 at a height of 294 feet (89.6m) above high water. The light comprised of twenty-seven Argand oil lamps, each with its own parabolic reflector which, in clear weather, could be seen at a distance of twenty-three miles (37km.) The tower and outer wall of the dwelling were whitewashed, thus making the station conspicuous during daytime.

Subsequent to a general lighthouse and light-vessel inspection by the elder brethren of Trinity House in July 1843, they reported seven months later that Old Head with Cape Clear was too high and often obscured by low cloud. They suggested removing the station towards the point of the headland at a lower level. Inspector Halpin, who had accompanied the elder brethren on their trip, agreed and duly visited the proposed site and reported favourably to the board in April 1845.

Statutory approval from Trinity House was obtained on 26 February 1846 and an inquisition was held in Kinsale on 4 October 1846 to determine the value of the ground required for the new lighthouse premises. £100 was placed on the seven acres, five perches plus a right-of-way to the old lighthouse site.

The complete station was designed by Inspector George Halpin and constructed under his supervision by tradesmen of the board. He marked out the site on Wednesday 20 March 1850, having travelled to Kinsale the previous day using the facilities afforded by railway communication. Fifteen months later, the tower was at the sixty-foot (18.2m.) level, dwellings were at the halfway stage and the compound wall was almost complete.

By 1853, the new station was finished at a cost of £10,430/3s./7d. The fixed

Old cottage lighthouse at the Old Head, with arched stone roof, possibly dates from the fifth or sixth century. A fire burned on its roof to warn mariners.

white light was established on 1 October 1853 at a height of 236 feet (72m.) above high water. The light source was a multi-concentric wick oil lamp at the focus of a first order dioptric lens with a range of twenty-one miles (33km.). It was visible from Charlesfort in Kinsale Harbour seaward to Seven Heads. The 100-foot (30.5m.) cut-stone tower was plastered on the outside from ground to balcony level and painted white with two red bands. The colour scheme was changed to black with two white bands during the summer of 1930.

When the present light was established, the 1814 light was discontinued. Its tower was reduced in height so as not to give the impression during daytime of a lighthouse, and the stones removed and set aside for constructing the Horse Rock beacon in Courtmacsherry Bay. The base for this beacon was partially constructed on Horse Rock and the granite slabs and circular cut-out can still be seen to this day upon this rock.

Early in 1854, Lord Bernard of Castle Bernard, Bandon, Co. Cork enquired why, since the new light was established, Courtmacsherry Bay was without a light. Inspector Halpin explained in his report to the board that the new light was a sea light and was not intended to guide vessels through the rocks and shoals of Courtmacsherry Bay. Also, if the latter were required, a local light on Land Point would suffice. Lord Bernard also directed his enquiry to the Board of Trade in London as a memorial from the grand jury of the county of Cork. George Halpin reiterated his remarks, this time to their lordships, who later in May suggested two forms of red sectoring over the bay. Whilst the inspector

The familiar lighthouse at the Old Head of Kinsale, commissioned in 1853. The light is 236 feet (72m.) above high water, giving a range of twenty-one miles (33km.). *Photo: Hans Koning Bastion*

still defended his reason for not lighting the bay from Old Head, stating also that the non-lighting gave an unmistakable warning to mariners, he did agree to having a red arc covering the bay with a dark sector across the entrance. The Board of Trade compromised with a red sector between Seven Heads and Horse Rock, and white to the north of the sector into the bay. The change was effected from 16 April 1855 and remained until the light was converted to incandescent flashing in December 1907.

Several letters were written in August and October 1868 from London to the Commissioners of Irish Lights in Dublin complaining of the exorbitant fee of £200. This was the annual cost of a lease from Lord Courcey for an acre of ground around the old lighthouse site, and they enquired if he would sell the piece of ground to Irish Lights. But he was not interested, and a suggestion was made that the Board of Trade in London should make a compulsory purchase of the property.

Towards the end of 1890, Inspector Captain Boxer recommended a fog signal for Old Head, and Sir Robert Ball, Astronomer Royal, was asked to report on the best light in his capacity as scientific advisor to the Commissioners. Sir Robert's recommendation was for the introduction of electricity, which was referred to the Board of Trade along with a proposal for a ten-wick oil burner from the engineer-in-chief, Mr W. Douglass. Their lordships would not commit themselves until Trinity House had given its sanction. By March 1891, the elder brethren stated they had no practical experience of a ten-wick burner where red and white light was involved but they recommended an eight-wick burner. During the following month, the inspecting committee stated that Trinity House should be informed that the divergence in the red sector would be slight and requested sanction for a ten-wick burner. Reluctantly, the elder brethren gave their sanction, as they could not justify the large expenditure on electrification. The Board of Trade sanctioned the cost of the burner, which went into operation in September 1892.

Three cannons were installed and established as a fog signal on 1 February 1893. Two successive reports were fired every ten minutes. A third keeper or fog-signalman was appointed to the station, who was at first in lodgings until another dwelling was built for him in 1895.

The Mercantile Marine Service Association in Liverpool wrote to the Commissioners in January 1903 enquiring whether they contemplated altering the obsolete and lower-powered light at Old Head, Kinsale. The enquiry was referred to the inspecting committee who, after almost two years, reported that sanction from Trinity House should be obtained to change the light to double flashing, incandescent vaporised paraffin and substitute cotton powder charge for the gun fog signal, altering the character to two successive reports every six minutes. Variations were considered, such as positioning the new lantern at the base of the tower, reducing the height of the tower and a new position on the head for the tower, but the end result was the existing lantern and granite blocking to be removed and replaced by the present iron lantern. Two small temporary semi-circular lanterns were attached to the outside of the tower whilst the new lantern optic-revolving apparatus and fog signal were being installed. The new light and fog signal were established on 17

December 1907. William Spence of Dublin supplied the lantern, fog-signal jibs and apparatus, Chance Brothers of Birmingham the bi-form first-order optic, and David Brown of Lockwood, Leeds the clockwork optic-rotation machine. The red sector over Courtmacsherry Bay was discontinued.

The character of the explosive fog signal was changed to one report every five minutes from 1 June 1934. When all explosive fog signals around the coast were discontinued in 1972, Old Head acquired the siren fog signal from the discontinued Poer Head fog signal-station (1970) with a character of three blasts every forty-five seconds. The siren was replaced by an electric horn with the same character in December 1985 and controlled by a videograph fog detector, obviously in anticipation of making the station unwatched. The optic was converted from vaporised paraffin to electricity on 25 April 1972 with a standby generating set in case of mains electricity failure. When the Daunt lightship was withdrawn, the radio-beacon navigational aid was transferred to two stations, Ballycotton and Old Head, on 28 August 1974, transmitting its morse identification signal 'OH' in a character lasting five seconds once every six minutes. Old Head is grouped with beacons at Ballycotton, Lundy (Bristol Channel), Flatholm (Bristol Channel), South Bishop (off St David's Head, Pembroke) and Tuskar.

Sadly, on 1 April 1987, the Old Head of Kinsale light was automated. The keepers were withdrawn and an attendant looks after the station.

Wells for All Sorts of Cures

Still standing today are the remains of Kilmore church holy well, named Tuibrin Righ an Domhnaig. This well is in the townland of Kilmore, its position approximately 100 yards directly south of Ballycatten fort. It was also the well that served the hamlet, fort and church of Kilmore. Several years later, people afflicted with sore eyes, ulcers and diseases of all descriptions came to this well where they would pray for the removal of their infirmities. After their visits, it was customary for them to leave some mementos, such as pieces of cloth tied to the bushes nearby, and relics were deposited there. Pagan beliefs and superstitions are rife in rural Ireland, nearly 1,500 years after Christianity and, as a race, we have proved to have a need to believe in something or place. If someone finds solace from such circumstances – spiritual healing, so to speak – it should be treated with respect.

When it was located in 1968 by myself, I found glass beads and broken egg-cups – used as eye optics – and coins, some dating back to the early nineteenth century. After much toil, it was clean again and accessible to the public. For once in my life, the power of prayer had won me over.

Toibrín Masmuis, in Rathrout, on the road from Ballinadee to Bandon, is one of the most famous spa wells in the south of Ireland. The water is reputed not to boil but will cure stomach complaints in man and beast. It's also said that an afflicted man dreamt three successive nights that if he dug near a gap where he would find the print of a horseshoe, he would get water to cure his ailment.

The water from this well certainly contains minerals and will keep fresh and effective for months – some say for years if uncorked. It is known as the surfit well. It must contain manganese or sulphur, as this would explain the boiling problem. People used to come from all parts of Cork and Kerry in years gone by to get cured.

Tobar na Groidte (Well of the Champions), near the Old Head of Kinsale, is said in legend to host a ghostly horseman at all hours of the night.

Tobar Ruadáin (St Rohan's Well) is near Courtapartin graveyard, just south of Sandycove village, and is supposed to be a cure for sore eyes. Pilgrims throw in a little white stone every time they visit. There is no other special pattern.

Tobar an Ceárdcan (Well of the Forge) was more than likely the castle well, being so close to Ringrone Castle. A group gathering seaweed one moonlit night saw a horseman galloping down the lane behind the castle. He stopped

Chalybeate well at Garrettstown, discovered in 1750 while a new canal was being cut to feed the Serpentine lake.

and galloped back again. 'Old Baron Courcey,' they said. More than likely, they were coming home from a late-night drinking binge in some sheebeen or pub.

Kilcoleman, near the Old Head, had its own holy well close to Bullen's Bay, though I cannot find a name for it.

At Garrettstown, there is a chalybeate saline spring but, as of yet, it has not gained holy status. The water is a crimson colour and is considerably strong to the taste. It's good for all sorts of complaints for which chalybeates is known to help. The well is unusual with its beehive-type hut covering it.

Miscellany

Lispatrick Burial Ground

Lispatrick burial ground is about halfway up the peninsula at the Old Head, and it was here that many a native before the arrival of the Vikings and Normans was buried. Later, the servants of de Courcey and the Bullens were laid to rest here.

In later years at this burial ground, many a Famine victim found their resting place. Unidentified bodies washed in by the sea were also placed within, as were still-born children and babies who died before Baptism, for they would not be recognised or deemed by the Church to be Christians, and were secretly buried at night. In all cases, the graves were unmarked.

Names

With so many families bearing the same name in the region, it was hard to distinguish who was who. Take one family – the Dempseys; some were called the Ger Ógs, and you had the Dónal Seán Ógs. Another family were called the Soggarts because the head of that family was well versed in religion and able to speak on these matters. Then you had Seán Dónal Mór, probably because the head of that family was a big person. Another family was called the 'Yanks' because one of that family had made a quick trip to America.

Schoolhouse

There was a tiny schoolhouse at the Old Head which is now demolished. The school was close to where the present Speckled Door pub is now situated. A later schoolhouse was built in the nineteenth century at the edge of the present beach and still stands to this day as a recreation holiday home for the Scouts.

The schoolmasters of the time were very grumpy. If pupils missed school without a good excuse, a roll book was issued and monitored by the police. All sorts of excuses were used, as some students attended class only a few days a week. Some would miss out for several weeks as they were needed to work on the farm, picking spuds or saving the harvest. More would not attend if the weather was bad because of inappropriate clothing. Girls stayed at home to help about the house. Corporal punishment was in force and teachers were given a free hand to beat the living daylights out of pupils. The walking cane and leather strap were the order of the day, and most households had one of these straps hanging on the wall by the front door – used to sharpen the cut-throat razor that removed the stubble off the face of the male elder on a Saturday night as he prepared himself for Mass the following morning – but it also served as a deterrent to the children of the household against misbehaviour. The mother only needed to cast her eye upon it to bring law and order about the house. A similar strap was used in schools in rural Ireland at the time and, indeed, in other more prestigious schools as well. When children returned home from school, they would be asked by their parents how many slaps did they receive today; if they owned up, in most cases, they received several more clouts from their parents and also ran the risk of bringing the wrath of their grandmother upon them with a swipe of a long, ragged dishcloth right into the puss (face).

A typical nineteenth-century school scene.

It's well worth mentioning that in the latter part of the nineteenth century, a schoolmaster in this area who was very impeded with arthritis had to remain seated in an armchair for most of the day, so he used to gather all the pupils around him in a circle to teach his class. When the dunce could not answer the question put to him, he was pushed forward by a few bigger fellows, gaffed by the teacher's walking stick and thrown across the teacher's knee for whatever punishment he might bestow upon the misfortunate fellow. Most of the chastised boys said afterwards that if the old schoolmaster was in good health he would have skinned them alive.

Years earlier, the same teacher – before he became immobilised with rheumatic pains – beat the living daylights out of a certain pupil with a portion of an old golf stick that he managed to retrieve from the teacher's cupboard. The pupil fled home with the teacher hot on his heels. When he had made the relative safety of his home, he threatened the teacher with a kettle of boiling water and thus ended his schooling. Another incident concerned one of the children of the coastguard. After a good flogging by the teacher at the school, this pupil took off, riding his donkey bareback, and headed back to the coastguard station, never to be seen at the school again.

The Old Head was home to a coastguard station and lighthouse, resulting in

A nineteenth-century life-saving rocket apparatus at Old Head. It went out of use in the 1970s.

a new breed of family living and attending school in the area. Some of these children were spoiled brats and caused much havoc with the local pupils. Fist fights were commonplace when football matches were played in the sandy warren between two local teams at the Old Head. (The football at the time would be part of a cow's bladder packed with straw or fine grass and stitched with a bag needle. When struck, it did not move very far and stuck to the ground where it fell.) These strangers would join in, only instead of kicking the ball, it was the shins and ankles of the locals that were kicked, and the end result was one big bloody row with skin and hair flying. When this was exhausted, they all went home only to build up a head of steam for the next day. You had names like Sleep, Day Knight, Twister Turner, Ryder, Chick, Auchland and Southworth. These coastguards and their families lived in the row of stone-slated cottages just above the present Speckled Door pub.

In 1908, a new, red-bricked station was built between the old and present lighthouse and was used extensively up until the late 1940s. Soon after, it fell into decay and was demolished a few years ago.

Rocket House
At the bottom of the headland at the Old Head, there is a boathouse where a small lifeboat was stored. This boat was later replaced with a four-wheeled rocket apparatus. This life-saving apparatus was the lifeboat of the land, and most prominent headlands around the coast were served by these rockets which were used extensively and brought many a sailor back safe to shore from his stricken ship before it was dashed to pieces on the jagged rocks.

Several times during the year, a number of training sessions would be carried out at the western end of the headland where a rocket pole was erected for test purposes. This pole would represent the mast of a ship, and about fifteen volunteers – agile men from the locality – would be drilled and trained so as to be prepared for the day when a ship would be in distress. If you were available and failed to answer a distress call – as is still the case – you were instantly dismissed. These men, aided by the coastguard, would be taught the way to send out ropes to the stricken ship – this was called a breeches buoy and was how the people were brought ashore from a vessel. For their services, each man would receive half-a-crown (2s./6d.) for each outing.

This four-wheeled rocket-carriage apparatus was drawn by two horses which transported all the rocket equipment, including ropes, ladders, lanterns, oil for the lamps, tripod, gun and base plate. The total compliment of rocket crew was fifteen, and they wore their numbers on their arm. Number one, who was in command, and two of the crew always rode on the carriage. When a distress call was received, the two horses – which were always kept in a field close by the station – were tackled up. The rocket carriage – always at the ready – struck off to the nearest point to where the ship was about to founder or had come ashore. The gun and its base plate would be set up and the crew would try and establish the identity of the ship. The degrees would be set and a very light line would be attached to the rocket harpoon. The line would also carry timber envelopes made out in several languages giving instructions to the crew of the ship regarding procedures for rescue.

When contact was made with the ship, the line was drawn on board, bringing with it several hundred yards of a much stronger rope which the crew of the stricken ship would attach to the mast or some other secure point on board. When this was complete, the rocket crew would send out a breeches buoy and each crewman was brought safely ashore.

A list of stores for the Old Head rocket life-saving apparatus, issued by the Board of Trade in London dated 1894, is very comprehensive. The inventory was in excess of 200 items, though some items were small, and it also stated that it had to be kept in the cart or wagon at all times and checked on a regular basis. Items on this list included the rocket, with pendulum, heaving lines, rocket lines, one set of drag ropes complete with shoulder straps (these might be needed if the apparatus had to be taken into a position the horses could not traverse), signal flags complete with staffs, snatch blocks, wire hawsers with cutters, tail blocks and swivel, handles for long lights, rope ladders with stakes, several straight ladders, two side lamps, lamp trimmer, hand signal, lanterns (red and white), oil for the lamps, water carrier, spare rockets, fuses, a total of twenty-five primers (some of which were used for detonating the long lights), a tripod for illuminating lights, three tally boards, spare coils of rope, belts, breeches buoy, hand barrows and small tools of all sorts. The inventory also included a spare set of shafts for the rocket cart, anchor, axes, pickaxe, shovels, spades, a tent and pegs, a cart cover and even a whip.

By the early 1970s, these rocket apparatuses had become outdated and replaced by a more modern method. Today, thankfully, the area is well served by a vibrant Coastguard and Cliff Rescue Service, and the eagle-eyed, famous Courtmacsherry lifeboat is close by.

Doras Brack

A little cove, at which many fishing boats were once moored, now consists of a small pier and slipway, and still to be seen close by is the remains of a large house known as Doras Brack, or 'La Porte de Differentes Couleurs' (the door with the different colours). Its name was later transferred to what is now known as the Speckled Door, a well-furbished bar and restaurant.

Bog, Sand Dunes and Old Head

A large bog and extensive sand dunes divide the Old Head from the rest of the mainland. At one time, this bog served two purposes: turf, though of poor quality, supplied fuel for households, and the large reeds that grew there were used to thatch the roofs of houses of which there were many in the area, some up to and as late as the 1960s.

A nine-hole golf course existed close to the beach up until the late 1940s but the shifting sands proved too much and it fell into disuse. Part of this golf course was developed into a very vibrant pitch-and-putt course during the 1990s.

The Old Head of Kinsale was always famous, both historically and as a landmark. Fortunately, its historic sites are still protected. It is home to one of the world's most famous golf links, constructed in the last years of the twentieth century and designed in keeping with its surrounds.

During the big storm of 1989, the beach close to the Old Head underwent a dramatic change. Thousands of tons of sand was swept away, revealing a mass bed of turf with rows of tree stumps protruding from this bed. Each tree looked as if it had been cut with a blunt instrument, perhaps cut down by the ancient peoples from the Old Head region many thousands of years ago.

Timmy McCarthy: Antarctic Explorer

In August 1914, Sir Ernest Shackleton sailed from Plymouth on the ship *Endurance* on his trans-Antarctic expedition. Several Irishmen served on his crew, among them Timothy (Thade) McCarthy from Kinsale, Co. Cork.

The little ship of 850 tons was loaded with men, dogs and stores, and it entered the ice pack in December 1914. By January, she was stuck fast in the ice and was soon after crushed like an egg. The crew had removed her three lifeboats onto the ice and for several months floated across the sea on ice until it started breaking up. They then launched the boats into the freezing water and, after a week's voyage, reached a large rock named Elephant Island. The nearest inhabited land was the Falkland Islands, some 600 miles north. To the north-east, 800 miles away, was South Georgia.

Shackleton was completely cut off from the outside world and felt that something had to be done to save his men, so he decided to embark on a journey over some of the world's stormiest seas. He took one of the lifeboats with him and set out on a course for South Georgia (the prevailing winds and currents meant he could not make the shorter trip to the Falkland Islands). He chose five men to go with him, among them Thade McCarthy. Shackleton had asked Thade to help make the lifeboat as seaworthy as possible, and the only timber available were a few timber packing crates. With these, a deck forward was made and the bow raised. McCarthy also helped to fit a mast from one of the other boats and to strengthen the keel. With six men carrying provisions for thirty days and a Primus stove, sextant, barometer, compass, candles and sleeping bags, they set out on their perilous journey on 24 April. After a nightmare journey of sixteen days, McCarthy sighted the cliffs of South Georgia.

Shackleton was loud in his praise for his crew who had sailed with him and singled out McCarthy whose cheerful optimism was an inspiration to all. After getting help at South Georgia, Shackleton rescue the rest of his crew from Elephant Island, bringing them safely back to civilisation. Eight years later, while on another expedition to the Antarctic, Shackleton died on board his ship *Quest*, and was buried in South Georgia. The little boat that McCarthy modified for Sir Ernest Shackleton made it to the Maritime Museum, Greenwich, London.

On returning home from South Georgia, Thade McCarthy joined the British navy. On 16 April 1916, he was drowned at the young age of twenty-nine when a German U-Boat sank his ship. Thade McCarthy, who was born in Lower Cove near Kinsale, had a brother named Mortimer; he sailed with Scott's expedition to the South Pole in 1912, and died in Newfoundland. The harpoon he had used when he sailed with Scott is in Kinsale Museum. Another brother, John, was killed in France while serving with the Australian army in 1914. In the dying years of the twentieth century, a monument was erected in Kinsale, a fitting tribute to the McCarthy brothers who all died far from their native land.

Denis Florence McCarthy

The numerical strength of the McCarthys in the southern portion of the island of Ireland is notable, and many have been distinguished in the military, cultural, religious and political history of Ireland. Denis Florence McCarthy was a great poet and wrote in the nation's newspapers, yet when the centenary of his death came about in 1882, there was hardly a mention of him.

Life and Death in Olden Times

Dying at a young age was not unusual. Life expectancy in feudal times was short for both male and female. Not so for a lady living across the Blackwater river in Co. Cork. She was the Countess of Desmond (Catherine Fitzgerald), and all the soft westerly and south-westerly air that she breathed had blown to her over Co. Cork. She lived to an age of at least 140 – some say 162 – and only died when she fell from a tree into which she had climbed to gather fruit.

Earliest mention of the old countess is found in Sir Walter Raleigh's *History of the World*. He mentions her as being known to him personally while he was resident in his estates in Co. Cork. He speaks of her as 'having been married in the reign of King Edward IV and as being alive in 1589 and many years afterwards'. Edward IV died in 1483, so even if the countess was married at the age of fifteen, that would make her age in 1589 to be 121, and Raleigh says that she lived for many years after that. The earliest date given for her death is 1604, making her a minimum age of 136, but you can add another few years to that total. Francis Bacon mentions her in his *History of Life and Death*, and when in his *Natural History* he is discussing teeth, he writes: 'they tell a tale of the old Countess of Desmond, who lived until she was seven score years old, that she did dentize twice or thrice casting her old teeth, and others coming in their place'. Of her death, it was written 'she might have lived much longer had she not met with a kind of violent death, for she needed to climb a nut tree, to gather nuts, so falling down, she hurt her thigh which brought on a fever and that brought death'.

Talking about trees, we had a man closer to home that lived in a tree. He was Tadhg Cronac. Folklore tells us that he was a highwayman and he lived near the village of Ballinadee, Co. Cork. All efforts to locate him failed until he left out his dog by mistake, thus resulting in his being captured. 'Shoot my son,' said he 'and I will tell you where my money is.' He feared his son would falter and betray the hiding place, and when his son was dead he simply remarked: 'Shoot myself now for man or mortal will never enjoy what I have risked my life to hoard.' His money is said to be buried in a field near the village.

Several years ago, a local man was going to a funeral across the fields. His stick stuck in a hole and he heard what he thought was the rattle of coins. Taking note of the place, he hurried on his way, but when he came back after the funeral he could not find the spot and so the earth retains its treasure.

Glossary

Territories: some of the ancient territories in existence from prehistoric times to the break up of the Gaelic order in the sixteenth century: *Breifne*: present Cavan and west Leitrim; *Corca Laoidhe*: south-west Cork; *Dál Riada*: north Antrim; *Desmond, Deasmhumhan*: Kerry and a large portion of Cork; *Muskerry, Muscraidhe*: north-west and central Cork; *Thomond, Tuathmhumhan*: most of Co. Clare with adjacent parts of counties Limerick and Tipperary.

Brehon Law: in Irish, *breitheamh*, genitive *breitheamhan*, a judge. The terms Brehon Law and Brehon system refer to the Gaelic legal system in force before the Norman invasion. The Brehons were divided into several tribes; their office was hereditary and their laws were in the ancient Irish language. Only those who studied in their schools could succeed the family Brehon. This system was not completely superseded until the seventeenth century.

Dál gCais: called the Dalcassians: embraced the main septs of Thomond.

Cenel Eoghain: clan name of O'Neill, descended from Eóghan, son of Niall of the Nine Hostages, located in Tyrone.

Eóghanacht: clan name of the descendants of Eóghan, son of Oilioll Olum, to which many of the main families of south Munster belonged.

Barony: a territorial division next in order of size to the county, each county comprising from five to twenty baronies according to its extent.

Galloglass: in Irish, *galloglach*, a heavily armed mercenary soldier usually, but not always, of Scottish origin.

Kern: in Irish, *ceithearnach*, an Irish soldier lightly armed.

One mark: 13s./4d.

League: three miles.

Escheator: feudal overlord of property.

Heckler: a person who dresses flax.

Windrow: long, thin pile of hay to catch the wind.

194

Sources and Bibliography

Manuscripts Dept., Library University of North Carolina, Southern
    Historical Collection, Desnouettes Letters.
Yale Manuscripts and Archive.
Cheltenham Art Gallery and Museum.
Edmund Burke Speeches on America.
Yale Gallery.
Rolf Loeber, *Biographical Dictionary of Architects in Ireland 1600–1720.*
Hibernian Journal, 1774.
Clerical and Parochial Records of Cork Cloyne and Ross, 1863.
Freeman's Journal, 1816, 1774.
Ancient and Present State of the County and City of Cork.
National Archives and Records Service, Washington.
Smithsonian Institution, Washington.
Peabody Museum, Salem, Massachusetts.
Dictionary of Canadian Biography, 1821, 1835, 1836, 1850, 1861, 1870, 1871
    1880, researched by Charles O'Sullivan.
Aristocratic Toronto, 1810–1915, Lucy Booth Martyn.
New York Mercantile Advertiser, 1822.
The Weekly Register, 1822.
Office of Public Works.
Merchant Sail.
Archives of Ontario, 77 Grenville Street, Toronto.
A Life of Propriety, Katherine M. J. McKenna, Professor of Women's Studies,
    Queen's University, Ontario, Canada, 1995.
Pears Cyclopaedia, 1928.
Cork City Library.
Ships of the Past.
Chronicles of the Sea, 1838, William Mark Clark.
Surnames of Ireland, Edward MacLysaght, 1985.
Smith's History Cork City and County, 1815.
Short History of Kinsale, Michael Mulcahy, 1966.
The Development of Lordship in County Cork, 1300–1600', Kenneth Nicholls,
Interdisciplinary Essays on the History of an Irish County, Cork History
    Society.
Great Battlefields of the World, 1998.

Timoleague and Barryroe, James Coombes, 1969.
How the Irish Saved Civilization, Thomas Cahill, 1995.
The Last Prince of Ireland, Morgan Llywelyn, 1992.
English Men of Letters, John Morley, 1882.
World History: A Chronological Dictionary of Dates, Rodney Castleden.
Dictionary of the Bible, Rev. John Brown.
Oxford Illustrated History of Ireland, R.G. Foster, 1989.
The Ancient World of the Celts, Peter Beresford Ellis, 1998.
Lovely is the Lee, Robert Gibbings, 1945.
History of the War in the Peninsula, Major General Sir W.F.P. Napier KCB, 1886.
Discover Dursey, Penelope Durell, 1996.
Bandon Historical Journal.
The Kinsale Record.
Southern Star.
Cork Examiner, extracts from the late Pádraig O'Maidin.
National Library of Ireland.
Cork Southern Reporter, 1822.
Discovering Cork, Daphne D.C. Pochin Mould, 1991.
Cork Executions, 1712–1911.
Lewis' Topographical Dictionary of Ireland, vol. ii, 1837.
Cork Historical and Archaeological Society, vol. xliv, 1939.
Journal Cork Historical Society, vol. i, 1892, vol. xx, 1914.
Griffith's Valuation, 1851–52.
History of the Diocese of Cork, Evelyn Bolster.
I.T.A. Reports, Seán McCarthy, 1942.
General History of Ireland, Sheathrún Céitinn (1570–1650).
Dictionary of Canadian Biography, vol. ix, 1861–1870.
Robinson Papers, Canada.
Logs of Irish Emigrants Proceeding to Canada, 1823–25.
A Frenchman's Impressions of County Cork in 1790, Sile Ní Chinneide.
General and Statistical Survey of County of Cork, vol. i, 1815.
Cork and County Cork in the Twentieth Century, Richard J. Hodges MA, 1911.
Castles and Fortifications of Ireland, 1485–1945.
Yale University Library.
Annals of Yale College History, vol. vi, 1805, 1815, Yale University Press, 1912.
Royal Irish Academy Proceedings, vol. xlix, Seán P. O'Riordain and P.J. Hartnett.
Archaeological Inventory of County Cork, vol. 2, East and South Cork.
History of Douglas, Con Foley, 1981.